Edouard Glissant and
Postcolonial Theory

Edouard Glissant
and Postcolonial Theory

STRATEGIES OF LANGUAGE
AND RESISTANCE

Celia M. Britton

New World Studies

A. James Arnold, Editor

University Press of Virginia
Charlottesville and London

The University Press of Virginia
© 1999 by the Rector and Visitors of the University of Virginia
All rights reserved
Printed in the United States of America

First published 1999

∞ The paper used in this publication meets the minimum require-
ments of the American National Standard for Information Sciences—
Permanence of Paper for Printed Library Materials, ANSI Z39.48-
1984.

Library of Congress Cataloging-in-Publication Data
Britton, Celia.
    Edouard Glissant and postcolonial theory : strategies of language
and resistance / Celia M. Britton.
        p.   cm. — (New World studies)
    Includes bibliographical references and index.
    ISBN 0-8139-1848-0 (alk. paper). — ISBN 0-8139-1849-9 (pbk. :
alk. paper)
    1. Glissant, Edouard, 1928–   —Contributions in political aspects
of language. 2. Glissant, Edouard, 1928–   —Contributions in postcolonialism. 3. Caribbean Area—Languages—Political aspects.
4. Postcolonialism—Caribbean Area. I. Title. II. Series.
P85.G57B75   1999
841'.914—dc21   98-48754
                                                          CIP

Contents

Acknowledgments

I WOULD LIKE to thank the British Academy for funding two research visits to Martinique and the University of Aberdeen for allowing me to take two semesters of research leave in order to write this book. I am also grateful to my colleagues in the French Department at Aberdeen for their support throughout this project, particularly Martin Munro for acting as my research assistant and John Roach for his help with the translations. Some of the material in chapter 4 originally appeared in an article entitled "'A Certain Linguistic Homelessness': Relations to Language in Edouard Glissant's *Malemort*," *Modern Language Review* 91, no. 3 (July 1996): 597–609. I would like to thank the editor of *The Modern Language Review* for granting me permission to reuse it here.

A Note on Translation

I HAVE translated into English all quotations from Glissant's novels and other writings, and given the original French text as well where I am analyzing his use of language. The page references following the quotations are to the most recent editions. I have quoted from the published English translations of the works of Fanon and of the parts of Glissant's *Le discours antillais* that have been translated by Michael Dash. I have made occasional minor amendments to these, signaled by square brackets, where the published translation is not sufficiently exact for my purposes. Dash translates some of Glissant's key concepts in a variety of idiomatic ways: *Relation* ("creolization," "cultural contact," "cross-cultural relationships"); *Être* ("original nature," "single culture"); *opacité* ("inscrutability," "obscurity"); *détour* ("diversion," "defensive strategy," "ploy"). I have replaced these with Relation, essence, opacity, and detour. I have also provided my own translation of quotations from the other parts of *Le discours antillais* and distinguished between them by prefacing the relevant page reference with *DA* for my translations and *CD* (*Caribbean Discourse*) for Dash's.

Abbreviations

The following abbreviations are used for titles of Glissant's books:

CC *La case du commandeur*

CD *Caribbean Discourse* (J. Michael Dash's translation)

DA *Le discours antillais* (author's translation)

IP *L'intention poétique*

IPD *Introduction à une poétique du divers*

L *La Lézarde*

Mah *Mahagony*

Mal *Malemort*

PR *Poétique de la relation*

QS *Le quatrième siècle*

TM *Tout-monde*

TTM *Traité du tout-monde*

Edouard Glissant and
Postcolonial Theory

Introduction

THE QUESTION of language is central to the colonial and postcolonial experience. The colonizing nations imposed their European languages on their subjects, but rarely to the extent of achieving total uniformity; colonial societies are almost always *mixed*-language communities. Language became an instrument of control and command, and anticolonial resistance therefore necessarily included as one of its dimensions resistance to the colonizer's language. But the colonizer's language also became an avenue of social promotion for an elite group of the colonized and a major element in ideological definitions of self and other. Both during the colonial period and in the aftermath of decolonization, language was and is a key site of conflict.

These are familiar generalizations and are more or less valid for all colonial and postcolonial situations. But along with the common features, the historical and geographical differences between colonies have created a variety of different language situations. Edouard Glissant comes from Martinique: it is a tiny island in the eastern Caribbean, one of France's oldest colonies, producing mainly cane sugar, originally by means of slave labor transported from West Africa. It has never become even nominally independent but was granted the status of a *département d'outre mer* [overseas region] in 1946 and was made subject to France's official policy of cultural assimilation. All of these factors affect the Martinicans' use of and attitude toward French and Creole and, therefore, affect Glissant's writing as well. But, as Glissant is well aware, the specificities of the Martinican situation only become significant if they are compared with other societies. Martinique, for instance, is typical of the Americas in its history of transportation and slavery; typical of the Caribbean but less so of mainland America in the virtual annihilation of its indigenous population; and atypical of the Caribbean in that it is not today an independent nation state.

The Caribbean acts as a particularly important context for Glissant's writing—fictional, poetic, and theoretical—and for his political activity. The Front Antillo-Guyanais, which he and Paul Niger founded in the 1950s, demonstrates his commitment to a political ideal of Caribbean solidarity as the best way to resist continuing pressure both from the European nations that originally colonized the islands and from the United States.[1] His promotion of the concept of *Antillanité* [Caribbean-ness] also expresses his enduring fascination with the cultural diversity of the Caribbean. *Antillanité* stands for the solidarity of a multiethnic and multilingual region in which different Creoles coexist with English, French, Dutch, and Spanish, so that, as Antonio Benítez-Rojo comments, "the spectrum of Caribbean codes is so varied and dense that it holds the region in a soup of signs."[2]

None of these languages, moreover, are indigenous to the region. Creole is a creation of colonialism; it arose out of the contact between European and African languages, but since the latter were lost with the first generations of slaves, Creole was forced to position itself solely in relation to the dominant European language, which it opposes while being continuously influenced by it. This double complexity—the multiplicity of languages in use and the lack of an autonomous, traditional indigenous language—is perhaps what gives such a sharp focus to the question of language in the work of many Caribbean writers.[3] As the Barbadian George Lamming writes, "the word colonial has a deeper meaning for the West Indian than it has for the African. The African, in spite of his modernity, has never been wholly severed from the cradle of a continuous culture and tradition." Lamming goes on to argue that "it is the brevity of the West Indian's history and the fragmentary nature of the different cultures which have fused to make something new; it is the absolute dependence on the values in that language of his coloniser which have given him a special relation to the word, colonialism." Thus, Edward Kamau Brathwaite's concept of "nation language," for instance, has much in common with Glissant's attempts to theorize and to forge in practice a new language use that will be both specific and adequate to the social realities of the Caribbean.[4]

What is not possible, Glissant argues, is to create a "new language" that will be unproblematically autonomous—distinct and separate from French—and unproblematically internalized as a "natural" mother tongue by the population. The continuing massive presence of standard

French in the island perhaps makes him more skeptical of a new language's chances of success than the comparatively optimistic Brathwaite's view of "nation language" or Lammings's confident assertion, made as early as 1960, that "I am not much interested in what the West Indian writer has brought to the English language; for English is no longer the exclusive language of the men who live in England. That stopped a long time ago; and it is today, among other things, a West Indian language. What the West Indians do with it is their own business."[5] But Glissant's insistence on the ambiguous and constrained nature of the struggle to build a new mode of expression is theoretically illuminating in a way that goes beyond Martinique's particular situation, if only because Martinique presents an especially acute case. Rather than establishing a "new language" alongside and outside the dominant one, a strategic relationship of resistance and subversion *to* the dominant language is negotiated from the inside. What is produced is a "counterdiscourse," in the sense in which Helen Tiffin writes: "These subversive manoeuvres, rather than the construction or reconstruction of the essentially national or regional, are what is characteristic of post-colonial texts, as the subversive is characteristic of post-colonial discourse in general. Post-colonial literatures/cultures are thus constituted in counterdiscursive rather than homologous practices, and they offer 'fields' of counter-discursive strategies to the dominant discourse."[6] Glissant coins the term *contre-poétique* for the same phenomenon; the problematic construction of a "counterpoetic" discourse in his novels and his theoretical texts is central to the concerns of this book. The issues addressed in the following chapters are thus: How does the colonized subject relate to a language initially imposed by the colonizer but subsequently, *to some extent,* subverted and reappropriated? And, what role can fictional representation play in this process?

In discussing these questions I aim to situate Glissant in the context of postcolonial theory. I refer to the work of Edward Said, Henry Louis Gates Jr., Antonio Benítez-Rojo, and the authors of *The Empire Writes Back*: Bill Ashcroft, Gareth Griffiths, and Helen Tiffin. The most extensive connections, however, are with Frantz Fanon, Homi Bhabha, and Gayatri Spivak. Fanon's relevance is in the first place a matter of biography; as a fellow Martinican and contemporary of Glissant, his perspective on colonialism—especially in *Black Skin, White Masks,* written before his political and professional involvement in Algeria—is very close to Glissant's, and Glissant explicitly acknowledges his influence. But Fanon was also the first writer to consider fully the articulation of the psychological with the socioeconomic in the context of colonialism and to argue for the necessity of integrating a psychoanalytic dimension into the overall analysis. The social features of colonialism have repercussions on the unconscious, in other words. These are particularly severe, Glissant argues, in the case of a *département d'outre mer,* in which domination by the metropolis continues, but in a far more covert and mystifying form than previously, and in which economic deprivation is not the main problem (Martinique is prosperous by Caribbean standards), but alienated identification with French culture is all the more pervasive.

Bhabha builds upon and reorientates Fanon's insights, arguing that not only colonialism but all subsequent forms of racial discrimination include unconscious determinations that cannot be understood without a psychoanalytical perspective.[7] Exploring the articulation of the political-discursive and the psychoanalytical, he writes, "such an articulation becomes crucial if it is held that the body is always simultaneously inscribed in both the economy of pleasure and desire and the economy of discourse, domination and power." Later in the same article he defines the "predominant strategic function" of colonial discourse as "the creation of a space for a 'subject peoples' through the production of knowledges in terms of which surveillance is exercised *and* a complex form of pleasure/unpleasure is incited."[8] His theorizations of the racial stereotype as fetish, of the split identification of the colonial subject, and of "unhomeliness" all provide important insights into Glissant's writing.

Spivak's provocative claim that "the subaltern cannot speak" counters the idealist view of the oppressed as full subjects capable of making their voices heard in the world and instead directs our attention to the complex and fragile textual effects of these marginalized subject-positions in dominant discourses. This results in an extreme problematization of the notion of "counterdiscourse," but not (as some critics have argued) in its exclusion. Spivak's work on epistemic violence, the semiosis of subaltern insurrection, political representation, and the position of the intellectual representing the "effaced itinerary" of the subaltern subject resonate with Glissant's representation of slavery as a "mute" world of "struggle with no witnesses" (*CD,* 159).

Apart from Fanon, all the postcolonial theorists I cite write in English, and their work is not widely known in the francophone world. Postcolonial theory has been developed mainly in the United States, Australia, and Britain. It includes considerable discussion of writers from the English-speaking Caribbean—Brathwaite, Wilson Harris, Derek Walcott, etc.—but, again apart from Fanon, has little to say about the writers and intellectuals of the French Caribbean. Glissant, who is undoubtedly one of the most important theorists of the French colonial experience as well as one of the greatest writers of the Caribbean, is virtually never mentioned.[9] This book is an attempt to remedy that omission, an omission that is all the more surprising given the extent to which Glissant's theoretical concerns overlap with those of other postcolonial theorists. Such major themes of postcolonial theory as the reappropriation of history, writing and orality, hybridity, subalternity, the problematizing of identity, and the colonial construction of the Other are central to his work, in addition to the sustained analysis of the problem of language.

The existence of these common concerns is obviously attributable, in the first instance, to the objective similarities of the colonial experience. But it also owes something to the fact that Glissant's intellectual development has, from 1946 (when he went to study at the Sorbonne and the Musée de l'Homme in Paris) onward, been intimately bound up with the successive versions of phenomenology, Marxism, and poststructuralism that characterized the Parisian intelligentsia in the 1950s, 1960s, and 1970s. These same movements have been central to the construction of postcolonial theory: Michel Foucault, Jacques Derrida, and Jacques Lacan, in particular, are essential reference points in the works of Said, Spivak, and Bhabha. The sense one has that Glissant inhabits the same general intellectual world as the anglophone postcolonial theorists is thus perhaps explicable in terms of their debt to French theory and the indirect links that this creates between their work and that of Glissant. There are also more specific connections, such as that provided by Fanon, for example, through his eclectic use of Marxism, phenomenology, and psychoanalysis; his prominence in Bhabha's work; and his influence on Glissant. A more recent example is Derrida's *Le monolinguisme de l'autre,* which gives an explicitly postcolonialist orientation to the question of the subject's relation to language and is based on a lecture he gave at a conference at Louisiana State University, co-organized by Glissant.

By juxtaposing anglophone postcolonial theory and Glissant's theoretical writing, I hope to bring out their similarities—and equally illuminating differences—and to show the significant contribution Glissant makes to this body of theory. But this book is above all a discussion of his novels, and this involves the relations between several other groups of texts. I of course look at the relationships between Glissant's novels and his theory, and between his novels and anglophone postcolonial theory. In addition, however, there are metropolitan French theorists, such as Gilles Deleuze and Félix Guattari, to whom he explicitly refers, adopting their notion of the "rhizome"; or Michel de Certeau, whom Mireille Rosello uses in her analysis of French Caribbean literature, which includes Glissant. There are the French Caribbean theorists, such as his collaborators on *Acoma*, the review he founded, but also figures such as Jacques André, René Ménil, Roger Toumson, Fritz Gracchus, and the *créolité* group (Jean Bernabé, Patrick Chamoiseau, and Raphaël Confiant), all of whom have written about Glissant's work as well as more generally on aspects of the islands' culture, language, and literature. Finally, there is the considerable body of existing critical literature on Glissant by Michael Dash, Suzanne Crosta, Richard Burton, Bernadette Cailler, and others. These categories of texts are distinct, and sometimes offer strikingly different perspectives, but to varying degrees they also interact consciously with each other.

The capacity of Glissant's novels to attract such a range of interpretations is in itself an indication of their richness and depth. The novels do not merely illustrate theoretical insights elaborated elsewhere (by Glissant or anyone else); they produce their own critique of the social situation in the island and their own representation of the defensive or subversive strategies that have evolved in response to it. Above all, through their structure and style—the adoption of elements of the "poetics" of oral Creole culture, or the refusal to allow a single individual authorial voice to dominate the text, or the insistence on its necessary "opacity" for the non-Caribbean reader—the novels themselves *constitute* strategies of language and resistance.

Glissant's writing falls into three main categories: poetry, novels, and essays.[10] I do not discuss his poetry at all here. Of the six novels he has published to date, I have little to say about *La Lézarde*, which came out in 1958. His second novel, *Le quatrième siècle* (1964), is more ambitious in terms of its scope—it traces the histories of two families from the arrival of their African ancestors on a slave ship in 1788 to the end of World War II—and it engages powerfully with themes that continue to remain central to the whole of his work: the loss of history, the trauma of transportation, the oral tradition and waning memories of the African past, and the growth of a new relationship with the geographical environment as slaves and maroons gradually implant themselves in the island. Some of the characters of *La Lézarde*—Papa Longoué, Mathieu Béluse, Marie Celat, and Raphaël Targin—reappear in *Le quatrième siècle,* and this pattern of recurrences is continued throughout subsequent novels.

But it is not until *Malemort* (1975) that the distinctively fractured, bitter yet expansive energy of his writing fully emerges, and that the questions of language and resistance to cultural as well as economic deprivation begin to dominate the text. *Malemort* is often described as the most pessimistic of his novels.[11] Glissant himself presents it as portraying a "banal example of liquidation through absurdity, in the horrorless horror of a successful colonization" and adds despairingly, "what can writing do about this? It can never catch up" (*DA,* 14). But it is also, in places, one of his funniest texts; a wild sardonic humor offsets the tragic lives of its protagonists and in itself offers a kind of cultural resistance. *La case du commandeur* (1981) is narrated by the same undefined and elastic collective "we" as is *Malemort*; and it picks up from *Le quatrième siècle* the idea of structuring the narrative according to the successive generations of a family, but with the difference that this principle governs only the first of its three parts and that it works backwards in time, from Marie Celat to the quasi-mythical "Odono," who was transported from Africa.

Mahagony has a more complex structure, with a number of different individual narrators participating in the reconstruction of the stories of three different figures. It is also thematically complex, in the sense that it occupies a transitional position in Glissant's work, between the problematic that dominates *Malemort* and *La case du commandeur*—and which is most centrally relevant to my perspective on Glissant—and the new, more optimistic stance that characterizes Glissant's most recent novel, *Tout-monde.* Moreover, it is the structural innovation of a plurality of differentiated individual narrators that enables the thematic transition to take place. That is, in *Mahagony* Glissant discovers the "relay": the principle that narrative is always multiple, decentered, and nonhierarchical. Different "voices" add their contribution to a collective text that is always in process—always unfinished and constantly expanding. They relate to each other on equal terms, and none of them are constrained by the narratives of any of the others. Like the previous novels, *Mahagony* still produces an analysis and critique of linguistic domination and still works in the materiality of the fictional text itself to elaborate a counterdiscourse that subverts the dominant discourse. But it also lays the groundwork for the abandonment of this double axis in *Tout-monde,* and it does so by opening up the possibility of a free, equal, collective participation in the construction of discourse. To this extent,

Mahagony offers an alternative model rather than a critique. The shift is one of atmosphere and emphasis more than of the substance of Glissant's analysis of neocolonialism in Martinique, but it is nevertheless striking. In simple terms, *Tout-monde* is not dominated by conflict, constraint, and struggle in the way that Glissant's previous novels are. (It is also the first novel not to be set entirely in Martinique.) This is not to say that conflict is resolved; rather, it is dissolved in the deliberately open-ended, ramified, heterogeneous, and dispersed (non)structure of the text.

The chronological progression in Glissant's novels cannot be understood without considering them in the light of the theoretical writing that he was producing over the same period. There are seven collections of essays: *Soleil de la conscience* (1956), *L'intention poétique* (1969), *Le discours antillais* (1981), *Poétique de la relation* (1990), *Faulkner, Mississippi* (1995), *Introduction à une poétique du divers* (1996), and *Traité du tout-monde* (1997). They cover a wide range of subjects and are not in any sense pure theory. Personal recollections and impressions combine with critical pieces on individual writers and artists; with sociologically orientated studies of aspects of Martinican family life, sexual relations, unemployment, etc.; and with a sensuous, poetic apprehension of the Caribbean landscape and climate. But certain dominant themes emerge: the position and responsibility of the Caribbean writer; the relationship between language and subjectivity for the diglottic peoples of the Caribbean, and Martinique in particular; and the history of colonialism in the Caribbean. And all of the essays are informed by a view of postcolonial reality that is both a political analysis of colonialism and a phenomenological exploration of the concept of the Other.[12] On the first page of the earliest volume, *Soleil de la conscience,* Glissant writes: "My intuition is perhaps that there will be no more culture without all cultures, no more civilizations that can make others their colonies, no more poets that can ignore the movement of History"; and this is still, forty years later, a good summary of Glissant's position. But his ideas have of course undergone considerable development since the 1950s. *Le discours antillais* is in some ways his most ambitious achievement—not only in its length (five hundred pages), but also in its determination to grasp the whole of the complex, multiply interrelated and overdetermined cultural reality of Martinique in its relation to France and to the rest of the Caribbean. Bringing together linguistic, psychological, literary, economic, and historical analysis, it is also the most politically combative of his theoretical works: the politics of cultural struggle against the alienating occultation of social reality that *départementalisa-*

tion has imposed on the Martinicans necessitate not only programs of action but thorough analysis. In its opening section Glissant defines "the object of my work" as "a matter of tracking down every manifestation of the multiple processes . . . that have ultimately woven for a people, that had at its disposal so many trained officials and individuals, the web of nothingness in which it is ensnared today" (*CD*, 2).

Poétique de la relation, published nine years later, continues the same project but with—as its title suggests—a wider focus and a greater emphasis on the elaboration of the philosophical concepts that underpin the political analysis. The anti-essentialist thrust of "Relation," its contestation of universal norms, the notion of "chaos," and the deconstruction of the traditional humanist notion of identity are the dominant themes in this volume. *Introduction à une poétique du divers* consists of the texts of four lectures given in the course of 1994 and largely restates the main ideas of *Poétique de la relation*, but with a number of new emphases. It is also closely connected to the themes of *Tout-monde*, which itself, although nominally a novel, contains substantial passages of authorial reflection on these ideas. Most recently, the *Traité du tout-monde* brings together a number of further reflections on the themes of Relation, chaos, and language and identity. The differences between the works of the 1990s and those of the 1970s and 1980s are, first, that Glissant now accords greater weight to the action of the *imagination* in creating freer societies, referring for instance to "the necessity, of course, of supporting political and social struggles in the places in which one finds oneself, but also . . . the necessity of opening everyone's imagination up to something different, which is that we will change nothing in the situation of the world's peoples if we do not change that imagination"; and, second, that he increasingly writes as though the values of Relation, chaos, and diversity have in fact already prevailed: "L'universel a basculé dans la diversité, qui la bouscule" [The universal has toppled over into diversity, which is knocking it about] (*IPD*, 66, 68).

This book is structured thematically rather than chronologically. Chapter 1 outlines those aspects of his theoretical writing that relate to the question of language and cultural resistance, and that are referred to in subsequent chapters, and it juxtaposes them with other postcolonialist theory. Subsequent chapters can be seen, in general terms, as moving from the more negative to the more positive aspects of the problematic. Chapter 2 is concerned with the basic predicament that generates the various strategies of resistance—the "lack of language," not just in the sense that there is no adequate language, but that what language there is, is experienced as "lack." The imaginary ideal of authentic language, in its changing and increasingly compromised formulations, is also traced chronologically through the novels. Chapter 3 presents Spivak's concept of subalternity—the claim that the subaltern cannot "know" or "speak" his or her situation—and discusses fictional representations of the subaltern in *Le quatrième siècle* and *Mahagony*. Chapters 4 and 5 are both based on Fanon's analysis of the psychological alienation caused by colonialism, Bhabha's development of this theme, and Glissant's related work in *Le discours antillais* on the "mimetic drive" and "verbal delirium." Chapter 4 examines six sections of *Malemort* in the light of these relationships to the white Other's speech and the psychic dislocations that they produce. Chapter 5 follows the theme of madness through its paradoxically more positive manifestations as the colonial subject pursues a desperate search for meaning in an attempt to come to terms with what Bhabha terms the "unhomeliness" of contemporary postcolonial society; the figure of Marie Celat is considered in detail in *La case du commandeur, Mahagony,* and *Tout-monde*. Chapter 6 looks rather at the more controlled and conscious uses of language as "camouflage"—as deliberate ruse and "rhetoric of indirection," to use Gates's phrase. Examples from *Le quatrième siècle, Malemort,* and *Tout-monde* are followed by a more sustained analysis of *La case du commandeur*. Finally, chapter 7 is based on the notion of "relayed" speech (as defined above) as this operates in *Mahagony* and *Tout-monde*. Chapter 8 provides a brief retrospective overview and a restatement of the central theme of this book: Glissant's exploration of the role that language plays in resisting colonial domination.

1 Concepts of Resistance

GLISSANT'S ESSAYS form a substantial body of work, intimately connected to his fiction and poetry, and of equal importance in the context of his work both as a writer and as a political thinker and activist. His critique of the Western tradition of humanist philosophy, which has much in common with similar critiques mounted by European Marxists, phenomenologists, and poststructuralists, often operates on a general philosophical level; but it is always combined with a deep sense of the specificity of the anticolonial struggle in the Caribbean. In this chapter I outline the four concepts most relevant to the question of language and resistance, and to which I refer frequently in subsequent chapters. These concepts are Relation, opacity, detour, and counterpoetics.

Glissant's theoretical work is a complex, ramified, proliferating, and constantly evolving body of ideas. But it is all underpinned by *la Relation*. The starting point for this concept is the irreducible difference of the Other; "Relation" is in the first place a relation of equality with and respect for the Other as *different* from oneself. It applies to individuals but more especially to other cultures and other societies. It is nonhierarchical and nonreductive; that is, it does not try to impose a universal value system but respects the *particular* qualities of the community in question, in a movement of "degeneralization" (*PR*, 75). But this does not imply a defense of cultures that jealously guard their uniqueness by shutting out the rest of the world; particularity is valuable only as long as it is outward-looking and related to other cultures and values. Thus, Glissant conceives of Relation as a system rather than as a number of separate, singular relations. It is, however, a fluid and unsystematic system whose elements are engaged in a radically nonhierarchical free play of interrelatedness.[1]

Relation is an anti-imperialist project. Glissant argues that Third-World societies are better placed to "enter into Relation" than the West, which, weighed down by its colonial history, still sees itself as the imposer of supposedly universalist norms on the rest of the world. The "discoverers"—that is, not only those who actually "discovered," subjugated, and settled in non-European societies but also those who continued the colonial regimes and especially those who legitimized them through the construction of bodies of knowledge such as ethnography[2]—are anxiously determined to cling to their conception of a world in which they dominate and control rather than "a world in which one is, quite simply, one agrees to be, with and among others" (*PR*, 128). But it is not impossible for the West to move away from its imperialist world view and to participate in Relation; paradoxically, this shift is inscribed in the very logic of colonialism itself and the contradictions that it produces. Not only did colonialism force very different societies into contact, and hence "relation," with each other—albeit in an extremely violent and unequal way—but in the long term, through the tensions and conflicts it caused *in the colonizing nations themselves,* it undermined the unity of the West, whose attempt to remain master of the world's destiny has proved "so futile that the West itself is breaking up into opposing intentions" (*IP*, 209). In this new situation, the diverse and divided communities of the West have no choice but to become involved with the rest of the world; what remains to be seen, of course, is whether this involvement will be a participation on equal terms or a continuation of the old domination (see *PR*, 205).[3]

Diversity is thus a prime value of Relation. In the section of *Le discours antillais* entitled "Sameness and Diversity" (*CD*, 97–104), Glissant argues that the universalizing force of Western humanism leads to a conception of the Other as mere fodder for its drive to reduce everything to "the same."[4] In contrast, recognizing the value of diversity allows the creation of a relation that sees the Other as equal and as a presence that is necessary *because* it is different: "Diversity leads to Relation: it is the modern implication of cultures in each other, through their wanderings, their 'structural' demand for absolute equality" (*DA*, 191). Relation operates within a totality based on diversity rather than unity. This totality is the opposite of totalitarian, because it needs the presence of all its diverse and equal elements.[5] Thus, "the Whole" is inclusive whereas "the One" is not: "We have argued that Relation is an open totality, always moving on from itself. In other words what we subtract from this idea . . . is the principle of unity . . . multiplicity in totality is total diversity"

(*PR*, 206). The totality is structured in a way that eradicates the hierarchical opposition between center and periphery.[6] Recent history, in particular anticolonial struggle, has allowed "peoples who yesterday inhabited the hidden side of the earth . . . to assert themselves in the face of a total world culture. If they do not assert themselves, they deprive the world of a part of itself" (*CD*, 99). Equally, the totality can never be fully known by any individual; Glissant describes it as a force field of possible trajectories, along which people move in a new, nonimperialist kind of traveling, which he calls "errance." The "errant" explores the world, aspires to know it in its totality, but realizes that he never will and that "in this resides the endangered beauty of the world" (*PR*, 33).

This infinitely open-ended, uncontainable aspect of Relation is characteristic of *Poétique de la relation* and *Introduction à une poétique du divers*, where Glissant places greater emphasis than hitherto on change; Relation is never fixed but remains an open, constantly mobile totality (*PR*, 206). Rather than a structure, it is seen in his more recent work as a dynamic *process* governed by principles that are themselves always being changed by the elements they govern (*PR*, 186). The same emphasis on movement and dynamism also leads him, in these later texts, to associate Relation with what he calls the *chaos-monde*. This concept of the "chaos-world" is derived from scientific chaos theory, which argues for the impossibility of explaining an entity (here, the totality of Relation) in terms of classical causality or analyzing it via a single system of measurement; whereas an alternative, perhaps more intuitive, way of conceiving it is possible: "the forms of the chaos-world (the incommensurable mixing together of cultures) are unpredictable *and guessable*" (*PR*, 152, emphasis added). Glissant illustrates this with two examples of the extraordinarily incongruous, and yet somehow unsurprising, "relations" of contemporary global culture and the difficulty we have in interpreting or evaluating them. What kind of significance should we attach to the fact that the Chinese students risking death in Tiananmen Square chose as their emblem a cardboard image of the Statue of Liberty? Or that during the Rumanian revolution people replaced the reviled portraits of Ceausescu and his wife that had hung in their homes by—of all things—photographs cut out from magazines of the characters from the U.S. soap opera *Dallas*? "Just asking the question," Glissant concludes, "means imagining the unimaginable turbulence of Relation" (*PR*, 153). Relation, which is "le chaos-monde qui (se) relate" [the chaos-world as it relates (to itself)/relates (i.e., tells) itself] (*PR*, 109), is thus multiply dynamic and radically heterogenous; no one norm can account for it. Glissant links it to the notion of the "rhizome" developed by Gilles Deleuze and Félix Guattari: unlike the root and the tree, in which all growth is structured from a single central point, the rhizome, which is indistinguishably both root and stem, proliferates randomly from many different nodes at once. Thus, the root is "absolute" or totalitarian; the rhizome is "relative."[7]

A similar use of chaos theory, but applied specifically to the Caribbean, is prominent in Antonio Benítez-Rojo's *The Repeating Island*. Here, too, the emphasis is on an unpredictable dynamic, an "attitude, whose end is not to find results, but processes, dynamics and rhythms that show themselves within the marginal, the regional, the incoherent, the heterogeneous, or, if you like, the unpredictable that co-exists with us in our everyday world." This dynamic transcends the opposition between unity and diversity and, thus, rather like Glissant's "totality," finds within diversity a *pattern* that allows common or "repeating" features to be discerned without reducing the phenomena to "the Same." Within chaos, in other words, "every repetition is a practice that necessarily entails a difference and a step towards nothingness." The "repeating island" is not a positivistic entity but a collection of overlapping, self-reproducing, self-generating *impulses*: as Benítez-Rojo puts it, "But what is it that repeats? Tropisms, in series; movements in approximate direction. Let's say the unforeseen relation between a dance movement and the baroque spiral of a colonial railing." The emphasis on diversity and unpredictability is reminiscent of Glissant's work of the 1990s. Benítez-Rojo, however, is more concerned than Glissant is, at least in his later texts, to find in the Caribbean chaos underlying common factors—however subtle or evanescent—that would allow the area to lay claim to a certain cultural specificity.[8]

Relation has a further major significance in that all of its features oppose it to the notion of "essence." To exist "in relation" is to be an element of an ever-changing and ever-diversifying process and to be nothing over and above this: in other words, to lack any permanent, singular, autonomously constituted essence. The cryptically titled "Ce qu'étant ce que n'est" [That which being that which is not] section in *Poétique de la relation* makes this point (199–202), but *Le discours antillais* situates it in a more concretely historical context, linking it to the experience of transportation from Africa to the Caribbean: "There is a difference between the transplanting (by exile or dispersion) of a people who continue to survive elsewhere and the transfer (by the slave trade) of a population to another place where they change into something different, into a new set of possibilities" (*CD*, 14). That is, transportation causes such a violent, fundamental break in experience and sense of identity that it destroys the idealist conception of being as permanent essence.[9] As Glissant writes in the earlier *L'intention poétique,* "We were not born; we were deported from East to West. A sailor's knife cut the umbilical cord. Slave fetters staunched the blood. There is no essence here, but only perdition" (191).

But this "perdition" has the positive consequence of opening up the possibility of Relation instead of essence; Glissant distinguishes between "a people that survives elsewhere, *that maintains its [essence],* and a population that is transformed elsewhere *into another people* . . . and that thus enters the constantly shifting and variable process of [Relation]" (*CD*, 15). Essence is revealed as complicit with the coercive universalism of the West. So, too, is the correlative notion of origin. The slaves in the Americas are irremediably cut off from their historical origins in Africa; for them, identity cannot stem from a secure knowledge of one's origin.[10] This idea is developed in *Poétique de la relation* via an opposition between *étendue* and filiation, in which, particularly in the Caribbean, the "space" of Relation has supplanted the linear timespan of filiation—that is, legitimacy established by tracing one's origin back through a chain of ancestors. Caribbean societies with their extremely mixed and disrupted populations do not subscribe to the "hidden violence" of filiation. But, equally, the preeminence of Relation is now spreading to the rest of the world as the old violence of filiation is being swept aside by a new kind of "anarchical violence arising from the clash of cultures, in which . . . legitimacy . . . disintegrates" (*PR*, 73–74).

Thus, the Caribbean is, in a sense, an exemplary case of a phenomenon that Glissant believes is now becoming the general condition of global society, as the "periphery," which has been so profoundly changed by colonialism, now in turn causes an equally profound change in the metropolitan "center." Eventually, Caribbean Creole may even be seen as exemplary of contemporary language in general. Creole is "variable," with no fixed form or essence. Moreover, since it arose out of the contact between different, fragmented language communities, it has no singular, "organic" origin but is instead "organically linked to the worldwide experience of Relation. It is literally the result of links between different cultures and did not preexist these links. It is not a language of essence, it is a language of the Related" (*DA*, 241).

As this implies, there is a logical connection between, on the one hand, the rejection of the Western values of origin and filiation and, on the other, the positive value attached to mixed, composite cultures. That is, Relation not only celebrates the diversity of the world's cultures but also places a particular value on the *internal* diversity of those societies that include a number of different ethnic communities, such as the Caribbean ("What is the Caribbean in fact? A multiple series of relationships," *CD,* 139). This is *métissage,* the mixture of races and cultures that sweeps away notions of racial purity and singular origin, and of which Glissant writes that "the poetics of *métissage* is the poetics of Relation" (*DA,* 251). Hybridity, the English-language equivalent, has been theorized in similar terms by other Caribbean writers, such as Wilson Harris and Edward Brathwaite. In reference to these writers, the authors of *The Empire Writes Back* present hybridity in terms of the privileging of "space" over "history, ancestry and the past," thus echoing exactly Glissant's opposition between *étendue* and filiation.[11]

The value of hybridity is a constant throughout Glissant's work, from *L'intention poétique* to his most recent writings. In an article on Caribbean societies written for the *Courrier de l'UNESCO* in 1981, for instance, Glissant restates his claim that the hybrid and composite nature of these societies makes them an almost "organic" case of Relation.[12] In his more recent texts, he has identified a kind of extreme degree of hybridity: creolization. This is hybridity as a self-conscious, general *principle* extended to human society in general and generating the same kind of dynamic multiplicity that characterizes the chaos-world. It is "hybridity without limits, hybridity whose elements are multiplied, and whose end-results are impossible to foresee" (*PR,* 46). *Introduction à une poétique du divers* reiterates this distinction between simple hybridity and creolization on the grounds of the latter's *unpredictability* (37). Benítez-Rojo's "repeating island" resonates with creolization, too: he writes of "an island that proliferates endlessly, founding and refounding ethnological materials."[13]

In a 1993 lecture, Glissant stresses even more explicitly creolization's opposition to essence: what it teaches us is above all that "Creolization is unpredictable, it cannot solidify, become static, be fixed in essences or absolutes of identity." Thus, identities and differences are always in process. Expressing much the same idea, Homi Bhabha writes, "The representation of difference must not be hastily read as the reflection of *pre-given* ethnic or cultural traits set in the fixed tablet of tradition. The social articulation of difference, from the minority perspective, is a complex, on-going negotiation that seeks to authorize cultural hybridities that emerge in moments of historical transformation."[14]

But perhaps the most significant aspect of hybridity lies in the way it redefines the relation to the Other. If contemporary social reality is hybrid in its very principle, then identity ("the Same") is never pure, and *neither is otherness.* The Other is never absolutely other. Pure otherness is a fantasy, which Glissant identifies as the basis of exoticism. Writing on Victor Segalen, for instance, in *L'intention poétique,* he argues that Segalen's wish to lose himself in a completely alien culture was a kind of bad faith; the fantasy of absolute otherness absolves him of the responsibility of examining his position in relation to it—of becoming aware of his own positionality as investigative subject, to use Gayatri Spivak's formula.[15] In reality, however, "the Diverse is given to everyone only as a relation, not as an absolute power or a unique possession." That is, otherness is relative because the relation to the Other is always, precisely, a *relation,* and "the Other is in me, because I am me. Equally, the I from whom the Other is absent (abstracted) perishes" (*IP,* 101). The same idea is reiterated in *Poétique de la relation* with a more concrete emphasis on the sociohistorical realities that have shaped it: "We 'know' that the Other is in us and has an impact not only on our development but also on most of our ideas and on the movement of our sensibility. Rimbaud's 'Je est un autre' ['I is an other'] is historically quite literally true. A sort of 'consciousness of consciousness' opens us up in spite of ourselves and makes of each of us the bewildered actor of the poetics of Relation" (39). Thus, even that most fervently ideological of colonizers, the famous seventeenth-century missionary Père Labat, wrote about his slaves with fear and repulsion but *also* with an embryonic, barely conscious sense of complicity: the history of missionaries' contact with the slaves was of course one of conflict, but it was also "a slow process of hybridization, involuntary or deliberate" (*PR,* 81).

Hybridity in turn leads to a conception of *identity*—individual or collective—that is radically different from that of traditional Western humanism. The static polarity of same and other gives way, in Relation, to a situation in which identity exists only as a shifting term in a network of multiple relations with the Others who constitute it. Glissant defines it as a *questioning* identity, in which it is the relation to the Other that determines the self, but in an open-ended way (*CD,* 169). It is based in interdependence rather than independence (*PR,* 157); hybridity, creolization, and the rhizome all reinforce this implication. Thus, creolization makes our identities dependent on all the possible "mutual mutations generated by this play of relations" (*PR,* 103). In similar fashion, the distinction between root and rhizome is exploited to recast identity in the terms of Relation (*PR,* 31). The section "Les écarts déterminants" [The determining distances] in *Poétique de la relation* systematically contrasts a list of features of "l'identité-racine" [root-identity] and "l'identité-rela-tion" [relation-identity] (157–58), and the rhizome becomes a figure for identity in creolized culture. As Glissant writes in *Introduction à une po-étique du divers,* it is to be seen "no longer as a single root but as a root reaching out to meet other roots" (23). The notion of identity as "root," based on a singular autonomous origin, has been the subject of numer-ous critiques in the context of poststructuralist thought in general, and this background informs Spivak's work on colonial and neocolonial ide-ology. What Glissant calls the "root-identity" is in Spivak's terms an ide-ological justification for a neocolonialist nationalism that serves the in-terests of a new indigenous ruling elite and deprives the rest of the society of a political voice, and it is in this context that she explores the problem of "subaltern" consciousness.[16] Glissant's position, especially as expressed in *Introduction à une poétique du divers,* is even more ex-treme: the conception of root-identity is held almost solely responsible for the genocides in Rwanda and Bosnia (96).[17]

    The humanist conception of identity also allows it to incorporate "naturally" a spontaneous and authentic language, which expresses it and forms an important element in its constitution. This simple equation between language and identity is contested by Glissant's "counter-poetics" and also by Spivak, who says, for instance, "One needs to be vigilant against simple notions of identity which overlap neatly with lan-guage or location." Derrida, too, shows how the position of those who cannot fully identify with any language, like himself as a colonial French Jew from Algeria, reveals the oppression inherent in the idealizing of the "mother tongue": "That was my culture, it taught me the disasters into which men can be plunged by an incantatory appeal to the mother tongue. Right from the start my culture was a political culture."[18]

Relation as a whole is also intimately connected to another of Glissant's main theoretical concepts: "opacity." Respect for the Other includes re-spect for the "opacity" of the Other's difference, which resists one's at-tempts to assimilate or objectify it. "The poetics of relation presuppose that each of us encounters the density (the opacity) of the Other. The more the Other resists in his thickness or his fluidity (without restricting himself to this), the more expressive his reality becomes, and the more fruitful the relation becomes" (*IP,* 24). Relation thus safeguards the Other's difference; it is "the welcome opaqueness, through which the other escapes me" (*CD*, 162). Therefore, just as I cannot reduce the Other to my norms, nor conversely can I *become* the Other, in the kind of exoticizing identification that Glissant attributes to Segalen (of whom he writes that "personally I believe he died of the Other's opacity," *PR*, 208).

Accepting the Other's opacity means also accepting that there are no truths that apply universally or permanently.[19] Relation and opacity work together to resist the reductiveness of humanism. *Le discours antillais* speaks of the need "to develop everywhere, in defiance of a universalizing and reductive humanism, the theory of specifically opaque structures. In the world of [Relation], which takes over from the homogeneity of [essence], to accept this opaqueness—that is, the irreducible density of the other—is to truly accomplish, through diversity, a human objective. Humanity is perhaps not the 'image of man' but today the evergrowing network of recognized opaque structures" (*CD*, 133). In this sense opacity becomes a *militant* position, so that Glissant can state unequivocally, "We must fight against transparence everywhere" (*DA*, 356), and claim that opacity is a right: "We demand for all the right to opacity" (*PR*, 209). Finally, on the last page of *Le discours antillais*, he equates opacity simply with freedom: "their [opacity], which is nothing, after all, but their freedom" (*CD*, 256).

More controversially, opacity is also a defense against *understanding*, at least in the hierarchical, objectifying way in which this usually operates between the West and the Third World—illustrated, for instance, in Benítez-Rojo's sardonic description of the mechanism whereby Western readings of the Caribbean project onto it "dogmas and methods" that are relevant only to Western societies, and so "they get into the habit of defining the Caribbean in terms of its resistance to the different methodologies summoned to investigate it."[20] The right to opacity, which Glissant claims is more fundamental than the right to difference (*PR*, 204–5), is a right *not to be understood*. In this section (entitled "Pour l'opacité" [For opacity]) of *Poétique de la relation*, he writes: "If we look at the process of 'understanding' beings and ideas as it operates in western society, we find that it is founded on an insistence on this kind of transparency. In order to 'understand' and therefore accept you, I must reduce your density to this scale of conceptual measurement which gives me a basis for comparisons and perhaps for judgements" (204). In other words, understanding appears as an act of aggression because it constructs the Other as an *object* of knowledge. In the etymology of the verb "comprendre" [to understand; the root of which, *prendre*, means to take], Glissant discerns a gesture of "taking" the world and bringing it back to oneself: "A gesture of enclosure if not of appropriation" (206).[21]

Spivak's term for this is "epistemic violence." She argues that it not only characterizes the imperialist project but also continues to operate in postcolonial societies to exclude and silence subaltern groups, that is, those outside the new bourgeois nationalist ruling class. Her question— "on the other side of the international division of labour from socialized capital, inside *and* outside the circuits of the epistemic violence of imperialist law and education supplementing an earlier economic text, *can the subaltern speak?*"—receives a largely negative answer: the subaltern cannot "speak" in the sense of directly and unproblematically making his or her voice heard within the dominant social discourse.[22] Thus, for Spivak as for Glissant, subaltern consciousness is opaque in that it cannot be "read" by the ruling groups. But whereas Glissant interprets this as a form of resistance, for Spivak it is merely a form of disempowerment. However, this contrast is in turn complicated by Glissant's equally strong sense of the difficult relationship the subaltern has with language per se—the "lack" of language considered in my next chapter—which can be seen as another formulation of the subaltern's inability to speak and one that is closer, although not identical, to Spivak's. But he also posits a dynamic relationship between the lack of language, as a passively determined condition, and opacity as an active strategy of resistance—a strategy that assumes lack and transforms it into a positive force (in ways that are discussed in chapter 2). This can be translated into Spivak's terms as follows: the subaltern's exclusion does not cause any problems for the dominant discourse as long as it remains invisible to that discourse, but if it can be made visible *as exclusion*, it will constitute a locus of resistance to the discourse's appropriation of it; it will become opaque, in Glissant's sense. Indeed, some of Spivak's own analyses of particular cases show this process in operation and thus counteract the impression of total powerlessness that her general formulations sometimes give.[23] Even so, Glissant's opacity is still a far more active, positive form of resistance than Spivak's theorization allows for. To sum up the difference simply, Spivak focuses more on the subaltern's inability to "speak" the dominant discourse whereas Glissant focuses more on the dominant discourse's inability to "understand" the subaltern.

Thus, Glissant's initially surprising idea that a relationship of not only respect, but also solidarity and affection, is possible and better without "understanding" the other (*PR,* 207) has wide implications for literature as well as for social existence. In his reading of the novels of William

Faulkner, for instance, he notes that the black characters are only ever represented from the outside; they are given no interior monologue, and their actions do not even seem coherent (*IP*, 169–70). But this, he argues, is precisely why the portrayals are valuable. In the first place, they are evidence of the author's honesty in recognizing the limits of his own understanding and "dramatically taking on board the Other's *opacity* to oneself" (169). More importantly, Faulkner's blind spot locates and reveals the "real density" (170) of the black Other's presence as it resists assimilation and confronts him with a barrier that he will never cross: "In other words, Faulkner's inability to delineate this character is *positive*" (170). This accords with Spivak's idea that one cannot retrieve the lost consciousness of the subaltern and also with her use of Pierre Macherey's claim that "what the work cannot say"—its blind spots, in other words—may be more significant than what it does say.[24]

Glissant even applies this principle of nonunderstanding to understanding of oneself—with further repercussions on the reworking of the notion of identity discussed above. Opacity means also that parts of myself are obscure and incomprehensible to me; accepting this fact means that I can give up the insistence on the transparent *unity* of the whole self—this, Glissant argues, is a liberating experience.[25]

As a strategy of protection, opacity sometimes takes the form of simple concealment: hiding from the oppressive Other. Thus, one image for it is the forest into which the slaves escaped and where the maroon communities lived, and which was "the first obstacle the slave opposed to the *transparency* of the planter" (*CD*, 83). But the forest is disappearing, and its loss is symbolically as well as literally destructive. In *Malemort* Glissant writes of "the vast leprosy of erosion of deforestation eating away at the great mountain wringing your heart with all the present woes and all the woes that are still to come" (179). The forest provided invisibility, in other words, but is no longer an adequate metaphor for opacity; the concept of opacity in general is part of a far more complex structure of seen and unseen, seeing and not seeing, that determines the relations between "discoverer" and "discovered."

In the first place, the colonizer's power obviously depends to a large extent on *surveillance*. He cannot control what he cannot see.[26] In *Le quatrième siècle*, the newly arrived slave "learned right from the first day that the master only really existed when he was looking at you; despite the permanent fear and the leaden hand that seemed to keep you forever down in the mud; that the master lost some of his power when he had turned his back on you, as though he could command only by imposing the flux of his gaze, which dried up as soon as he turned away from you" (79). But, as the immediate, face-to-face nature of this encounter implies, the master's power depends also on the slave seeing that the master sees him; that is, the colonizers exercise their domination not only by seeing but by being seen, and by being seen to be powerful. And, since the masters were heavily outnumbered by the slaves, it was the *individual* figure of the master that had to inspire fear and obedience. As Fanon puts it, the master had to be an exhibitionist: "The settler pits brute force against the weight of numbers. He is an exhibitionist. His preoccupation with security makes him remind the native [*colonisé*] out loud that there he alone is master." The extraordinary ostentation and visual extravagance of colonial life (in clothes, architecture, etc.) in the period of slavery was a strategy of intimidation; as Roger Toumson writes, "The system of terror calls for a system of sumptuous extravagance."[27]

But the relationship between colonial master and slave is not limited to a purely rational exercise of power. It is widely recognized (since Joseph Conrad's *The Heart of Darkness,* if not before) to include also a dimension of unconscious desire and fear. Similarly, in "Poetics and the Unconscious" Glissant makes it clear that opacity is not simply a practical, rational strategy on the part of the colonized, but a constituent of their collective unconscious (*CD*, 159). It is thus not surprising that the interchangeability of the two forms of power—that is, surveillance and intimidation, seeing and being seen—and the ease with which one crosses over into the other are also reminiscent of the reversibility of the psychic drives analyzed by Sigmund Freud. Indeed, one of Freud's main examples is the relation between voyeurism and exhibitionism, the two closely connected variants of the scopic drive. Sight and visibility, in the colonial relationship, relate to a domination that goes beyond conscious, rational concerns of imposing or eluding control and includes a strong element of unconscious fantasy. Power and pleasure merge together, in the way outlined by Bhabha in his analysis of "the peculiar visibility of the nature of colonial power," to result in a form of exhibitionism that exceeds the narrowly practical aim of imposing control. Significantly, it is this exhibitionism, rather than the colonizer's powers of surveillance, as common sense might dictate, that is given in "Poetics and the Unconscious" as the reason for the colonized subject's desire for opacity. This desire is provoked not by the *gaze* of the master but by the exaggerated "transparent" *visibility* of his presence—not the master as all-seeing, but the master as seen: "The only source of light ultimately was that of the transcendental presence of the Other, of his Visibility—colonizer or administrator—of his transparency fatally proposed as a model, because of which we have acquired a taste for obscurity, and for me the need to seek out [opacity]" (*CD*, 161).[28]

The oppression inherent in the master's gaze is repeated in that of historically later types of "discoverer," such as the ethnologists for whom the colonized peoples are merely visible objects of knowledge. But it is significant that, in his discussion of this relationship in *L'intention poétique*, Glissant states that the colonial subject's desire is not to escape the master's gaze, but to participate in the scopic *exchange* on equal terms. He writes, "We hate ethnography. . . . The distrust that we feel toward it is not caused by our displeasure at being looked at, but rather *by our obscure resentment at not having our turn at seeing*" (128, emphasis added). The problem is, in other words, the inequality and lack of reciprocity of the relation, in which those who are seen cannot themselves "see" those who see them.

Pursuing the psychoanalytic dimension of the colonial relationship—that is, its imbrication, alongside political and economic motivations, in unconscious fantasy and desire—reveals a further sense in which opacity resists the domination of the discoverers. This depends upon Bhabha's analysis—already suggested in the work of Fritz Gracchus—of the racist stereotype as *fetish*. Bhabha argues that the stereotype is the result of a complex unconscious dynamic, which derives from the *ambivalence* at the root of all colonial power: both civilizing mission and violent subjugation. Thus, the stereotype is "the primary point of subjectification in colonial discourse, for both the colonizer and the colonized." He notes the irrational, compulsive, and ever-renewable quality of racial stereotypes and sees them as the product of the same mechanism of *disavowal* that Freud defined in relation to the sexual fetish. That is, just as the fetish is a defense against the anxiety aroused by the man's knowledge of sexual difference, the racial stereotype represents an attempt to disavow racial difference insofar as this poses a threat to the white person's own sense of identity. Bhabha argues that the racist stereotype in fact exists to *reduce* racial otherness—that is, to reduce its power to challenge the legitimacy of the "civilizing mission"—by containing it in fixed and controllable forms. But this fixity is never fully achieved, because disavowal, in its constant oscillation between two contradictory beliefs, always reactivates the knowledge, and hence the anxiety, that it is trying to suppress. The production of stereotypes is thus a never-ending process: "the process by which the metaphoric 'masking' is inscribed on a lack which must then be concealed, that gives the stereotype both its fixity and its phantasmatic qualities—the same old stories of the negro's animality, the coolie's inscrutability or the stupidity of the Irish which *must* be told (compulsively) again and afresh, and are differently gratifying and terrifying each time." The same instability inherent in disavowal accounts for the subject's *ambivalence* toward the fetish, which according to Freud is as much an object of aggression as of love. Similarly, racist stereotypes cover a wide range, "from the loyal servant to Satan," as Bhabha puts it, and are as often patronizingly affectionate as they are overtly hostile.[29]

The phantasmatic nature of the racist stereotype, its ambivalence, and its compulsive, unstoppable dynamic mean that it cannot be countered by logical argument or empirical experience—or by simply replacing a negative image with a positive one. (Thus, the Martinican René Ménil writes: "We are not 'the opposite' of our colonial image, we are *other* than that image.") Nor is there any escape from it: Bhabha notes that the main difference between sexual fetishism and the racial stereotype is that the former is secret while the latter, marked by skin color, is totally visible. It is here that the strategy of opacity becomes relevant, because if Bhabha's analysis is correct, then opacity provides the only possible mode of resistance to the stereotype. That is, it confronts the stereotype's attempt to fix racial difference with a self-representation that cannot be fixed because it is deliberately unintelligible. We have seen the results of this in Faulkner's opaque representation of the black characters in his novels—where, moreover, Bhabha's claim regarding the *fear* of racial difference generating the stereotype is closely echoed in Glissant's description of the effect of the countervailing opacity: "But this opacity is terrifying, and it is impossible for America to wish to recognize it as its own: it would be to admit to a fundamental barrier: to come face to face with one of the doors opening onto savagery" (*IP*, 170). Opacity, then, transforms the status of the colonized subject's visibility from a source of vulnerability—the kind of vulnerability to which Fanon refers when he writes that "the black man has no ontological resistance in the eyes of the white man"—to the active production of a visible but *unreadable* image.[30]

There is also another sense in which opacity, at least as far as Martinique is concerned, cannot be reduced to simple invisibility or concealment. In *Le discours antillais* Glissant makes an important distinction between those colonies that have a "hinterland" and those that do not (*CD*, 102–4). In its literal, geographical sense, the absence of a hinterland in the tiny island of Martinique made it more difficult for the slaves to escape and for the maroon communities to survive on the scale that they did, for instance, in Jamaica or Haiti. But there is also no *historical* "hinterland" in Martinique or in any community whose population was transported: that is, there is no indigenous culture into which the colonized people can retreat, as they could in colonial India or Africa. In this situation, opacity cannot mean simply hiding, because there is—culturally as well as literally—nowhere to hide. Opacity therefore has to be produced as an *unintelligible* presence from within the *visible* presence of the colonized.

The most crucial dimension of this cultural hinterland is language. In colonies where there were indigenous languages that the colonizers could not understand, these provided a "naturally" opaque protection for the colonized. In the Caribbean, however, the only available language was Creole, and it was equally available to both master and slave. It therefore became a question, for the slaves, of developing within the common language strategies for nevertheless eluding the master's comprehension. They gradually formed a particular usage of Creole, which the master did not understand but did not realize that he did not understand.[31] Camouflage is inherent in the basic structure of the language. An emphasis on loudness and a jerky, accelerated delivery that appears to be meaningless or even nonsensical in fact serves to communicate, secretly, the real meaning: "Creole is originally a kind of conspiracy that concealed itself by its public and open expression. . . . this form of nonsense . . . could conceal and reveal at the same time a *hidden* meaning" (*CD*, 124–25). The relation to the Other here consists of outwitting him and protecting oneself from him by secrecy and cunning—Glissant lists "the ruses of creole" (*DA*, 235). Creole thus developed as a subversive language whose purpose from the start was not simply to communicate but also to conceal its meanings, thereby turning the master's language against him. In this sense it is a typical form of opacity.

Because of these same features, however, Creole is also an important example of the *detour*, which is another of Glissant's major theoretical concepts. In many of its manifestations, the detour overlaps with opacity, but whereas opacity is above all an ethical value and a political right, the detour is more tactical and ambiguous. It is essentially an indirect mode of resistance that "gets around" obstacles rather than confronting them head on, and it arises as a response to a situation of disguised rather than overt oppression and struggle. Glissant argues that the real power behind the oppression of the Martinicans has never been the settlers in the island, who with the collapse of the sugarcane market soon lost all economic power and became economically and politically dependent on metropolitan France, but the French government itself: "[The detour] is the ultimate resort of a population whose domination by an Other is concealed: it then must search *elsewhere* for the principle of domination, which is not evident in the country itself: because the system of domination . . . is not directly tangible. [The Detour] is the parallactic displacement of this strategy" (*CD*, 20). If the enemy cannot be attacked directly, the confusion is such that opposition is not coherent and organized; it is not even entirely conscious. Thus, the detour is itself marked with the alienation it is trying to combat. It is both an evasion of the real situation and an obstinate effort to find a way round it.

In the case of Creole this ambiguity has very specific and concrete effects on its structure and usage. As the vernacular language of the island, it is a principal site of resistance. But it has no autonomous origin; unlike the "primordial" languages of Africa, it was constructed out of the unequal, conflictual relation with the colonial language. "Creole is also a concession made by the Other for his own purposes in his dealings with our world. We have seized this concession to use it for our own purposes . . . but having seized it does not make it into a means of self-expression" (*CD*, 166–67). And Glissant claims that the origin of Creole—as the language of the master's command and power as much as of the slave's struggle and identity—has marked its very structures. Thus, for instance, many of its particular strategies for concealing its meanings from the *békés* [the white inhabitants of the island, descendants of the original settler community] depend upon exploiting the image that the latter have of it. Since they see it as simplistic and infantile, picturesque but incapable of expressing rational abstract thought, these are the features that it will deliberately exaggerate and use as camouflage. In "a systematic process of derision: the slave takes possession of the language imposed by his master, a simplified language . . . and makes this simplification even more extreme. You wish to reduce me to a childish babble, I will make this babble systematic, we shall see if you can make sense of it" (*CD*, 20).[32] Equally, other characteristic features of Creole, such as the importance of sound and rhythm or the use of concrete images rather than abstract concepts, are not innocent or natural but deliberate and constrained reactions to the white Other and his language (*CD*, 126). On the basis of all these limitations, alienations, and distortions, however, the "ruses" of Creole are nevertheless effective; the language functions through its pervasive ambiguities, simultaneously expressing and hiding its meanings, so that "one never knows if this speech, while delivering one meaning, is not at the same time being elaborated precisely in order to hide another one. . . . In other words, if it is a case of speech as message or, at the same time, speech as screen" (*DA*, 355).

This two-edged quality is fundamental to the detour in all its manifestations, linguistic or otherwise. It may take the form of popular religion (*CD*, 22), emigration (*CD*, 22–23), or "marronnage" (*PR*, 83), or something else. It also covers the actions of Caribbean intellectuals and political activists who react to the impossible situation in their own islands by carrying on their political work elsewhere: Marcus Garvey, George Padmore, and above all Fanon, who for Glissant is the most significant example—"a grand and intoxicating" detour (*CD*, 25). All these phenomena have in common the fact that in them the borderline between blind, compulsive reaction and clever ruse becomes blurred. Spivak's central contestation of the "heroic" *knowing* proletarian subject and her counterclaim "that the subaltern's own idiom did not allow him to *know* his struggle so that he could articulate himself as its subject" is relevant here. The detour is not a freely chosen, rationally planned autonomous act of opposition, but neither is it simply an evasion. In an interview given on the publication of *Le discours antillais*, Glissant stressed that "the use of the Detour does not in any sense mean an escape from reality. In the Caribbean, one of the traditional forces of opposition in complicated situations is the ruse."[33] *Le discours antillais* itself states that "no, it is not . . . a conscious strategy of flight in the face of reality," but a few lines further on adds: "Its deception [ruse] is not therefore systematic. . . . It is an 'attitude of collective release' [*échappement*] (Marcuse)" (*CD*, 19, 20). This apparent contradiction is better seen as an indication of the irreducibly ambiguous nature of the detour—the result of an "entanglement of negativities accepted as such"—in which it is not possible to make a clear-cut distinction between active and passive, choice and constraint, or even victory and defeat. Madness, for instance, in the form of delirious speech, becomes a tactic of survival (*CD*, 19, 129).

A similar emphasis on the ambiguous and reactive nature of opposition occurs in other representations and analyses of French Caribbean society. The introduction to Mireille Rosello's *Littérature et identité aux Antilles*, for example, develops the implications of the "entanglement of negativities" in terms of the difficulty of judging the effectiveness of such ad hoc, alienated, and compromised modes of struggle. This problematic, insofar as it affects writers, is the central theme of her book. Rosello asks, "which are the oppositional tactics that risk sabotaging completely the attempt at change because they are too similar to the means used by the established power?" but also demonstrates the efficacy, in certain situations, of "mimetic opposition," arguing that "by taking over the enemy's prejudices and using them for their own ends the Caribbean people have sometimes succeeded not only in exposing the contradictions of the system which oppressed them, but also in making themselves heard in a context in which their voice had been outlawed."[34]

Rosello uses Michel de Certeau's concept of *la tactique* to explore these complex modes of action and reaction, and although she does not explicitly make the connection, the similarity with Glissant's detour is very striking. De Certeau's "tactic" operates where no autonomous basis for action exists: "The tactic has no place other than the place occupied by the other. It insinuates itself there, in a fragmentary fashion, without taking it over entirely, and without being able to keep it at a distance."[35] Rosello comments further, in a sense similar to Glissant's definition of the detour in *Le discours antillais,* that the tactic "is in fact a form of struggle appropriate to a specific situation in which there is not an overt struggle between two factions each of which aims to take power, but rather a (suppressed) opposition on the part of those who are suffering from the established order." Unable to overturn the relations of oppression, it aims to destabilize them and to turn the master-slave opposition into "an unbalanced situation, never static, always in the process of being redefined."[36]

Equally, just as the nature of the detour makes it inherently difficult to determine what counts as success or failure, liberation or constraint, so too the tactic will often seem ineffective or absurd because we are unable to see "what the notion of strategy can become when there is no longer any difference between passivity and struggle, courage and submission, rebellion and suicide, suicide and fight to the death." Rosello develops this ambivalence into a critique of heroism and martyrdom, arguing for the unobtrusive ruses of survival shown in, for instance, Simone Schwarz-Bart's *Pluie et vent sur Télumée miracle* as against the glorious but damaging martyrdom promoted by Aimé Césaire's *Et les chiens se taisaient.* As these two examples suggest, the detour-tactic also redefines the significance of women's role in the liberation struggle, as physical strength and direct confrontation become less important than the traditionally "feminine" tactics of ruse and indirectness. In fact, Glissant has expressed the view that Caribbean women are better able to deal with the obscured, camouflaged reality of the society than are the men. (Historically, some of the most successful campaigns against the plantation owners were based on poisoning carried out by the mainly female cooks in the masters' kitchens.) Thus, Rosello stresses the importance of women writers and female heroines. But she also uses Glissant's novels as examples of the deconstruction of the opposition between heroic maroons and cowardly slaves. His undermining of the myth of (largely male) heroism, which other critics have also commented on, is perhaps more evident in his later fiction but can be seen as rooted in the concept of the detour.[37]

Moving beyond the French islands, we can find a related sense of the detour or diversion as a typically Caribbean tactic in a further development of Benítez-Rojo's "chaos." He contrasts it with the notion of apocalypse and contextualizes the contrast in terms of Cuban responses to the exemplarily apocalyptic moment of the 1962 missile crisis. The section of *The Repeating Island* entitled "From the apocalypse to chaos" describes how the Cubans themselves defused the apocalypse simply by refusing to see it as such and by dissolving it, so to speak, into the low-key unheroic rhythms of detour and accommodation. Benítez-Rojo comments, "The choices of all or nothing, for or against, honor or blood have little to do with the culture of the Caribbean." Stark choices and heroic stances cannot survive in the Caribbean, which he argues is the ambiguous realm "of waves, of folds and double-folds, of fluidity and sinuosity. It is . . . a chaos that returns, a detour without a purpose, a continual flow of paradoxes; it is a feed-back machine with asymmetrical workings." All of these emphases—folds, fluidity, sinuosity, etc.—are equally characteristic of Glissant's detour. But Benítez-Rojo's version is far less constrained and far more optimistic; it works, ultimately, to sublimate and defuse *social violence*—hence the rituals of carnival, for instance, are an exorcism of the violence arising from inequality and oppression.[38] Glissant's detour, on the other hand, while certainly an attempt to deflect or evade social violence, would not claim to be transforming it into something else.

As we have seen, the Creole language is a major form of detour. More generally, Martinican attitudes to language per se are, according to Glissant, characterized by a similar combination of constraint, ruse, confusion, and indirectness. French, imposed by the colonizers, still remains a source of hostility and insecurity; it does not fulfill the need for an adequate language that the speaker can "naturally" identify with. But— and here Glissant disagrees fundamentally with *créolistes* such as Chamoiseau and Confiant—*nor does Creole*. This is partly for the historical reasons discussed above: Creole was never the slaves' own, autonomous language, and Glissant states unequivocally: "Creole was not, in some idyllic past, and is not yet our national language." Those who claim that it is, he argues, are evading the issue of the Martinicans' ambiguous and problematic relation to language and hence, also, to themselves (*CD*, 167).[39] But an equally weighty reason is Creole's present-day marginality as a means of communication, which he attributes to economic factors. The plantation system was not succeeded by any autonomous economic production in Martinique, in which Creole would have remained and been consolidated as the natural means of communication through which the production was carried out. Instead, an economy (or "pseudo-economy") based on metropolitan subsidies and service industries such as tourism can function only in French: "Creole cannot become the language of shopping malls, nor of luxury hotels. Cane, bananas, pineapples are the last vestiges of the Creole world. With them this language will disappear, if it does not become functional in some other way" (*CD*, 127).

Thus, he concludes, in "the French Lesser Antilles . . . the mother tongue, Creole, and the official language, French, both produce in the Caribbean mind an unsuspected source of anguish" (*CD*, 120). In other words, there is no existing viable language that can be unproblematically assumed as one's own. Here the distinction Glissant makes between *langue* and *langage* is important: "I call [*langage*] a shared attitude, in a given community, of confidence or mistrust in the [*langue* or *langues*] it uses" (*CD*, 120). *Langage*, in other words, is a collective subjective practice of and attitude to a *langue*; for the Martinican community, the relationship is a tense and ambivalent one.[40]

This idea is already present in *L'intention poétique*, but it is given a sharper focus in *Le discours antillais*.[41] The quotations in the preceding paragraph come from a section in *Le discours antillais* entitled "Natural Poetics, Forced Poetics," in which, having established the significance of *langage*, Glissant puts forward his notion of "counterpoetics" (which he also refers to as "anti-poetics," "forced poetics," "constrained poetics"). This is the strategy that comes into play when a harmonious practice of the *langue* is impossible: that is, an attempt to build a *langage* on the basis of an antagonistic or subversive relationship to the *langue*, which the subject nevertheless has to use. The Caribbean speaker has to "force his way through the *langue* toward a *langage* that may not be part of the internal logic of this *langue*. Forced poetics emerges from this opposition between a *langue* that one uses and a *langage* that one needs" (*DA*, 237).[42]

This opposition itself arises from a lack of social, and *hence* also verbal, autonomy.[43] Counterpoetics, Glissant claims, is the act of a community whose means of expression do not spring directly and spontaneously from its autonomous social agency: "Self-expression, a casualty of this lack of autonomy, is itself marked by a kind of impotence, a sense of futility" (*CD*, 121). It is, therefore, only a partial, temporary solution to a problem that ultimately requires profound sociopolitical change in Martinican life as a whole. It is a constrained and contradictory response to a constrained and contradictory social situation—which, Glissant suggests, is too tense to last forever (*CD*, 133–34).

Counterpoetics is thus a form of detour that relates to language used in cultural production—namely, writing but also the oral tradition of folktales and even the ambiguous kind of verbal performance he calls "routine verbal delirium" (*DA*, 363). It works toward the construction of a *langage* that, while in no sense *natural*, might be a more effective means of expression. It is thus a detour around the problem of the lack of a natural authentic language: that is, a compromise solution but simultaneously a critique of the supposed plenitude and immediacy associated with the notion of an authentic language.

The section on *langage* in "Poetics and the Unconscious" (*CD*, 166–69) places an even clearer emphasis on its strategic, "forced" construction by means of a counterpoetics that contests the French language from within. It is a question of "forg[ing] . . . based on the defective grasp of two [*langues*] whose control was never collectively mastered, a [*langage*]"—and the end of this sentence underlines the paradoxical combination of determination and indeterminacy that always characterizes the detour—"through which we could *consciously face our ambiguities* and *fix ourselves firmly in the uncertain possibilities* of the word made ours" (*CD*, 168, emphasis added).

It is a detour also in the sense that it acts with, and is constrained by, a constant awareness that it is in principle *impossible*. Glissant defines forced poetics as "any collective impulse toward a form of expression that, as it asserts itself, simultaneously confronts the *lack* that makes it impossible—not as impulse, which is always present, but as expression, which is never achieved. . . . Forced poetics can be found wherever a need for expression confronts something impossible to express" (*DA*, 236). *Le discours antillais* returns frequently to this idea of *lack* underlying the speaker's and writer's relationship to language; the counterpoetics is itself marked by the lack that it forces itself to find a way around.

It has, also, the same lack of lucidity and control as does the detour. In "Poetics and the unconscious" Glissant describes it as the repressed, subversive underside of everyday alienated speech, of which it is the "unconscious rhythm," expressing an "instinctive denial that has not yet been structured into a conscious and collective refusal" (CD, 163). However—and this is equally typical of the devious operation of the detour—the lack of conscious knowledge and control is itself a (different) kind of knowledge and efficacy. The counterpoetics of the Creole folktale, for instance, is "primarily locked into [the detour]—that is, into an *unconscious body of knowledge* through which the popular consciousness asserts both its rootlessness and its density" (CD, 132, emphasis added). The range of practices cited as examples of counterpoetics illustrates this ambiguous mixture of ruse and compulsiveness: from the lucidity of the novelist to the uncontrolled obsessions of verbal delirium. But Glissant is careful to stress how little separates these two activities: "It's the same struggle to clarify our collective memory . . . to embed our words in a shared poetics. Verbal delirium is a desperate reaching towards a syntax, an explanatory order, a relationship with the world. . . . Is that not also, apart from the despair, the status of the writer in our countries?"[44]

Moreover, counterpoetics sometimes succeeds in turning lack itself into a means of opposing the dominant language of the French other. "Poetics and the Unconscious" is based on the idea that the Martinican speaker is by definition "limited by a poetics that is incapable of *realizing* anything from a collective and time-honored body of knowledge. This poetics produces, on the contrary, in fits and starts a kind of [nonknowledge (*non-savoir*)] through which an attempt is made to deny the Other's total and corrosive hold. An anti- (or counter-) poetics" (CD, 159). In other words, the oppressor's power and knowledge are combatted not mimetically—with a countervailing but similar power and knowledge—but by an unconscious ruse that makes unconsciousness itself ("instinctive denial," "nonknowledge") into a form of subversive negativity. In this case, then, the detour does not use the adversary's weapons against him but unbalances him with something so radically different that it cannot be assimilated into his system of knowledge.

Here again a central example is the folktale, where, in what Glissant calls the "pathetic lucidity of the Creole speaker" (CD, 129), the community's material and social "lacks" are translated into a form of expression that makes of its own lack—of knowledge, of conceptual abstraction, formal eloquence, and ease—a derisive undermining of these very qualities. For instance, to convey the splendor and opulence of a castle solely by the bald statement that it has two hundred and ten toilets is to mock the value of splendor and the value of its conventional literary representation (*CD*, 131). The counterpoetics of the creole folktale is "a tense discourse that, woven around the inadequacies that afflict it [*tramant le manque dont elle pâtit*], is committed, in order to deny more defiantly the criteria for transcendence into writing, to constantly refusing to perfect its expression. The Creole folktale . . . fixes expression in the realm of the derisively aggressive" (*CD*, 129).

There are also simpler and more positive ways of attacking the French language, through parody and so on, and Glissant's own novels contain many examples of them. But he also analyzes, again in "Poetics and the Unconscious," one particularly concrete case of a collective subversion of French: bumper stickers warning "NE ROULEZ PAS TROP PRÈS" [DON'T DRIVE TOO CLOSE] were spontaneously transformed by literally cutting them up and rearranging the pieces into a number of creolized variants: "PAS ROULEZ TROP PRÈS," "PA ROULÉ TROP PRÉ," and even "ROULEZ PAPA" [GO, DADDY, GO!] (*CD*, 163–64). This, Glissant argues, illustrates all the features of counterpoetics: mocking the language that one nevertheless uses, transgressing its rules, subverting its original meaning, resisting an "order" from elsewhere, and beginning to form one's own "counterorder" (*CD*, 165).

Glissant's formulation of counterpoetics has similarities with the two concepts of abrogation and appropriation defined in *The Empire Writes Back* in relation to cultures that had English as the colonial language. There are two significant differences: abrogation and appropriation are "two distinct processes," in contrast to the contradictory unity of counterpoetics; and counterpoetics is the collective practice of a community and takes many different linguistic forms, whereas abrogation and appropriation are concerned only with literary language and the problematic situation of the individual writer in postcolonial society. But the basic sense of a conflictual yet necessary relationship to the colonial language is central to both formulations. Abrogation is the act of breaking away from the language, and also from the aesthetic values and cultural norms, of the colonial power; it "involves a rejection of the metropolitan power over the means of communication." But abrogation on its own would merely lead to the attempt to replace the prestige and power of the colonial language with that, newly created, of an indigenous language (in the non-Caribbean former colonies that have one).

Appropriation, the second phase in this dynamic, is "the process by which the language [i.e., of the centre] is taken and made to 'bear the burden' of one's own cultural experience, or, as Raja Rao puts it, to 'convey in a language that is not one's own the spirit that is one's own.'"[45] Ashcroft, Griffiths, and Tiffin see this being achieved, fairly simply, by infiltrating the dominant language with elements of local and vernacular speech patterns: for instance, standard English is "contaminated" with Indian languages, and a new Indian English results. Thus, taken in isolation, neither abrogation nor appropriation approaches the complexity or the power of Glissant's concept. Abrogation is simply the rejection of standard English, and appropriation is simply its adaptation to a specific colonial context (that nevertheless has the advantage of making it impossible to think of language in terms of purity or authenticity). But the fact that they operate together brings them closer to counterpoetics. *The Empire Writes Back*, for instance, describes the "gap between 'worlds', a gap in which the simultaneous processes of abrogation and appropriation continually strive to define and determine their practice"—reminding us of the "lack" underlying counterpoetics—and continues: "This literature is therefore always written out of the tension between the abrogation of the received English which speaks from the centre, and the act of appropriation which brings it under the influence of a vernacular tongue, the complex of speech habits which characterize the local language, or even the evolving and distinguishing local english of a monolingual society trying to establish its link with place." A comparison of the theorizations of this phenomenon in Glissant's works and *The Empire Writes Back* allows us to go beyond the Martinican context to see it as a feature of postcolonial societies in general and, at the same time, highlights the differences between these societies, in particular as regards the existence or lack of a viable indigenous language.[46]

The value of Glissant's concept of counterpoetics, however, is that it is not restricted to literary language, but is a collective response to the impossibility of a natural autonomous "own" language. As such, it is a strategy of both resistance and accommodation. It forges its own *langage* out of the tension of its relationship to the dominant language, which it simultaneously subverts and restructures. It can be seen at work in a variety of practices of language, some of which are represented in Glissant's novels; one such practice is, of course, the actual writing of those novels. Thus, both Glissant and his characters are engaged in counterpoetics; both of these levels of discourse are analyzed in subsequent chapters.

2 The Lack of Language

GLISSANT'S ANALYSIS of the Martinicans' relationship to language concludes that there is no given available language in which they can fully articulate their sense of themselves and their specific social and material reality. Counterpoetics arises as a response to this situation, where "a need for expression confronts something impossible to express" (*DA,* 236). In this chapter I examine the representations of this impossible situation in Glissant's novels. It generates a range of different strategic reactions—in both the writer and the fictional characters and discourses—which are discussed in subsequent chapters. But the basic initial predicament of a *lack* of language itself needs to be elucidated. Why is it that "the subaltern cannot speak"?

Language is an important dimension of Relation, and the novels return repeatedly to the theme of the Martinicans' "voice" failing to reach the outside world. Since they lack an effective language, Glissant's characters cannot make themselves heard. In *Malemort,* for instance, "nobody heard is there a place anywhere in the world where you can hear those who have no voice" (133). The collective narrator of *La case du commandeur* wonders "were we alive? No one trembled at our cries" (52). In *Le quatrième siècle* the reason given for the "death" of the people's speech is "because the world, to which they listened in desperation or resignation, had no ears for the absence of their voice" (305). The question of language thus rejoins the larger issue of the possibility of Relation, which depends upon the Other being able to hear, and agreeing to listen to, the subject's voice. For Mathieu in *Le quatrième siècle,* the importance of Papa Longoué's remembering and retelling their history (in this instance, the episode of the slave market) is not in order to accuse their enemies or to claim revenge but to *give themselves a voice*: "It seems to me a light would be lacking from the light all over the world if we didn't draw up the account of the market. . . . A voice would be missing in the sky and the light, that's why I'm here beside you in your silence: for the voice: not for the accusation suffering death" (67–68).

In *Le discours antillais* Glissant identifies two main causes of this lack of language: the community's history and its socioeconomic situation. Glissant argues that an economy run from and for metropolitan France undermines the Creole language: "With the disappearance first of the plantation system, then of the traditional crafts (coopers, tanners, cobblers, joiners, small shopkeepers, etc. . . .), with the decline of the 'basic' crafts (fishing, for example . . .), with the standardization of business . . . within the logic of this system Creole actually loses its *raison d'être*. . . . A language *in which* nothing is made any longer (so to speak) is a language under threat" (*DA*, 173–74). In other words, for Creole to survive in any real sense, it must be the language people use every day at work, rather than just possessing a cultural value as folklore—however energetically this may be encouraged. We find an echo of this in *La case du commandeur*, in connection with the loss of traditional local technical skills, marginalized by economic changes (162–63). The disappearance from everyday vocabulary of the names for these technical processes is a symptom of Martinique's acute lack of economic self-sufficiency. As if attempting to halt or compensate for the loss, Glissant then gives another list of the technical terms associated with the deserted sugar factory (*CC*, 164).[1]

In a similar fashion, the historical factors that have created the present language situation are evoked in the novels, particularly in *Le quatrième siècle*. The transported Africans arriving in Martinique had their own languages, but these could not survive for long the disintegration of the original communities and the new realities of their situation in Martinique. The old slave in *Le quatrième siècle*, for example, speaks to the newly arrived Béluse in their shared African language but has to revert to Creole to describe the features of their new situation (71). Longoué's learning Creole from Louise is an important part of his coming to terms with his new life on the island: "so he allowed her to give him something: the new way of speaking" (110).

Fragments of the African languages do survive, and they acquire a sacred, magic significance as part of the ritual of the *quimboiseur* [sorcerer]—which Liberté, for example, inherits from her father, reciting "the bits of words (*ni temenan kekodji konon*) that Melchior had taught her; the scattered traces of the language or rather languages that had condensed in the *Rose-Marie*'s hold and then evaporated in the wind here" (CC, 106). This is one aspect of a process that had begun much earlier; the very fact that African languages were gradually lost as a functional form of communication meant that they simultaneously acquired a quasi-ritual significance, becoming the symbols of an original identity and also a symbolic refusal of colonial reality. Thus, in the encounter between Longoué and the master from whom he escaped, Longoué speaks in the African language that he has not used for ten years (QS, 122–23); and when Aa, the equivalent maroon figure in *La case du commandeur*, is finally captured and tortured to death, he too defiantly speaks to his torturers in his African language (139–40). Thus, African languages remain important—and, indeed, become fetishized—as a kind of symbolic mother tongue, but since this symbolic prestige depends on their being incomprehensible, they cannot provide any real solution to the problem of expression and communication. Their value is rather that they constitute a version of opacity; indeed, Glissant suggests that his childhood experience of this kind of ritualistic language may have been the unconscious inspiration for his theorization of opacity in general.[2]

The slaves' loss of their mother tongue is then compounded by what Glissant calls the *mutisme* of slavery: "Slavery, a struggle with no witnesses," "the implacably silent [*muet*] world of slavery" (CD, 161). The muteness of slavery is in some sense the extreme case of what Spivak calls "the effaced itinerary of the subaltern subject," and it is equally an extreme version of epistemic violence—backed up by extreme physical violence.[3] Not only were the slaves often deliberately separated from others who spoke the same language, but the psychological shock of transportation reduced them to a silence that was then actively reinforced by their masters. Glissant links their muteness with their alienation from their bodies, which did not belong to them: "the alienated body of the slave, in the time of slavery, is in fact deprived, in an attempt at complete dispossession, of speech. Self-expression is not only forbidden, but impossible to envisage" (CD, 122).

This kind of muteness is not exactly the same phenomenon Spivak is concerned with. Her subaltern subject's inability to "speak" is a theoretical metaphor for a social position; it is not the *literal* silence of Glissant's slaves, and it does not have the same close relationship to the body. For example, we may compare the "historically muted subject of the subaltern woman" with the physically mute slave woman of *La case du commandeur*, who was raped and impregnated by sailors on the boat and killed her baby and then herself: she refused to learn Creole and never spoke (CC, 131–37).[4] The two are not identical. One could perhaps see Glissant's literally silent slave as a metaphor for Spivak's metaphorically silent subaltern. The disjunction of levels between theory and personal experience that this implies, however, has consequences that are relevant for the rest of this chapter. That is, the historical and economic determinants of the situation are on the whole less central to the novels' representation of the lack of language than the way in which this is *experienced* by speaking subjects—both individually and collectively. There is a difference of level or perspective between the theoretical analyses and the fictional mise-en-scène of this theme. *Le discours antillais* argues forcefully that the "lack" is not *inherent* in a certain people's use of language but is the consequence of the way that language is situated within a worldwide network of discourses of unequal power. Edward Said's analysis of the discourse of orientalism and its ability to impose silence on the object of its representation is illuminating here, insofar as it applies equally to the Caribbean colonies. Said speaks of "the muteness imposed upon the Orient as an object. . . . The Orient was therefore not Europe's interlocutor, but its silent Other." But the effectiveness of orientalism, its "sheer knitted-together strength," is inseparable from "its very close ties to the enabling socio-economic and political institutions" of European imperialism. It derives, in other words, from the relative positions of the two cultures, and "in a quite constant way, Orientalism depends for its strategy on this flexible *positional* superiority, which puts the Westerner in a whole series of possible relationships with the Orient without ever losing him the relative upper hand."[5]

Thus, the social, economic, and cultural structures that have caused the Martinicans' lack of language extend far beyond Martinique itself and involve the global context of colonialism; the "silence" imposed on Martinique results from its position in relation to other societies and not from its own intrinsic characteristics. Glissant's Relation, understood as a theoretical concept, also implies this. It implies, in other words, that the language situation in Martinique—the phenomenon of lack of language—is a consequence of Martinique's *exclusion* from active participation in, precisely, Relation as a global political reality. Relation itself theorizes the Martinicans' inability to enter into Relation. Therefore, the Martinicans' perception that they are cut off from Relation is not inaccurate; but the very fact that it is true means that they are also cut off from the "relational" or positional understanding of their particular situation that it could provide: namely, that their inability to "make their voice heard" is primarily a consequence, and only secondarily a cause, of their position in relation to the rest of the world.[6] That is, the analysis is not spontaneously evident to the speaking subject who experiences the lack.

On this theoretical level, Spivak's conception of subalternity is entirely relevant. Exclusion from Relation can be seen as exactly the condition of the subaltern, who is excluded from the discursive construction of history as narrative: "The ways in which history has been narrativised always secure a certain kind of subject position which is predicated on marginalising certain areas. The importance of deconstruction is its interest in such strategic exclusions"; "the subaltern is necessarily the absolute limit of the place where history is narrativised into logic." The result of this exclusion, similarly, is that the subaltern cannot *know* his or her conditions. Glissant's novels, like the stories of Mahasweta Devi that Spivak praises, exemplify this representation of subaltern consciousness in which "the development of character or the understanding of subjectivity as growth in consciousness is beside the point"; one thinks especially, perhaps, of the fractured, alienated subjectivity of Dlan, Médellus, and Silacier in *Malemort*. The subject's experience is an emotional one of personal alienation and impotence, and it is inevitably an *imaginary* version of the real situation: "imaginary" in the Lacanian and Althusserian sense of the individual's unmediated implication in fantasy and ideology.[7]

The novels, then, give more prominence to the individually experienced impossibility of expression. This manifests itself in the first place as a kind of repression: not only emotions but also insights are repressed because they cannot be articulated. It produces physical tension: "the body jerking, suddenly braced in the impossibility of saying anything at all" (*Mal*, 126), thus echoing the dual bodily and verbal alienation that Glissant ascribes to the condition of slavery.[8] It affects relationships: Pythagore and Cinna Chimène gradually grow apart because they cannot see that "their apparently contradictory statements were the sign of an identical unease, and that the reason they found it hard to live together was that they felt the same burning, bore the same hole in their heads. But it is true that . . . a cane-cutter and a field negress . . . could not have expressed such profound torment, even though they shared it" (*CC*, 41).

But by far the most important subjective aspect of the lack of language is the repression of the *past*. While in Glissant's novels historical *events* do figure, rather peripherally, in connection with the language situation (as outlined above), he devotes much more space to describing the present-day community's inability to know and to come to terms with those past events, and it is this repression that is shown as having the strongest connection with the inadequacies of language.[9] The unconscious pressure of a traumatic past is a recurrent issue in *Le discours antillais* ("The past, to which we were subjected, which has not yet emerged as history for us, is, however, obsessively present," *CD*, 63), but it assumes even greater importance in the novels, particularly in *Malemort* and *La case du commandeur*.

The word "Odono," which haunts *La case du commandeur*, illustrates powerfully this connection between the lack of language and the repression of history. Apparently meaningless, muttered by seemingly mad people in the street, this opaque word is in fact the forgotten name of the ancestor of the Celat family. But in its opacity it functions as a kind of marker or placeholder for "missing" meanings in general, and so it comes to stand for the collective repression of the past: "the obstinate stammering of the word (not even a word, a repeated flash of sounds) *Odono Odono*" (40). Its referent—which is never fully established, it is one or the other of two brothers—is less important than its role as a symbol of what has been repressed but can be recovered: "the legend . . . creates multiple Odonos in the hearts of those who walk without knowing, eat without thinking, drink without being thirsty" (142).[10]

Malemort contains a restatement of the same theme, but with the addition of a third term: the geographical reality of the island, in its concrete and particular materiality. There is a triangular relationship between history, language, and the country. The traumatic nature of Martinican history produces a subjective repression of the past, "something impossible to express," which erodes the language; but, equally, it is responsible for an alienated relationship to the island itself to which the slaves were forcibly brought and to which their descendants have therefore never felt that they belonged; and, finally, both these alienations mean that the language cannot adequately articulate the contemporary physical reality of the island. This vicious triangle, so to speak, is gradually and painfully explored in a long passage in *Malemort* (69–71), revolving around "the impossibility of naming the things of everyday life and the necessity of doing so in order to survive" (70). The passage appears in the fourth section, which juxtaposes two years: the first morning of the maroon Longoué (here called "the Negator") on the island in 1788 and the journey to the sea made by Dlan, Médellus, and Silacier in 1939, just after war has been declared. They are in fact retracing the steps of Longoué, but without realizing it, because the one hundred and fifty years separating the two itineraries are a blank, a "break" in time: "these hundred and fifty years fallen into the abyss" (67), "this break of a hundred and fifty years which had cracked open between the first innumerable long-ago and the second all too easily enumerated present" (69). The abyss of forgotten time has swallowed up any desire to remember, and at the same time it has rendered words meaningless or even caused them to disappear altogether:

> Cette casse de cent cinquante années . . . où les mots (et les significations) s'étaient pétrifiés comme d'une absence de quoi que ce soit à dire ou à désigner, où toute volonté de se souvenir de la première nuit et du Négateur s'était comme dessouchée des têtes et des ventres, où le mot mantou et le mot calloge le mot vezou—sans compter tant d'autres qui avaient vécu la vie raide des êtres clandestins menacés secrets—avaient peu à peu terni et disparu. (69)

> [This break of a hundred and fifty years . . . in which words (and meanings) had fossilized as though from the absence of anything to say or to denote, in which any will to remember the first night and the Negator had as it were been uprooted from heads and bellies, in which the word for mangrove crab and the word for rabbit-hutch the word for cane syrup—not to mention the many others that had lived the inflexible lives of clandestine threatened secret beings—had little by little faded and vanished.]

The next paragraph continues the same theme but with an additional emphasis on the conflict between language as a form of organization ("a language a way of arranging things in the indistinctness of time and dark merged together," 69) and the almost overwhelming weight, disorder, and sensuous profusion of the world that language has to try to express:

> La difficulté . . . d'avoir à *articuler,* autour des racines mauves, des fours à charbon sépulcraux dans leurs hardes de pluie, des fosses d'igname haut balancées, des plaques à cassaves sans yeux, des bâts de mulet en trapèze, des zébus lourds à la charrette, des chaudières rapiécées, des jambières de haillons sur la ligne de coupe de cannes, autour des cases sous les manguiers ou des bourgs de planchettes marquetés de terre grise, *quelque cri que ce fût qui pût réellement se nouer en forme de langage.* (69–70, emphasis added)

> [The difficulty . . . of having to *articulate,* around the mauve roots, the charcoal ovens like tombs shrouded in rain, the pits of yams slung up high, the eyeless cassava boards, the trapeze-shaped mule yokes, the Brahmin-oxen slowly dragging the carts, the patched-up boilers, the ragged

leggings along the line where the cane is being cut, around the shacks under the mango trees or the villages of wooden planks dappled with grey mud, *any kind of cry that might really form itself into language.*]

The "something impossible to express" of counterpoetics is given a more precise content here: it is the concrete particularities of day-to-day existence—work, homes, etc.—that are so difficult to express in a language that has, so to speak, come adrift from them. The next paragraph links the contradiction of counterpoetics more explicitly with the historical discontinuity, juxtaposing "the gap thus embedded in the very rust of existence" with "the impossibility of naming the things of everyday life and the necessity of doing so in order to survive" (70). The following paragraph starts by reiterating the feeling of emptiness and impotence— "in this emptying out where the expiring of the voice and the body's gesture had left us with this clumsy awkward stammering"—and goes on to restate the connection between language and the past: "it was also to exert voice and memory at the same time." But the text then brings in a new term that can perhaps be seen as synthesizing the preceding list of disparate, random items—"the mauve roots, the charcoal ovens, etc."; this is the geographical reality of the island that, variously called *terre, pays, paysage,* or *territoire,* is such an important point of reference in all of Glissant's writing. The paragraph continues: "voice and memory at the same time, harnessed to the same cyclone of words and of *land,* then to go down through the *country* and see it at last and *shout it out just so that it can go on*" (70, emphasis added).

These three closely interwoven elements—language, history, and landscape—are all central to Glissant's concerns and recur in different combinations throughout his writing.[11] But the physical reality of the island is also always placed in relation to the outside world and the Martinicans' *desire* to be connected to the rest of the world and to enter into "Relation" with it. From this point until the end of the chapter, this outward movement (ironically made possible by the outbreak of war and the call for Martinicans to join up) is dominant—and is seen as the only possible solution to the lack of language: "Trying with a single leap all piled up on the same bank to join up with the world which had finally joined up with them (immobile incarcerated), to touch it not with gestures actions facts not with a sentence a word but by the very effort whereby they drove themselves, past so many questions, to *fill in at one and the same time the white hole of time and the pallid absence of a language*: trying, trying" (71, emphasis added).

This passage also makes it clear that the "lack" of language is not just a question of missing items—words that do not exist, whether they are the lost names of traditional work processes or terms for socially irrelevant emotions (Gani and Tani in *Mahagony,* for instance, are in love, but "anyway there was no word to designate what one might have thought was love or affection," 69). It is also the fact that the language they do use is experienced by them *as* lack, blighted by a kind of nothingness because it has no real connection either to its speakers or to the reality it is supposedly expressing: elsewhere *Malemort* claims that "we can name nothing, we have been worn down in ourselves without noticing it, reduced not so much to silence as to that unraveled absence that is ours, in which neither the caricatures of speech nor the muteness itself mean anything any more" (163).

Those who have no effective language are of course very vulnerable to domination or manipulation by those who have, and there are many examples of this in the novels. The social violence that underlies the lack of an "own" language is made entirely concrete in *Malemort,* for instance, when the strikers in the cane fields confront the police, and hence also the exemplarily alien "language of the jeeps":

> Il fallait parler aux jeeps dans le langage des jeeps c'est-à-dire expliquer devant les fusils les mitraillettes balancées à bout de bras que la langue ne permettait pas d'exposer les problèmes qu'il faudrait reprendre dans le parler qu'il aurait fallu reprendre dans le parler quel parler le dur mélange de terre rouge pointée d'épines amères de gras luisant en feuillage de sables empierrés de fruits en ortie, le concassement de mots arrachés à la douleur comme denture à vif sur la mâchoire des bois des cannes des cacaos des cafés, mêlés à l'orgeat au mabi amer, le trébucher de la bouche encombrée de boues pourries de crachats blancs, la saccade du corps soudain cambré dans l'impossibilité de dire quoi que ce soit et qui ne se déliait parfois que dans le goût strident d'un chanter interdit. (126)

> [You had to speak to the jeeps in the language of the jeeps that is explain in front of the rifles the machine guns held swinging loose that the language did not allow you to present the problems that you would have to begin again in the speech that you should have begun again in the speech what speech the hard mixture of red earth studded with bitter thorns of shiny slime and foliage of stony sand of fruit and nettles, the chopped up words torn out of pain like teeth ripped from the jaw of wood of cane of cocoa of coffee, mixed with barley water and sour mabi,[12] the stumbling of the mouth full of rotten mud and white spit, the body jerking, sud-

denly braced in the impossibility of saying anything at all and which could only be relaxed occasionally in the strident taste of a banned song.]

Here the difficulty is *enacted* in the text, in the perceptible sense of the struggle to convey something, the lack of abstract concepts, the way the need and the impossibility are both experienced through the body (teeth, mouth, "body jerking, suddenly braced"), the close links with the land, and the peculiarly fractured language that results.[13] Later in the same episode, one of the policemen starts shooting at random into the crowd of strikers, who are now in the town. At first the text again "tries" to describe the scene "in its own words," but the language literally breaks up into fragments:

> Le brigadier Tigamba était comme une ortie une éruption il criait il vomissait la rue était un détritus ravagé Tigamba ne voulait rien entendre il arma sans viser tira dans les corps découpés sur la baie de lumière de la savane, roulé, cassé, tambouré, vitre, grillage, dalot, roulé dos couteau tombé dalot, roulé, maté.

> [Sergeant Tigamba was like a nettle an eruption he shouted he choked the street was laid waste like a garbage heap Tigamba wouldn't listen he drew his gun without aiming shot at the bodies outlined in the bay of light of the open space, rolled, broken, hammered, window, fence, gutter, rolled back knife fallen gutter, rolled, overpowered.]

Then, almost as though acknowledging defeat, the text suddenly switches into an ironic discourse of normality—Tigamba resuming his everyday life as though nothing had happened:

> Tigamba qui ne serait ni inquiété ni poursuivi qui continuerait à faire chaque matin sa tournée au marché aux poissons où il prélèverait ses deux kilos de poisson rouge et de temps en temps les coulirous ou les balarous à faire frire. (129–30)

> [Tigamba who would be neither troubled nor prosecuted who would continue to take his morning stroll to the fish market where he would collect his two kilos of red snapper and sometimes a few coulirous or balarous to fry up.]

As in this example, the oppressors are usually middle-class mulatto or black characters. But where, unlike here, their own speech is reproduced in the text, we can see how acutely it is affected by the insecurity and alienation that arises from their attempts to internalize and reproduce white French cultural values. (This phenomenon, which Glissant calls the "mimetic drive," is the central topic of chapter 4.) Their speech thus suffers from its own lack.[14] Ironically, it is often just this hollow, insubstantial quality of the *oppressors'* language that effects their domination of others. For instance, Mycéa is reduced to silence by her headmaster's verbal attack: "This speech which she would not have been able to contradict but which a painful positioning of her childish body rejected. Only her body, for she certainly didn't know what it was that, behind the ritual that the headmaster was performing for himself more than for his wide-eyed pupils, hit her like a rock. She was quite unable to locate in her mind the exact place where the flow of his words suddenly veered off toward stretches of nothingness" (CC, 44).

Not "having a language" makes it impossible to relate on equal terms—or even at all—with people who are socially different from oneself, whose language is more powerful. But it is specifically the "nothingness" of the headmaster's words that attacks her "like a rock"—the very emptiness and lack of connection to concrete reality that Glissant elsewhere characterizes as a feature of the inadequacy and, in a real sense, the impotence of language. But this abstract, "unreal" discourse, however alienating it may be for its subject, is also a means of mystifying and intimidating others. In *Le quatrième siècle,* Mathieu contrasts the wordless subaltern "universe of cane, clay and straw" with the socially superior "saying people," whose speech is *nevertheless* also a "nothingness": "saying people [*des gens disants*] whose speech he felt was nothingness, smoke already turning blue in the gulf of the great sky" (305).

A more extended illustration of this idea that the lack of one's own language makes it impossible to resist being dominated or manipulated by the other's *equally alienated* speech occurs in *Malemort.* Silacier is silently eavesdropping on a conversation between Lesprit, the mayor's secretary, and his equally middle-class and educated friends. The aptly named Lesprit's witty, fluent, and elegant French has the same quality of "nothingness" as that of Mycéa's headmaster; it "covers up" and implicitly denies the existence of "the canefields and their persistent marshy smell, the Lézarde river and its water gradually drying up, the schoolboys lined up once a week to receive their quinine" (82–83). The list continues for another whole page of the heterogeneous objects that, as we have already seen, Glissant uses to evoke the chaotic social and material reality that language cannot adequately express, and the passage concludes, "his endless speech had rubbed away gnawed away the firm contours of things, leaving this pasty mushy pomposity" [*concluant à cette suffisance pâteuse sans accident ni pointe ni croc*] (82). And for this reason Silacier cannot get any purchase on it; he is simply hypnotized by it: "Silacier . . . rocked himself in the hammock of words" (84); "and Silacier bumped along gently on the wave of words . . . he didn't notice the time passing, cocooned as he was in this tapestry of words" (96–97). He actually hates Lesprit for his corruption, his exploitation of the people of the town, and in particular for his involvement in the murder of an election candidate several years ago—but Lesprit's eloquence, confusing and overpowering him, in effect cheats him of his hatred: "The hate inside him was, without him realizing it, deflected from Monsieur Lesprit who was its true object. . . . Through his foliage of spellbinding words Monsieur Lesprit escaped, safe" (84).

The subjectively experienced lack of language evokes as its counterpart a strong *desire* for language. The question arises as to what form this desired language takes. How is it represented in Glissant's novels? The speaking subject's experience is one of lack—of not having a language that one can fully and unproblematically assume as one's own and that therefore "naturally" coincides with one's sense of identity (what I call the language-identity equation in chapter 1). Thus, a lack of language can also be experienced as a lack of *self*. It follows that the desired ideal language will have precisely the characteristics that will make good the lack and fill the emptiness of the self. The language will bestow plenitude on the self by forming an indissoluble part of the self's identity. It represents the ideal of an "authentic" language that can be spontaneously assumed as one's own, as a true and unmediated expression of one's identity.

The characters in Glissant's novels often express the desire for such a language. But this does not necessarily mean that the novels endorse the ideal of an authentic language. This issue is particularly important because in Glissant's theoretical writings he argues *against* the equation of a single identity with a single language (which thereby becomes "authentic"). The concepts of counterpoetics in *Le discours antillais* and of creolization in *Poétique de la relation* and *Introduction à une poétique du divers* both make this argument, but on different grounds. *Le discours antillais* presents a situation in which the historical trauma of transportation has permanently *excluded* the possibility of an essentialist conception of a natural, authentic mother tongue equating with a natural, authentic identity. The response to this situation, Glissant claims, is counterpoetics, which, rather than fantasizing about a lost natural language, works to confront, subvert, and partially *reappropriate* the language of the oppressors—but in the knowledge that what will result will be a constrained, compromised, and "unnatural" social construct. In "Poetics and the Unconscious" Glissant states clearly the limitations of the reappropriated language: "an antipoetics, deliberately [shaping a *langage*], with a more limiting, less developed, less free function" (*CD*, 168). But counterpoetics, wresting a *langage* from the colonial *langue*, is the only honest and realistic solution. *Poétique de la relation*, on the other hand, centers on a critique of the notion of identity itself (reiterated in *Introduction à une poétique du divers*), redefining it in plural and relational terms (as described in chapter 1) and promoting an ideal of multilingualism in the context of creolization. Nevertheless, both positions are opposed to the notion of authentic language; by introducing a theoretical break between language and subject, they counter the language-identity equation.

However, Glissant's early novels do underwrite the ideal of authentic language. In *Le quatrième siècle* Mathieu has the full weight of the narrative discourse behind him when he realizes how the people "could vanish . . . enclosed in their death which was in reality their farthest horizon, for the simple reason that their speech was dead too" (305). In other words, they are dead *because* their speech is dead—a very straightforward form of the equation—and his discovery that "the voice itself was *denatured*" implies an ideal of naturalness that reinforces the notion of authenticity (305, emphasis added). In *La Lézarde* language is only a marginal issue, but here too, in the context of the election campaign, the "voice" of the people (*voix* is sometimes indistinguishably "voice" and "vote") is seen as an assertion of their identity and struggle for political liberation. Conversely, political action results in a "liberated language," which is also emotionally fulfilling: its argument "is not based on cold logic, but warm reassurance" (219). The fact of having "freed" language is itself a political victory; after the election, Mathieu comments: "So, we haven't done much. But there it is. You could say that we can speak now" (215).

In this novel, language is thus seen above all as a means of achieving political freedom. The relevant connection is between language and action; the people are alienated from action because they are alienated from their language. It follows that language can only be effective in enabling and promoting action if it is an authentic element of collective identity: an *unalienated* language is seen as a necessary condition for collective action. *Le quatrième siècle* describes the beginnings of this process as the cane-cutters' gradual and hesitant discovery—*through* its articulation in language—that they are capable of social agency:

> Already strong enough to describe the action or to predict it; but in broken fragments, in cryptic sayings, and never guessing that they bore it within them. . . . Weaving, from one proverb to another, . . . the voice thick with mystery from which their clarity would emerge. . . . Without daring to believe that . . . they could perhaps feel the future action running through their sentences. Action: the drive that already fitted the words together, or rather, the articulation (unsuspected syntax) of their disjointed conversations. (176–77)

In *La Lézarde* and *Le quatrième siècle,* then, written in 1958 and 1964, respectively, Glissant represents the gap between subject and language as a form of alienation and, thus, as something that can and must be overcome to create an authentic language. Even here it is important to note that the explicit emphasis is on the relation between language and action, rather than between language and identity, and that it is collective rather than individual: identity, by implication, is not even in these early texts a matter of inward-looking singular definition. But the view of language is still substantively different from the formulation given in counterpoetics, which Glissant develops later in articles written during the 1970s and revised for inclusion in *Le discours antillais* in 1981.

Malemort and *La case du commandeur* were written in the 1970s, and in these two novels the question of language and identity—that is, the proposed solution to the problem of the lack of language—is presented in terms that are basically congruent with counterpoetics, while still placing more emphasis on the imaginary (in the Lacanian sense) level of experience. Not only does *La case du commandeur* contain few explicit formulations of the "desired language," but in it we find that the theoretically posited break between subject and language is given—for the first time in the novels—a positive value, through its being staged in a phantasmatic context as magic. As a child, Cinna Chimène runs away into the forest, where she has a magical experience that revolves around the idea of a "break" in her voice, that is, of losing control of her words:

> Alors elle souffrit la première cassure dans la voix—non pas la voix qu'on lève à tout venant sans y penser mais la lame qu'on murmure dans la tête et qui retentit derrière le cœur avec le bruit d'une ravine qui débonde—et elle vit les mots défiler au-devant d'elle et la traverser, tout de même que si elle n'avait été qu'une véranda noire ouverte dans cette

nuit: *Poussé Odono la belleté de la bête tu mas annoncié tifille tifille vini éti éti icite ou cé la bête qui a fait l'annoncement. . . .* Ainsi pour la première fois brisant en elle la barrière entre tant de mots différents contraires, elle défrichait la nuit. (64–65)

[Then she suffered the first break in her voice—not the voice one raises anywhere without thinking but the murmuring swell in one's head, echoing behind the heart with the sound of a gushing ravine—and she saw the words go filing past in front of her and through her, just as though she had been nothing but a black veranda open in the night: *Grown Odono the beautifulness of the beast you annunciated me littlegirl littlegirl come here or its the beast who made the announcement. . . .* So for the first time breaking through the barrier inside her between so many different contrary words, she opened up the night.]

Suzanne Crosta interprets this episode as a manifestation of voodoo, in which the "break in the voice" is a sign of possession. Cinna Chimène, finding herself uttering strange alien words, is thereby able to "externalize in words the things excluded from her existence," and Crosta comments that "what is important in voodoo is the eruption of an other voice."[15] In other words, the possessed subject is *traversé* by language—language "goes through" her—rather than being in possession of it as a component of identity (the kind of interior monologue suggested by "la lame qu'on murmure dans la tête"), but this is an illuminating and liberating experience, breaking down barriers in language and enabling the child to "open up" the surrounding darkness.

Overall, however, questions of language figure more prominently in *Malemort,* which accords a central importance to fictional representations of strategies for appropriating the Other's language (discussed in more detail in chapter 4). But this does not mean that *Malemort* simply illustrates with fictional examples the theoretical definitions of counterpoetics. There is a difference of approach, and once again it relates precisely to the status of the characters' *desire* for language. The force of this desire—the lyrical, plaintive, bitter, desperate, or despairing evocation of a "new" language—has the effect of simplifying definitions of its object, so that it sometimes seems as though the text as a whole is underwriting the ideal of authentic language, which *Le discours antillais* contests. The opening chapter of the novel, for instance, links it with the "natural" physical self-expression of dance, which makes Dlan feel that "you stammer in the confused trembling the first naked daring of the new language" (20). Nor does *Malemort* distance itself from the desire by placing or qualifying it in any way: it pervades the whole text. Thus, the "new language" at times *appears* to be something more (more immediately desirable, perhaps) than the constrained and compromised construct of counterpoetics.

But a closer examination of the novel shows that this is not the case. Rather, the workings of counterpoetics itself have become invested with an emotional force and lyrical poignancy that is more usually associated with the simpler appeal of authentic language. In fact, the text makes it quite clear that the new language will *not* spontaneously come into being as the expression of a liberated identity but will be the result of a deliberate act of construction—"the materials with which to build another language," "organize this wind-skimmed foam from which our language will emerge," and so on (161). This new language is thus a process of reappropriation—with the difficulties and compromises that this entails—rather than of creation. But the detour, forcing a *langage* out of the resistance to the dominant *langue,* is itself, in the novels with their more subjective perspective, assumed by the speaking subject as an object of identification and so invested with positive value on an imaginary level. Roger Toumson describes the Caribbean subject's ability to assume and experience nonauthenticity and dispossession as a kind of authentic identity: "Struck by the fictional nature of his ego, the subject migrates elsewhere. He perceives himself as residual, lacking identity. But he remains capable of producing a critique of his own resentment. So he reaches a new synthesis: that of identity from within non-identity, of the experience of lack as experience of being in its maturity."[16] A similar strategy is at work on the more specific question of the subject's relation to language; its effect is to infuse dispossession with an essentially *ironic* kind of imaginary plenitude that has a very powerful emotional resonance precisely because of its forced and compromised nature.

Even the apparently hopeless position of Silacier, for example, generates its own detour of resistance. While he is succumbing to Lesprit's dazzling mendacious eloquence, Silacier nevertheless still retains, on some not-quite-conscious level, an accurate sense of what is happening to him and his potential ability to resist it. (This is discussed in more detail in chapter 4.) This ambivalent resistance follows exactly the dynamic of counterpoetics, which thereby acquires the poignancy of a heroic personal struggle. The text elucidates Silacier's position by means of what is, in effect, a definition of counterpoetics, in that it shows how the "lack" of his language is also paradoxically what gives it its own peculiar (and limited) efficacy: "This suffering this uncertainty of the words themselves, of their meaning, but also of their use, which push the language to the limits of derision but through luck or by way of compensation give it its particular sense—a sense unnoticed, incomprehensible for anyone who has not gone around and around in this hollow of land creased with hills in the north and salt marshes in the south" (*Mal, 95*).

In this way the novels of the 1970s shift the theoretical concept of counterpoetics into a slightly different perspective that accords more importance to its repercussions on the imaginary level of individuals' experience. In Glissant's two most recent novels, *Mahagony* and *Toutmonde,* the position with regard to language and identity changes yet again. On the one hand, the link between the two is broken far more definitively than previously—not under the disguise of voodoo as in *La case du commandeur* but in an entirely general fashion, and in *Mahagony* in particular, it is broken in favor of a more clearly strategic use of language (this is analyzed in detail in chapter 7). The characters in *Mahagony* are all to some extent distanced from their discourse; they move through a number of different discourses, which they use with a flexibility that eliminates the distinction between their own and others' language. The urban Ida, for example, when she goes to live with her fiancé's family in the country, starts to speak like them and finds that "I'm used to their way of talking now, I can imitate it fairly easily, well no, it comes fairly naturally to me" (161), thus erasing any difference between natural speech and artificial imitation. Also, the theme of lack of language is simply much less important in *Mahagony*. This novel, written in 1987, seems to be moving on to a new problematic, where the emphasis is on an interconnected but differentiated plurality of discourses. From this point of view, the novel anticipates the new theoretical developments that will be explored in *Poétique de la relation,* in which the importance given to plurality in the form of creolization, and the emphatic rejection of singular identity, lend a wider significance retrospectively to the plural narrative structures and discourses of *Mahagony*. Conversely, the notion of counterpoetics has disappeared in *Poétique de la relation*. The latter's critique of an idealist notion of identity, although it is relevant to the notion of authentic language and, therefore, in principle also relevant to the notions of lack of language and counterpoetics, is not explicitly connected to either of these. Creolization offers a different framework, within which the lack of language and the subject's relation to language cease to be relevant because language has become so fluid and diverse that it can no longer be seen as having any role in the constitution of subjectivity.

Tout-monde follows closely *Poétique de la relation* in its development of a view of language as a radically plural phenomenon: the new "chaotic" reality of the *tout-monde* undermines the autonomy of any one language by mixing them violently together: "You can hear the world's languages as they meet on the wave or on the mountain, all these languages crashing into each other like the crests of furious waves" (20). The ultimate form of global Relation means that one can no longer speak a language that is clearly demarcated from all the others: "The airplane has mixed up the languages, here you are in the presence of all the languages in the world, you will have to shake up the one you use, you can't just let it trot contentedly along, and if you speak another language as well . . . then you summon up the clash . . . in which, through each other, these languages are revealed to themselves and to the world they live in" (267).

The notion of one's "own" language has ceased to be even a desirable fantasy. The most notable illustration of this is the character Stepan Stepanovitch, whose lack of any viable mother tongue would in an earlier novel have been presented as a source of frustration and powerlessness. In *Tout-monde*, however, he is presented as *celebrating* his freedom from any such attachment; and his limited and idiosyncratic use of French is, equally, shown to be an exuberantly effective means of communication: "Stepan écrire vrai bon français, quand il faut! Écrire pas difficile, quand il faut! Stepan décidé pas une langue bonne pour parler! Pas une langue vaut la peine! Cacher langue! Stepan puissant pour cacher langue! Même à l'oral des examens!" [Stepan write proper good French, when he must! Write not difficult, when he must! Stepan decide no one language good to speak! No one language worth it! Hide language! Stepan strong to hide language! Even in oral exam!] (356).

The notion of lack thus gives way to its opposite: to a proliferation of languages, none of which is permanently assumed by a subject. It is difficult to determine whether this is solving the problem or merely evading the issue of *inequality* in Relation and its consequences on language use. Glissant has suggested that counterpoetics is a transitional stage (*CD*, 133–34); for it to be genuinely superseded, the power relations of neocolonialism would presumably also have to be transformed at least to the extent of creating greater social autonomy in Martinique. What is clear is that it is his writings of the 1970s and early 1980s—*Malemort, La case du commandeur, Le discours antillais,* and, to a lesser extent, *Mahagony*—that most powerfully present the ideas of struggle, resistance, and strategy.

3 Subaltern Language

The Unmarked Path

THE PRECEDING chapter discusses the ways in which Glissant's novels depict the impossibility of "authentic" expression and its various social and psychological consequences. But this lack of language also has consequences for the *representation* of the characters. If they cannot speak for themselves, how can anyone else speak for them or even speak about them without objectifying them? We return here to Spivak's problematic of the representation of subaltern consciousness.[1] This chapter examines two of Glissant's novels—the early *Le quatrième siècle* and the much later *Mahagony*—in the light of Spivak's theorization of subalternity and her claim that the subaltern cannot speak or know his or her social condition.

The term "subaltern" is first found in the work of Antonio Gramsci.[2] Gramsci established the concept of hegemony—the claim that the ideology of the dominant class in any society becomes the dominant ideology of the whole society; that is, those who do not belong to the class whose interests it serves will nevertheless subscribe to it. This kind of ideological "capture" of a society accompanies political power and economic dominance, but Gramsci makes a basic distinction between power based on domination and power based on hegemony. Thus, it is important to note that hegemony is an ideological or, in the poststructuralist framework, discursive reality and that it is not correlated with any one particular class.

The subaltern, for Gramsci, is the nonhegemonic subject, excluded from the dominant ideology's representation of the society and its history, and therefore from the possibility of representing himself or herself as a political agent. Gramsci's example of subaltern consciousness is the Italian peasantry. He is primarily concerned with theorizing their entry into hegemony, which he sees as taking place via an alliance with the

revolutionary proletariat in the northern cities of Italy. When the notion
of subalternity is applied to a colonial situation, as in Spivak's work, it
has to be modified to some extent; the logic of the subaltern subject's entry into hegemony becomes far more tenuous because of the epistemic
violence inherent in colonialism.[3] It is important to bear in mind that
Spivak's use of the term "subaltern" refers solely to the *colonized* subject
who does not belong to the nationalist bourgeoisie that becomes the
dominant class after independence.

To claim, as Spivak explicitly (and Gramsci more implicitly) does,
that the subaltern cannot know his or her collective situation conflicts
with a certain conception of class-consciousness as inherent and spontaneous, in which the oppressed have an almost instinctive awareness of
themselves as a collective with common interests and common enemies.
In "Can the Subaltern Speak?" Spivak argues carefully against this conception, using Karl Marx's famous text *The Eighteenth Brumaire of
Louis Bonaparte* to show that class-consciousness is an "artificial," historically specific construct. This complicates the question of political
representation: if there is no transparent continuity of collective interests
and individual consciousness, then an oppressed group will not "naturally" throw up its own leader capable of articulating its real interests.
Instead, "working on the structural principle of a dispersed and dislocated class subject" in his analysis of peasant proprietors in postrevo-
lutionary France, Marx demonstrates how "the (absent collective) consciousness of the small peasant proprietor class finds its 'bearer' in a
'representative' who appears to work in another's interest."[4] The efficacy of political leadership is therefore conjunctural—a result of the particular historical situation—rather than inherent.

Spivak links this question of class-consciousness to the relationship
between political representation (*Vertretung*) and representation in the
artistic or philosophical sense (*Darstellung*). She argues that translating
both concepts as "representation" has obscured some of the meanings
of Marx's texts in their English translations. Put simply, it is the difference between speaking *for* someone and speaking *about* someone. Distinguishing between the terms reveals, precisely, their complicity in
action: one cannot represent (speak for) any community without producing a particular representation *of* it; and, conversely, "[theories of
ideology] must note how the staging of the world in representation—its
scene of writing, its *Darstellung*—dissimulates the choice of and need
for 'heroes', paternal proxies, agents of power—*Vertretung*."[5]

Representation is intractable and problematic; but once one abandons the idealist notion of spontaneous class-consciousness, both *Vertretung* and *Darstellung* are revealed as unavoidable.[6] "Can the Subaltern Speak?" begins with a scathing critique of "the first-world intellectual masquerading as the absent nonrepresenter who lets the oppressed speak for themselves"; it is, Spivak argues, the difficult responsibility of the first-world intellectual to analyze and represent the texts of subalternity in order to trace in them the ways in which the subaltern subject is discursively constructed.[7]

The concept of subalternity thus contests the idealist and "heroic" view that sees the oppressed as having an unalienated, unmediated, and accurate understanding of their collective situation in history and society, and the ability to articulate their understanding and to communicate it to others outside their own situation. The subaltern cannot know his or her social condition. In the first place this is simply a corollary of the general poststructuralist model of subjectivity that Spivak uses. This model consists above all of a critique of the sovereign subject—the notion that the subject exists outside the determinations of ideology and the unconscious, that it is essentially conscious, unified, and capable of full self-knowledge. In this sense, subaltern consciousness is exemplary of consciousness in general: "It is the subaltern who provides the model for a general theory of consciousness." However, according to Spivak, the very theorists who are most committed to the critique of sovereign consciousness often fail to extend its implications to the subaltern, so that "only the dominant self can be problematic; the self of the Other is authentic without a problem. . . . This is very frightening."[8]

But the poststructuralist model, if used coherently, also enables us to see how the subaltern subject does have specific ideological determinations, different from those of the hegemonic subject. This model sees subjectivity as constructed within discourse—as subject-effect within the "social text."[9] Spivak uses Foucault's definition, from *L'Archéologie du savoir*, of subject-positioning in discourse, and she stresses the fact that the "'I'-slot is a sign. It may for instance signify a sociopolitical, psychosexual, disciplinary-institutional or ethno-economic provenance. Hence, Foucault uses the word 'assigned': 'The position of the subject can be assigned.'" Thus, the subaltern subject is assigned a different subject-position from that of the hegemonic subject. The hegemonic subject is "inside" the dominant ideological discourses of the social text and can therefore represent itself (in both senses) within them. This is different from saying that it has access to true self-knowledge, but it means that its self-representation is effective, because it is readable within the dominant discourse. The subaltern subject cannot effectively represent itself, because the position it is assigned is, for the most part, one of exclusion: "subaltern consciousness is . . . always askew from its received signifiers, indeed . . . it is effaced even as it is disclosed." It is in this sense that the subaltern cannot "speak."[10]

In the case of the colonized subaltern, more than just marginality is at issue; the exclusion of the subaltern is the result of a specifically imperialist project of "the constitution of the Subject as Europe." This is the root of all epistemic violence—what Spivak calls the "remotely orchestrated, far-flung and heterogeneous project to constitute the colonial subject as Other. This project is also the asymmetrical obliteration of the trace of that Other in its precarious Subject-ivity." The history of imperialism can thus be equated with "the epistemic violence that constituted/effaced a subject that was obliged to cathect (occupy in response to a desire) the space of the Imperialists' self-consolidating other." That is, the place of the Other within hegemonic Western discourse is not only constructed by the Western subject but constructed *in order to* "consolidate" the West's representation of itself, while at the same time the traces of that consolidating role are themselves obliterated.[11]

There are thus two interlinked problems for the intellectual who—like the Indian-based Subaltern Studies group Spivak analyzes—tries to investigate the issue of subaltern consciousness.[12] The first problem is that it is not possible to retrieve the lost "pure consciousness" of the subaltern, because any such possibility implies an essentialist view of consciousness in general. Hence, the dangerous political naïveté of attempts to "let the oppressed speak for themselves," which Spivak critiques in greater detail in "Can the Subaltern Speak?" in relation to a text by Foucault and Deleuze: to claim that there is a place beyond representation "where oppressed subjects speak, act and know *for themselves,* leads to an essentialist, utopian politics." The belief that one has recovered the true voice or consciousness of the subaltern in fact results—because it is an illusion—in an "insidious objectification" of the subaltern, which "would . . . control him through knowledge even as they restore versions of causality and self-determination to him."[13]

Therefore, the investigating intellectual can only try to represent and analyze the assignment of subaltern subject-positions within the social text. Here the second problem arises: namely, the traces of the subaltern —unlike those of the hegemonic subject—are very largely obliterated.[14]

To convey the nature of this "effaced itinerary of the subaltern subject," Spivak borrows a phrase from Pierre Macherey: "The point is not to recover a lost consciousness, but to see, to quote Macherey, the itinerary of the silencing." Macherey's insight that "what the work *cannot* say is important, because there the elaboration of the utterance is carried out, in a sort of journey to silence" implies that, in analyzing a text, we have to pay as much attention to its omissions and exclusions as to what it includes: the subaltern subject-position may be recoverable only through its negative traces.[15]

What are the consequences of all this for the *literary* representation of the subaltern and for critical analysis of such representations? First, a distinction must be made between a psycho-realist representation of the subaltern that stages an "authentic voice" speaking to the reader with the weight of narrative authority and a representation of the subaltern as subject-position in ideological discourse.[16] It also means locating in the text those rare moments of fracture when the subaltern subject-position, through its very ex-centricity, levers open one of the ideological closures of the dominant discourse. The critic's work, in other words, is to uncover the subject-position assigned to the subaltern in the text and to show how this may involve deconstructing a Western logic of representation and self-representation.

Glissant concurs with Spivak's refutation of the "heroic" model of natural, unalienated class-consciousness, at least as far as Martinique is concerned. He repeatedly stresses the lack of any such consciousness throughout Martinican society, which he explains in Marxist terms as the result of the lack of any autonomous economic production (as described in chapter 2).[17] The "total alienation of the system of production" distorts all social relations; it splits the classes' real but unacknowledged social function from their manufactured self-image and makes it impossible for them to have a realistic sense of their situation, while conversely inflating "the importance of appearance and 'rôle' (as opposed to a real function)" (*DA*, 288).[18]

But in other ways Glissant's own theoretical account of the lack of language, as described in chapter 2, does not accord with Spivak's concept of subalternity. The divergences highlight the enormous differences between Martinican society and the Indian colonial history on which most of Spivak's work is in fact based. In the first place, transportation has resulted in a less hierarchical society in contemporary Martinique: there never were any dominant indigenous groups comparable to the traditional Indian ruling class and its complex and often successful accommodations with the imperialist power. The vast majority of the island's population are the descendants of slaves. Thus, Glissant explains the subaltern's inability to know and to speak in primarily psychological rather than class terms as the collective repression of the trauma of slavery. He writes, for instance: "Fanon says that he does not want to be the slave of slavery. To me that implies that one should not be content with *ignorance* of the historical phenomenon of slavery; that one must not suffer its persisting trauma on a compulsive, unconscious level. To overcome it one must explore it projectively. The slave is above all someone who does not know. The slave of slavery is above all someone who does not want to know" (*DA,* 129). Secondly, the maroon communities of runaway slaves, as depicted by Glissant, constitute an oppositional discourse that, while never politically effective, is more autonomous than Spivak's formulation allows for, implying as it does an all-pervasive hegemonic social text. Finally, unlike India and indeed most of the Third World, Martinique is not today an independent state and is therefore not *post*colonial in any real sense. It has never experienced a mass independence movement led by a nationalist bourgeoisie; in fact, there has never been a nationalist bourgeoisie of any importance, since the majority of the middle class historically looked to assimilation with France. In both Martinique and India, the economic exploitation of the subaltern is of course carried out by the same complex of neocolonial, multinational companies; but the *political* exclusion of the Martinican subaltern is not, as it is in postindependence India, effected by an indigenous nationalist ruling class but by an assimilated bourgeoisie in collusion with metropolitan France. Therefore, the subaltern's ideological struggle is in principle still against assimilation with France.

It is therefore not surprising that the main thrust of Glissant's position is against assimilation, appropriation, and objectification, as the discussion of Relation and opacity in chapter 1 makes clear. Glissant is so aware of the dangers of "speaking for" the Martinican people (see, for instance, the satirical treatment of the "visiting experts" in *Malemort,* 198–99) that, at least in his earlier work, he conversely underwrites the notion of "letting the oppressed speak for themselves."[19] However, given his professed reluctance to speak for the Other, there is something almost provocative about the way in which his novels so frequently stage the "voices" of *female* characters: Mycéa in *La case du commandeur, Mahagony,* and *Tout-monde;* Adélaïde and Eudoxie in *Mahagony;* and Anastasie, Marie-Annie, and Artémise in *Tout-monde.* His more recent texts contain a different theoretical emphasis as well: *Tout-monde,* for instance, picks up an earlier recurrent image of the subaltern colonized peoples emerging from the darkness of "the hidden side of the earth"— not, however, into the pure light of consciousness this time but into the glare of television publicity: "Already the summoning of all those countries who had waited in the night, on the other side of the visible face of the earth, who had brought this far their load of unknown suffering, of undeclared privations, but who were soon going to enter *the television of the world* and cross that dividing line between night and day, invisible and visible, ignorance and knowledge" (137, emphasis added).

If the world has become a television program that the subaltern watches and on which he or she is represented, then both the subaltern's knowledge of social reality and the West's knowledge of the subaltern are defined as the product of the ideological discourse of the media. Indeed, elsewhere in *Tout-monde* Glissant presents with a vigorous irony the very notion of the authentic voice of the oppressed, seeing it as a seductive object for the "mastery" of the Western intellectual in a way that echoes exactly Spivak's analysis of Foucault and Deleuze's "Intellectuals and Power": "We observe how many ex-masters, and especially intellectual masters, adore listening to the words of their ex-oppressed, when these words stoutly close in on themselves and resound with allegedly primordial authenticity" (*TM*, 158).

My discussion of *Le quatrième siècle* and *Mahagony* will thus argue that the subaltern subject is not presented as a psycho-realist consciousness but as a subject-position in discourse, discernible mainly through a range of representational *detours*: through the limits and "silences" of the text as Macherey suggests, or through its differentiation from other subject-positions, or through the pressure points exerted on the dominant discourse by the subaltern's very exclusion from it. This will also involve discussion of the ways in which both novels engage with the problem of political representation.

Since this centers on the maroons, some preliminary comment on this group is needed. The maroon is at once the most potent and the most ambivalent figure in the popular imagination of the Caribbean. The community of runaway slaves in the central hills of Martinique never attained the dimensions that it did in the larger islands but was still a significant factor both in the daily lives of the slaves and in the periodic uprisings, which were often led by maroons. The maroon figured as the only source of outright resistance to the planters and the only alternative to slavery, but also as a demonic stealer of children and a violator of women, or as a kind of romantic brigand. He is thus both a hero and a

source of fear. In *Le quatrième siècle* these two attributes come together
with the suggestion that the slaves' fear of the maroon may *also* be a fear
of freedom itself: the image of revolt is threatening to those who do not
dare to revolt, and they fear him *because* "for the people living on the
plantation the maroon was the personification of the devil: that is, he
who refuses" (150).

In *Le discours antillais* Glissant traces the historical decline of the maroon from the political and cultural resistance of the early period ("the
basic cultural opposition to the new order imposed on the slave"),
through the planters' successful indoctrination of the slaves with the
idea that the maroon was nothing more than a violent criminal bandit,
to the internalization of this idea by the maroons themselves: "What is
even more significant is the fact that the maroon ends up being what
they had claimed he was, and that he starts behaving like an ordinary
gangster" (*DA,* 104). For Glissant the maroon is the *Négateur* [Nega-
tor]: the one who refuses the values of colonialism. But it is striking that
the only entirely positive representation of a maroon leader in his fiction
is the eighteenth-century character A-aa in *La case du commandeur.*
Later maroons are shown far more ambiguously, either as lone individual rebels who are unable to represent any collective struggle or as de-
spisers of the slave community who collude with the masters against the
slaves. (Historically, for instance, the maroon communities sometimes
concluded treaties with the plantation owners in which they would agree
to return any new runaways in return for being left alone.)[20]

Nevertheless, Glissant states unequivocally that "the fact remains,
and we can never emphasize it enough, that the maroon is the only true
popular hero of the Caribbean . . . an indisputable example of systematic
opposition, of total refusal" (*DA,* 104). Thus, on the one hand, Glissant's representation of the maroon goes against Spivak's contention of
the silencing of the colonized subject. On the other hand, however, the
dislocations Spivak analyzes in *Vertretung* are dramatically illustrated
by the maroon: in the absence of any effective political organization
among the slaves or, later, the mass of agricultural workers, the maroon
represents their only possibility of political leadership, but he is a leader
whose interests and ideological position are in many ways opposed to
theirs. It is perhaps significant that, as Régis Antoine points out, Glissant
is very cautious about representing maroon speech; unlike other, more
romantic versions, his maroons are limited to fragmentary and opaque
utterances.[21]

In *Le quatrième siècle*, the character Papa Longoué has the status of narrator throughout the novel. (This is not the case in the other novels in which he appears.) He tells the story of the Longoué, Béluse, and Targin families to the adolescent Mathieu Béluse. As such, his role appears to contradict Spivak's thesis of subalternity because he seems to be a clear example of the subaltern—he is poor, illiterate, rural, and marginal—and yet he can "speak" and "know" his situation, in that he is shown as giving an authoritative account of his people's history. Moreover, he gives it to Mathieu, who is presented as a typical young, urban, westernized intellectual; and Mathieu, although he argues with him, ultimately acknowledges his authority. This then seems to reproduce the scenario that Spivak criticizes, of the liberal "nonrepresenting" western intellectual letting the oppressed subject speak for himself. However, a closer examination of the text reveals that this is not exactly the case.

In the first place, Papa Longoué does not fit neatly into the category of the subaltern. He comes from a maroon family, and he is also a *quimboiseur* [sorcerer]; that is, he belongs to the African counterculture, which retains at least a relative and local authority, and he is a dominant figure within it. Although Papa Longoué always stresses his own and his people's ignorance—"we were so ignorant, ignorant of ourselves which is the most terrible of all" (159)—he is nevertheless shown to possess a kind of knowledge that is still culturally sanctioned locally and that allows him to represent (in both senses) his people. It allows him, for instance, to construct an alternative to the official colonial history, in the "four centuries" of the novel's title that start with the first Longoué's arrival in 1788.[22] But the text repeatedly stresses the fact that this African-based tradition is dying out. Papa Longoué is the last of the *quimboiseurs*; he has reached "the end of the road"; he dies toward the end of the novel; and we are told that what he has communicated to Mathieu is not knowledge or understanding as might be expected, but just "the faceless bodyless anxiety which was his lot" (310, 314). The narrative, in other words, enacts a kind of fall into subalternity.

What is more important, however, is the way in which the actual discursive structure of the novel reveals the limits of Papa Longoué's narrative voice. The text switches repeatedly from passages of his speech—*telling* the story to Mathieu—to passages of impersonal narration, which are nevertheless by various indirect means attributed to him.[23] This ambiguity in his status as narrating subject has two consequences. It denies him a psychologically realistic presence in the novel, since we are not always sure whether he is speaking or not, and it carries the strong implication that he cannot in fact "know" and "speak" his people's history, since in order to tell this history the text has to supplement his words with a different, subjectless narrative discourse.

But it is not only Papa Longoué's voice that is circumscribed and undermined in this way. The impersonal narration that reveals the gaps in his voice, by the act of filling them in, is itself shown to be incapable of representing the totality of the narrative. Its conventional fictional realism from time to time gives way to a kind of abstract, "poetic" discourse, which is much less usual for fiction; it is as though certain aspects of subalternity cannot be represented within the dominant code of conventional fictional discourse, and, as a result, the text is unable to remain within a single consistent discourse. The most sustained examples of this occur, significantly, when the text is representing the subaltern subject in its slow and difficult movement toward political consciousness. One of these passages is a mise-en-scène of a cane-cutter who is not a realist character but an anonymous, archetypal "man": "the man: no longer Melchior or the Targins, and not Mathieu or Papa Longoué, but that indistinct figure (called Sylvius, or Félicité or Ti-Léon) who knew in his flesh the real weight and the size of a sugar-cane leaf" (256). The passage describes how "the man," whose horizon of knowledge is limited to the canefield and who cannot "speak"—"pinned down between the two ends of the cane plant, had not had a single moment in which to raise his voice, had not found a single silence in which to temper his voice so that he might then brandish it like a weapon" (258)—is nevertheless advancing politically, in the sense that he is beginning to realize that he cannot trust any of those who claim to be acting on his behalf. While he is still just a "spectator by the roadside," he is at least now "a spectator who wouldn't be duped . . . in whose eye that sly trickle of gloomy knowledge was always wavering" (258). All of this strongly suggests that, in order to speak of the subaltern subject, the text has to move out of its normal fictional frame of reference: "the man" is not an individual character.[24]

A different example of "what the text cannot say" in *Le quatrième siècle* concerns the representation of slave uprisings. The Subaltern Studies group is centrally concerned to establish the hitherto dismissed role of subaltern insurgency in India's struggle for independence, and in "Can the Subaltern Speak?" Spivak comments at some length on the semiosis of insurrection. If the disorganized, largely leaderless, and inevitably defeated collective action of the subaltern is to be read within the social text as an "utterance," who is transmitting it to whom? Almost by definition, the "utterance" constituted by insurgency cannot be integrated into dominant narratives of colonial history: "it seems to me that the whole of a non-narrativisable subaltern insurgency is in fact the reason why it is called subaltern by people like Guha: it is not within capital logic that these oppositions occur." This is their weakness, but also, Spivak suggests, their strength: "I think that their strength is that they're non-narrativisable."[25]

In this paradoxical spirit, one can read *Le quatrième siècle*'s inability to represent slave uprisings within the norms of traditional realist fiction as a sign of their disruptive force. It suggests, in other words, that these uprisings cannot be contained within the limits of the main narrative discourse of the novel. Several insurrections are referred to in the course of the narrative;[26] but they are never presented as *scenes*—as particular, singular events involving known individual characters, as in the key dramatic scenes describing Longoué's escape, Anne's murder of Liberté, or the hurricane, for instance.[27] We are told, briefly, that Longoué, Béluse, Anne, and Liberté participated in the insurrections, but we are not given any concrete detail of what happened. The same generalizing, abstract quality attaches to them as to the above-mentioned passage describing the cane-cutter's growing political consciousness. Individual motives for joining the uprising are either obscure (Béluse "not even asking himself why he had previously joined up with the rebels," *QS*, 114) or trivial ("Anne fought on the plantation owners' side for the simple reason that Liberté had followed a band of maroons," 137). The only interpretation Glissant gives of the utterance of insurgency is made in entirely general, extra-diegetic terms: "The revolt of a slave is nothing to do with hope . . . it inaugurates that most muted and painful of actions (of operations): taking root" (117).

In addition to merely summarizing the revolts from a distance, the text emphasizes their repetitiveness: "when *for the nth time* fighting broke out everywhere" (232); "a flare-up of revolt which *once again* shook the country" (137); "*each time* the despised, the slaves, the shackled agreed to die" (171); and so on (emphasis added). Thus, rather than singular, exceptional events that stand out against the monotony of daily life, they are simply a recurrent part of it. This comes across strongly in the following passage:

> This then was the situation on the two plantations when the revolt broke out everywhere. There is nothing to say about it, except that it was slavery: revolt is normal, wherever the slave finds a machete, a hoe, a stick. Just as one cannot completely describe the state of slavery (because of

that tiny but irreducible piece of reality that no description, no analysis will ever manage to include: the enfeebled mind waking up to pain, sometimes getting exasperated as the days pass, only to fall back into the everyday, the accepted, which is even more horrible than the spasm of damnation) so too there is nothing to say about this kind of revolt except that it is the *merry-go-round* of suffering. (117)

Moreover, the point is made explicitly in the context of the *unrepresentability* of day-to-day subaltern slave consciousness—"that tiny but irreducible piece of reality that no description . . . will ever manage to include"—and what is most striking here is that the uprisings are unrepresentable *in exactly the same way*. The text conflates the everyday and the unrepresentable: the revolts are *insignificant* in both senses: unremarkable but also unmeaningful. They form an "unreadable" part of the social text; later in the same passage, Glissant distinguishes between the middle-class political agitation in the towns and the completely separate violence of "the man enslaved to the masters' land," which is outside words, that is, nonnarrativizable: "His action was freed from the momentum of words" (118).

Insurrection, in other words, which is the only form of political action open to the slaves, cannot be made intelligible within the boundaries of conventional realist fictional discourse, and this "silence" is another indication of the irretrievability of subaltern consciousness. In "Can the Subaltern Speak?" it is in fact the major and crucial example: "When we come to the concomitant question of the consciousness of the subaltern, the notion of what the work *cannot* say becomes important. In the semioses of the social text, elaborations of insurgency stand in the place of 'the utterance.' The sender—'the peasant'—is marked only as a pointer to an irretrievable consciousness. . . . 'The subject' implied by the texts of insurgency can only serve as a counterpossibility for the narrative sanctions granted to the colonial subject in the dominant groups."[28]

The lack of organized leadership in the slave uprisings raises the related question of the *political* representation (*Vertretung*) of the subaltern. For Gramsci, the Italian peasants' only hope of victory was through an alliance with the organized proletariat in a revolutionary party. But in Martinique no such alliance was available. The claims of the legitimate political parties to represent the slaves, or later the agricultural workers, are false and self-serving; "the man," mentioned above, learns to see through their claims and to realize the futility of casting his vote (257–58).[29] The slaves do not see the constitutional efforts of the liberal bourgeoisie to abolish slavery as representing them (117–18). But neither are they able to act in their own name. An insurrection coincidentally taking place at the same time as the Franco-Prussian war takes as its slogan "Long live Wilhelm!" for the simple reason that he is an enemy of France; Mathieu asks: "And why not 'long live us'?" and is told: "Why not long live us—because you're surrounded by the sea: so if it's Wilhelm that it throws up on the sand, you take Wilhelm with his number, and you carry him on your head so as to be able to run forward" (232).[30]

If the urban political classes cannot represent the slaves or the agricultural workers, the only other possibility is the maroon community. But, as we have seen, the relationship between slaves and maroons is extremely ambivalent. When Louise is first taken up into the hills by Longoué, she looks for salvation to the maroons of Saint Domingue, whom she has heard about from the planters—Saint Domingue is "the supreme refuge where the maroons were organized and their word was law!" (108). Similarly, the maroons saw themselves as leaders, rescuing the slaves by inspiring and supporting their uprisings; thus, led by the first Longoué, "they all went down and burned a few plantations, to help the people down there who had risen up" (109). But the maroons have much less to lose than the slaves; Longoué can simply retreat to the hills and wait for the next occasion: "The revolt, bloodily put down, kept him busy for a few weeks. . . . When they finally realized that it was all over, that so many men and women were being massacred, he decided: 'It'll have to wait for another time'" (109). The maroons' superiority, in his eyes, over those who passively accept oppression means that his solidarity is mixed with a certain contempt: "Perhaps he thought the slaves were unworthy of his help . . . *why didn't they all join the maroons?*" But Glissant makes it clear that this arrogance is based on a false sense of autonomy; the maroon cannot see that his existence is actually dependent on the existence of the slave community: "He did not know how useful their struggle and their suffering was. He did not understand that they could not have come up en masse. The forest would not have been big enough to give them all shelter, let alone food. He did not know that their torment, and even their acceptance, were, therefore, protecting him" (109). The maroons' fighting, however brilliant and courageous, is also a kind of self-indulgence and almost an exploitation of the slaves, who suffer the reprisals; later the text refers to the way in which "the despised, the slaves, the shackled agreed to die in order that the proud, the untamed, could make their spectacular gesture of fire and battle" (171).

But it is not only the slave community that assures, indirectly, the survival of the maroons. The maroons' relationship with their enemy, the planters, changes over time from one of total opposition to a kind of hidden complicity. On one level this is simply because the planters realize that the existence of the maroons is not causing them any major problems: they can be accommodated within the plantation economy, and so they leave them alone (150). But, more insidiously, *Le quatrième siècle* also implies that there is an ideological complicity between the two sets of "lords" [*seigneurs*], based on their common contempt for the dominated slaves. It follows, therefore, that the status of both is undermined by the abolition of slavery: the masters no longer own the slaves, and the maroons lose the distinction of not being slaves. In other words, the slaves function as the self-consolidating subaltern Other of both masters and maroons, enabling both to define themselves as free, powerful, and superior. Thus, the "dark truth" of abolition is "that the lords, lords of the plantations or maroon-lords of the forests, would be forced to renounce their pact of splendor" (201).

The maroons, therefore, although at times they provide a form of heroic and very visible leadership for the slave uprisings, cannot act consistently as the slaves' political representatives because it is not in their interest to form a permanent political alliance with them. This disjunction has further repercussions on the representation (*Darstellung*) of slaves and maroons in the novel. To the extent that the maroons are not subalterns—either because they are popular heroes or because they share features of dominance with the planters—they seem to be easier to represent in the narrative discourse. Thus, Mathieu complains on several occasions that Papa Longoué talks about the maroon Longoué far more than he does about the slave Béluse. Béluse remains in the shadow; his subaltern consciousness has no "force," and it is difficult to find the words with which to talk about him: "I understand that Béluse isn't strong enough, we're always leaving him, he can't make us stay with him, I can even see that he doesn't give us any words, our speech drags when we try to make contact with what he was doing" (86).[31]

In summary, the narrative of *Le quatrième siècle* poses the problem of the representation of subaltern consciousness by implicitly revealing the limits of its own capacity to represent. It posits a subaltern narrator, Papa Longoué, who turns out to be only ambiguously subaltern and only ambiguously a narrator. The breaks and fade-outs in his voice are supplemented by an impersonal narrative, but this in turn cannot portray the key phenomenon of subaltern insurrection within its own well-established norms of fictional realism. The novel addresses the question of the subaltern's lack of political representation and demonstrates how the maroons, insofar as they do not represent the subaltern slave community, can more easily be incorporated into the dominant narrative discourse.

The other examples of the representation of subaltern consciousness that I discuss below are from *Mahagony* and all concern twentieth-century characters. First, the figure of Maho is relevant as a "degenerate" twentieth-century version of the maroon. Maho's story is a reworking of a central incident (based on a real event) in *Malemort,* set in the 1930s, in which the plantation foreman, Beautemps, suspects his woman, Adoline, of having been unfaithful to him with the planter who employs them both. Beautemps shoots the planter but only succeeds in wounding him, then flees to the hills and eludes the police for seven years until they finally surround him, whereupon he shoots himself rather than face capture.[32]

In *Mahagony* we learn that Beautemps's nickname is "Maho." He is described as "the last maroon of the century" (87). As such, he typifies the ambivalent status of the latter-day maroon. In *Malemort* he is presented as a hero—"soleil ensoleillé de sa seule force" [sun sunlit by its own force alone]—who was protected by the people and who remains in popular memory as an example of courage and resistance: "That force uprooted out of emptiness . . . and suddenly (yesterday or today or seven years ago) re-rooted in several memories, in the quivering acceptance of those who had not leapt out of the break, the gulf of oblivion" (54, 55). His death is movingly recounted as a brave and tragic gesture of defiance in the face of a cowardly band of policemen (58–61). At the same time, however, it is made clear that the people support him out of fear rather than solidarity: he is "that maroon who was terrorizing the workers" (44). But, again, Glissant is careful to elucidate the complex reasons for this fear. It is not because the people think that Beautemps will attack them if they refuse him food or shelter; rather (as in *Le quatrième siècle,* discussed earlier), the very admiration that his rebellion inspires is inseparable from a sense of shame at their own inability to rebel and fear of what might happen if they did:

> Because this force that weighed on him, secretly entered *them,* because they were suspicious of the incredible fact that a man could hold out alone against so many mobilized forces, because of course they rejected

the very idea of such a refusal to give in, of such a fight (whose success they attributed to *savage* forces), and because they all detected in him the old figure of the maroon for whom they still felt such panic-stricken fear, the maroon who expected neither love nor pity because his real function was not so much to remain free as to contest wherever he went the love and the pity that they all found themselves obliged to deal in just in order to survive and make life bearable. (45)

Here the text gives a cogent analysis of one of the difficulties of *Vertretung*: the very attributes that designate an individual as a potential political leader simultaneously prevent the people from identifying with him to an extent that would make collective action possible. For a community as politically entrapped as the plantation workers in this period, heroism is a deeply ambiguous quality. Maho thus represents a very late phase in the historical degeneration of the maroon, as *Malemort* again makes explicit: "he wasn't a Negator, he was forced to be merely a criminal a murderer and even when they called him a maroon it wasn't to build statues of him at the corners of war memorials it was to light up the night of fear in the children's hearts . . . *if Beautemps catches you and carries you off*" (56).[33]

By the time Beautemps/Maho reappears as one of the three central figures of *Mahagony,* his heroic qualities have almost completely disappeared. Here he is represented as "a fat overseer puffed up with jealousy" (92), more cruel and more stupid than he was in *Malemort,* both in relation to Adoline—since in *Malemort* there is no mention of the savage beating he inflicts on her when he believes, wrongly, that she was not raped by the planter but willingly slept with him—and to the people in general, whom he despises and whose attitude to him he cannot understand. Maho here, more subaltern than hero, cannot know his situation; he cannot consciously assume the role of leadership that would, perhaps, be possible given his objective status as popular icon of revolt: "But Maho . . . never guessed what a phalanx accompanied his wandering throughout these seven years. Concentrating more and more on his chosen task, which was to become wilder, rougher, more pitiless, more rapidly dirty and shabby, more crudely criminal, he had no idea of the dreams he had revived from a vertiginous past, nor of the proud inadmissible temptations that he implanted in the timid heads of the plantation workers" (*Mah,* 119).[34] In fact Mathieu, who narrates this section of *Mahagony* and engages in an argument with the "author," criticizes the earlier representation of Beautemps given in *Malemort* as being too "poetic"—"wrapped . . . in a veil of mystery and poetic confusion" (120). Glissant is in effect criticizing himself, in retrospect, for having subscribed to the myth of the hero rather than trying to understand the impact of Maho's actions in the present. Significantly, this coincides with a shift in his position on "letting the oppressed speak for themselves." In *Mahagony,* this view is now attributed to the "author" of *Malemort* and is challenged by Mathieu. That is, it is the "author" who is put in the position of saying that representing the oppressed is a form of assimilation and exploitation: "that the overseers turned maroons or the child prophets hadn't suffered their lives just so that we could exploit them in the form of palely accurate narratives." And, conversely, it is the more authoritative Mathieu who argues, in line with Spivak, that we have a responsibility to represent and analyze the "texts" of the oppressed: "I put it to him that we could understand the mutations that Maho had so weightily embodied, and that in so doing we would give a sort of useful echo to what had been a turbulent mortal agony" (121).

There is, however, an even more recent, and more diminished, version of the maroon in *Mahagony*—the adolescent Mani. The narrative concentrates on the last seven days of his life, which take place in the late 1970s. Mani and a friend, Filaos, get involved in a confrontation with some off-duty soldiers (149–50), the soldiers kill Filaos, Mani avenges him by going back and killing two of the soldiers on separate occasions. Mani goes back a third time to kill another soldier and is never seen again. His grandmother says that he is dead; his body is never found, and the assumption is that the soldiers killed him and the incident was covered up by the army (151, 155, 158).

Mani exemplifies the subaltern who cannot know or speak his situation. Marie Celat describes him simply as "le désordre" [disorder, disturbance] and sees him as typical of the internalized chaos of present-day Martinique: "But I think the disorder has now got into our heads and bodies. Not just imminent madness [*la folie en souffrance,* literally madness in suffering], but everything that you cannot even guess at, which drives you to savagery or despair" (135, 136). Mani, in other words, is wild and unpredictable because he cannot think straight. He does not spontaneously know himself but makes unconvincing attempts to construct an identity based on a disparate collection of out-of-date film stars: "He walked like Tarzan, he cut his hair like Ramon Novarro, he talked to women like Clark Gable. Except that it's not easy for a young black man with no moustache to play Captain what's-his-name in *Gone with the Wind*" (136).

No one knows why he acts as he does, not even his girlfriend Annie-Marie, who is the only person to whom he is really important. No one, therefore, can *represent* him, in either sense of the word. Annie-Marie juxtaposes this double impossibility (of *darstellen* and *vertreten*) when she says of him: "Who knows his reasons? Who has spoken for him?" (153). Marie Celat's daughter Ida assumes the role of Spivak's responsible intellectual representing the subaltern subject when she researches nineteenth-century uprisings in the north of the island. She knows, however, that the only names she can retrieve are those few "official" leaders, for the most part not themselves slaves, whose names have been recorded, and not the infinite number of "those who have never been entered on a court register, field niggers, who could be dealt with summarily" (160). And it is with the latter that she associates Mani, saying two pages later: "I think of Mani . . . his name isn't on the court registers" (162).

The way in which Mani is represented in *Mahagony* is determined by his inability to "speak for himself." Rather than claiming to reveal a full consciousness, the text approaches "this unapproachable young man" (171) through a number of detours, never reaching him but tracing his "effaced itinerary," to use Spivak's term. He is one of the three principal figures around whom the structure of *Mahagony* is elaborated. But with all three, the emphasis is on the difficulty of retrieving even the objective facts of their lives, let alone their consciousness. Thus, although they are in one sense central figures, they act as "holes" in the text rather than as substantial characters. The difference between Mani and the other two is that they—the nineteenth-century "child prophet" Gani and the outlaw Maho—are at least locally famous; they become folk heroes and acquire the ambiguous prestige of the typical maroon hero, whereas Mani remains completely obscure. He can thus be seen as an extreme case of the subaltern represented through his negative traces. This is achieved by first positioning him as a central character, through the novel's overall tripartite structure and through the attempts by Marie Celat, Ida, and Mathieu to reconstitute his story—but then by *subtracting* as much as possible from the representation of him. He is seen as unknowable but not mysterious; he has none of the aura that surrounds the "child prophet," for instance. Mystery is a form of plenitude: Gani possesses a secret knowledge that renders him potent. But Mani, as far as we can tell, has no secrets and no power. He is unknowable simply because he is outside discourse, a kind of blind spot in the social text. This has a number of consequences.

In the first place, he is not a coherent fictional character; he has contradictory attributes that cancel each other out. Ida says that she is afraid
of him (147), and then that she is not (162); he looks on her with contempt, and then calls her his sister (147); Odono describes his life as "an
organized rout" (149), a kind of contradiction in terms. But the most
striking and important feature of the text's construction of Mani is the
extent to which he is represented negatively through his *difference* from
other characters. This operates on two axes: he is different from Gani
and Maho but also from the contemporary Marny, a well-known criminal who was on the run at the same time.[35] All these others are represented in popular tradition. Gani consciously adopted the status of
leader, even though he was only a child. Maho and Marny did not, but
both inspired forms of rebellion in their communities, in Marny's case
even producing a quasi-political rhetoric in his supporters: "Annie-Marie
come with us the people commands" (154). None of them, of course,
was the leader of an organized political movement, and none of the uprisings with which they were associated was successful; but as individual
subjects they are "narrativized," in Spivak's terms, whereas Mani is not.

The differences between Mani, Gani, and Maho also stem from the
temporal progression within the novel. In the first place, the difficulty of
reconstructing the lives of Gani and Maho is due to their remoteness in
time: they belong to the past, and their obscurity results from the uncertainty of memory, the lack of records and so on, that is one of the most
resonant themes throughout Glissant's fiction. Conversely, the fact that
fragmentary traces of them have survived confers on them a kind of
prestige; their distance in time contributes to the aura of mystery surrounding them. Mani, on the other hand, is not mysterious or distant
but banally contemporary, and his obscurity is of a more elusive nature.
Equally, the transition from past to present marks the degeneration of
the maroon as hero. As Catherine Mayaux comments, referring to the
passage in *Le discours antillais* in which Glissant discusses this historical
phenomenon, "only Gani in *Mahagony* is a hero in the strict sense; each
of the other two characters is a derivative of his predecessor and embodies a further stage in the degradation of the concept of heroism."[36]
Mani's *marronnage* is simply a desperate and isolated gesture; the text
sums it up as "going on the run out of pure defiance, with no hope that
he could keep it up or gain a victory" (171). Although, insofar as he is
avenging the murder of his friend by the French army, his crime could be
seen as both more noble and more political than Maho's, it makes no
impact of any kind on the community.

Mayaux writes that one index of Mani's lack of heroic status is the fact that he is confused with the common criminal Marny.[37] But I would argue that it is his *difference* from Marny that is significant and that the confusion between them is paradoxically a sign of that difference. Marny at the age of eighteen stole a car, together with two accomplices, and was sentenced to prison for four years; released after two, he blamed the accomplices for having portrayed him as the ringleader and for not giving him, on his release, some money they had promised him. He decides to kill one of them in revenge but ends up killing three other people, more or less by mistake; arrested by the police, he escapes and despite a massive police hunt manages to evade recapture for nine days. This attracted a great deal of publicity and popular support; he became a symbol of revolt, and his escape nearly caused a mass riot: "with Marny on the loose, the general commotion, the revolution close at hand" (*Mah,* 170). People protected him, just as they had protected the earlier maroons, by giving him food and refusing to tell the police where he was hiding. When he was finally recaptured, he was deported to France to defuse the situation. *Mahagony* stresses the "public" status that he thus acquired, describing him as "a public figure . . . whose slightest gesture is known to everyone here" (192).

Marny's period of time on the run from the police coincides with that of the fictional Mani. Moreover, Mani at first covers his traces by shadowing Marny (171). Later he goes off on his own; but even then they both coincidentally ask the same fisherman, Maître Palto, to smuggle them across to Saint Lucia, and then both fail to turn up as arranged (156–57). In other words, Mani is *masked* by Marny, not only in that the army uses the Marny affair to distract attention from the killing of Mani, but more generally in that Marny's publicity initially shields but ultimately obliterates the "trace" of Mani, who remains silent and unknown.[38] As Ida comments: "Two explosions cancel each other out. What had been seen in the town, magnified by public rumor, blocked out what was stirring in the irretrievable unknown. Marny's newsworthiness drove Mani's obscurity even deeper underground" (158). Mani and Marny are thus separated by the opposition between public fame and anonymous isolation. But the "masking" effect is only possible because in other ways—their social marginality, their actions and the time and place in which they carry these out, and even their names—they are nearly identical. They are, as it were, superimposed on each other in the text: Mani is the shadowy double of Marny: "The trajectory that everyone knows about is blurred by an unreal trajectory," and he himself says: "We are doubles: one who makes a lot of noise, one whom nobody knows about" (171).

The text, then, represents Mani not as an individual in his own right but via the detour of his almost imperceptible difference from his two predecessors, and above all from Marny. His *differential* identity is made curiously literal in the near-doubling of their names, which when spoken are distinguished only by the *r* in Marny. But even this minimal difference exists only in standard French, because Martinican French lacks the phoneme *r*. So when Annie-Marie says "I must find Mani," the response is: "What are you talking about, Marny is in the Clarac hospital" (154). For Marie Celat, the overlap of the names serves simply to confuse the issue further: "Ida, you don't see that it's in order to disturb us. To obliterate the traces. To give you double vision. To add to the disorder" (142). But one could perhaps argue that the imperceptible difference signaled by the missing *r* in Mani—the phoneme that exists only in the elite discourse, the prestigious sign of Frenchness—serves also to figure Mani's exclusion from that discourse.[39]

The "Artémise, selon Adélaïde" chapter of *Mahagony* is one of the versions of Maho's story. In it we learn that in addition to his official concubine, Adoline, he is also loved by Artémise and by the washerwoman, Adélaïde, who becomes his housekeeper for a while before Adoline moves in, and who narrates the chapter. Adélaïde and Artémise are unambiguous examples of the colonized subaltern woman, who is doubly excluded, by gender as well as by class position, from the hegemonic discourse, which is exemplified here by the speech of the white nuns who run the local hospital.[40] I intend to show how their colonial Christian discourse imposes its construction of female sexuality, but also how revealing the subject-positions of Adélaïde and Artémise produces a kind of fissure in this discourse. As a further stage, I will show how Glissant's representation of Adélaïde and Artémise also deconstructs Western notions of identity and desire; the women *take each other's place* in a circulation of desiring female subjects around Maho as their common object. Finally, the same deconstructive process undermines the opposition of subject and object that is fundamental to self-representation in the dominant discourse.

At the outset, the three women are very clearly positioned as *socially* different in relation to *sexuality,* as defined by the Christian discourse. Adoline is the respectable wife; she is superior to the other two (Adélaïde refers to her as "madame Adoline"), because her body is the exclusive property of one man, Maho. Artémise is the "opposite," the sinful adolescent slut who will have sex with anyone on the plantation and then becomes a prostitute in the port. Underlying this opposition is, of course, the common Christian presupposition that the female body is an object of male property and exchange. Adélaïde herself represents a neutral term in the opposition, because she has no sexual relationships. She is socially inferior to Adoline but superior to Artémise because she is respectable; as washerwoman and Maho's housekeeper, she represents the "honest poor." She is, however, secretly in love with Maho. She exchanges her labor for her keep but also for the chance to live in relative, if nonsexual, intimacy with the object of her desire: "listen[ing] to him when he wasn't talking" (95).

The dominance of the Christian discourse of sexuality is clearly signaled by its privileged textual status, in that it is given the only piece of direct speech in the whole chapter:

> Il faut pardonner ma chère. Les pouvoirs du démon sont inépuisables, la miséricorde de Dieu aussi. Comment voulez-vous, avec cette chaleur de luxure. . . . Nous n'avons pas eu le temps de la policer, ni le pays avec, il y faudra cent ans au moins, au moins nous dirons des neuvaines pour son âme. La pauvre fille est bien punie. (99)

> [We must forgive, my dear. The devil's powers are inexhaustible, but so is God's mercy. What can you expect, with this lubricious heat. . . . We haven't had the time to civilize her, let alone the rest of the country, it will take at least a hundred years, at least we can say novenas for her soul. The poor girl has been punished enough.]

The nuns' hypocritically forgiving condemnation of Adoline's fall from virtue, their assumption that it is their duty to supervise her morals, and the cliché about the effect of the tropical climate all mark this utterance as typical of the discourse and also serve to link Adoline's sinfulness to that of the whole society: both need to be "policed," and the civilizing mission will take at least another hundred years.

Maho himself has an ambiguous relation to the Christian discourse, splitting apart its sexual and racial parameters. That is, in rejecting Adoline he is on the one hand subscribing to the Christian notion of female fidelity, but by trying to kill the white man responsible for her supposed infidelity, he transgresses the doctrine of the civilizing mission, and the church rejects him, refusing to give him a Christian burial (103–4).[41]

But the representation of Artémise produces a clearer, albeit mute, contestation. There is no attempt to represent her consciousness. She never articulates her position in any way; at no point are we told what she is thinking or feeling, and she remains unknowable in much the same way as Mani is. It is not her sexual activity per se that undermines the Christian discourse: it can be unproblematically represented in it as sinful and typically Caribbean. For instance, her only (indirect) contact with the nuns occurs when she attacks a would-be lover and the nuns calmly patch him up: "One day she bit one of them's balls, he was in hospital for a week, the Sisters chattered away as they bandaged him" (101). Nevertheless, she acts as a silent, opaque locus of resistance to the dominant construction of female sexuality in two specific ways, both of which are in fact related to her speechlessness. The first of these occurs when Maho rides past as she is having sex with someone, and he notices her for the first time:

> Sa tête tourne comme une mécanique pour suivre le géreur qui passe. Il passe sur le mulet, les yeux du géreur les yeux d'Artémise se suivent par-dessus le han-han du fornicateur, le géreur disparaît sans dire un mot, comme s'il n'avait pas vu. Alors elle rit tellement que le coqueur est dé-monté. Elle s'arrête aussi sec. On dit depuis ce jour elle a perdu la voix. Sûr certain, elle pousse comme un cochon des bois, houin-houin, elle ne dit pas autre mot. (97)

> [Her head turns like a clockwork toy following the overseer as he goes past. He rides past on his mule, his eyes her eyes following each other above the fornicator's panting, the overseer disappears without a word, as though he hadn't seen her. Then she laughs so hard that the fucker is thrown off his stride. She stops just as suddenly. They say that was the day she lost her voice. No doubt about it, she grows like a wild pig, grunting, she doesn't say another word.]

This is the moment she stops speaking. Before that, however, she *laughs*. The laugh remains completely opaque; we do not know what it means, but we do know that it "démonte" ("throws," but also "takes apart, dis-mantles") the male exploiter of her body. Artémise's laugh here is reminiscent of the ending of "Draupadi," when the tortured and multiply raped heroine reduces the army officer to unreasonable terror by laughing at him: a moment that Spivak defines as "the menacing appeal of the objectified subject to its politico-sexual enemy—the provisionally silenced master of the subject-object dialectic."⁴² The laugh, then, reveals both Draupadi and Artémise as *subjects* in discourse, momentarily positioned in such a way as to be able to "démonter" the dominant discourse.

Secondly, Artémise's speechlessness defines her as an animal—a "cochon des bois" [wild pig]. In the context, animality is also strongly associated with sexuality (her "houin-houin" echoing the "han-han" of the "fornicator"), and, since she is a woman, with female sexuality in particular. (A further sense of "démonter" is perhaps relevant here, suggesting that she is a horse throwing off her male rider.) Thus, the image of animality brings together the inability to speak and female sexuality, and so by implication positions the latter outside discourse.

Another version of the equation of speechless animality and female sexuality is used to convey the related idea that the latter is unknowable by man. Maho's mule acts as a metaphorical equivalent to all three of "his" women: he rides the mule as he "rides" the women. It is first associated with Artémise (supposedly sterile, like a mule) "attached to the tail of that mule" (118). But when Maho flees after wounding the planter, it is Adélaïde who wonders what has happened to the mule and imagines it being eaten by the "giant" who is a mythical version of Maho (101), just as he is eating the food left for him by the women, which is the main expression of their love for him. The last paragraph of the chapter, however, reveals that the planter now possesses the mule, just as he allegedly possessed Adoline, and is beating the mule just as Maho beat Adoline when he thought the planter had possessed her. (Earlier, moreover, when Adélaïde imagines how Maho imagines the planter having sex with Adoline, he still has his riding boots and spurs on (99)). But the sense of the metaphor becomes clear only in the very last sentence: a question that situates both men in terms of their inability to *know* any of the women: "What does he think, that one, on an unnatural mule who he doesn't even know?" (105).

The most textually explicit fracturing of the Catholic discourse is effected by Adélaïde herself, in a process that develops gradually in the course of the chapter. In the first paragraph (94) she describes herself as a respectable and self-respecting woman who can look people in the eye. At first she uses biblical language to condemn Artémise (who is, for instance, "sterile by the grace of God," 97) and by implication to contrast herself with Artémise. But as her narration progresses, she moves closer to the other woman, and this very striking rapprochement leads to and is marked by a subversive reappropriation of religious terms. Thus, the money Artémise earns through prostitution is a benediction (107); the mahogany tree that shelters Maho once he is on the run from the police is a tabernacle, and the food that both Artémise and Adélaïde bring him there is "disposé à la Sainte Table" [laid out on the Holy Altar] (101); the work that Artémise and Adélaïde do in order to make enough money to buy the food is a "sacerdoce" [holy vocation] (102); and all three women are finally referred to as "la Trinité du manger" [the Trinity of food] (104).

Adélaïde's realigning herself with Artémise in a movement that simultaneously fractures the dominant Catholic discourse can also be traced through what happens to Adélaïde's voice. When Maho moves Adoline into his house, he dismisses Adélaïde, and this rejection results in her losing her voice (98). This consequence is juxtaposed with a description a few lines later of Artémise running through the streets "without a word without a cry," just after we learn that she stopped talking on the day that Maho saw her having sex with another man. There are several references to Adélaïde's inability to speak during the period from her dismissal by Maho to his death (100, 101). But after his death, both women recover their voices; Artémise talks passionately to his corpse (104), and the nuns persuade Adélaïde to join the church choir, telling her: "Adélaïde vraiment vous avez une voix *bien placée*" [Adélaïde, you really do have a well-pitched voice] (104, emphasis added). It would appear, in other words, that Adélaïde has been brought submissively back into the Catholic fold and that it is on these terms that her voice has been restored—literally given a "place" by and in the Christian discourse. But this assumption is immediately contradicted by the text, which makes it clear that the *power* she acquires through being in the choir is a power that she turns against the church. Far from identifying with the other church officials, she looks down on them and sees herself as controlling them: "When I'm singing my body rises up, I look down on the acolytes the deacons the canon, they look like a procession of ants. My voice sweeps them along like a wind" (104). Moreover, she "turns" her singing toward Artémise, whom she imagines running through the church (as she used to run through the streets): "I sing for Artémise . . . from up in the Choir I see her running in between the Latin words the smoke of the incense" (104). That is, she inserts Artémise into the ritual Christian discourse like a kind of wedge that breaks it open.

But Adélaïde's move toward solidarity with Artémise also signifies a change in her representation of herself and her feelings for Maho, and this has other, less direct repercussions on the dominant discourse's representation of identity and desire. Artémise openly desires Maho right from the start, while Adélaïde's desire is initially kept a secret. Therefore, Adélaïde's move toward Artémise is also connected to the ability to assume herself as a sexually desiring subject. It is effected in the first place on the level of sight and visibility. At the beginning of her narration, Adélaïde asserts her virtue and respectability by saying: "I can look people in the eye," while Artémise, conversely, is a shameful *object* of vision, "an outrage for the eyes" (94). But if others could see Adélaïde's desire for Maho, she would lose her respectability, and so her desire has to remain invisible; she arranges to become his housekeeper in such a way that it appears to be an accident: "No one *saw* that it was my intention" (94–95, emphasis added). This gives her a certain status and a respectable cover for her feelings. But when he gets rid of her, her secret desire for him intensifies to the point that its necessary invisibility seems to spread to the whole of her identity, and she becomes invisible to others: "No one looks at me, even without a word, without a start" (98). Significantly, this immediately follows the exchange of looks between Maho and Artémise, quoted earlier: "his eyes her eyes following each other above the fornicator's panting" (97), thus contrasting Artémise's visibility and overt sexual desire for Maho with their opposites in Adélaïde. Similarly, Adoline, the object of Maho's desire, looks through her as though she does not exist (100).

The situation changes when Maho is on the run, and all three women are helping him by leaving food by the mahogany tree. Explicitly comparing herself to Artémise, Adélaïde says she does not care who sees her going up into the hills: "Whoever looks at me, I don't give a fuck, Adélaïde has her vocation too" (102). Finally, after Maho's death, the policemen who had been tracking him for seven years say that they saw her bringing him food in the woods: "Adélaïde, we saw you, you were the last of the Trinity of food" (104); and this would seem to constitute a very oblique recognition of her as being, like Artémise, a desiring subject. It also recognizes her as an *opaque* presence, resistant to the forces of law and order.

The movement that brings the two women together also operates through the connection between female desire and female work. They are initially opposed in that Adélaïde, the washerwoman, is "clean" while Artémise, the prostitute, is "dirty"; Adélaïde uses the river to wash clothes in while Artémise bathes in it to show off her naked body to the men, "but didn't scrub very hard" (95), as Adélaïde observes disapprovingly. Nevertheless, they are both working for the same reason, in order to earn enough money to feed Maho. Adélaïde admits that they earn an equivalent amount: "She made three francs a day, sometimes five. So she earned as much as I did in the river. A hundred and twenty-five francs a month, I assume she didn't labor on the sabbath let's hope not" [*je suppose elle ne besogne pas le dimanche il faut espérer*] (101). The fact that this appreciation of Artémise's earning power is immediately followed by the first use of the religious discourse ["besogner"] to be slightly but distinctly sardonic, shows yet again how solidarity with Artémise goes hand in hand with a distancing from the Catholic representation of female sexuality. The next sentence makes a far more concrete connection between the two women in terms of their work: "Each time I turn a pair of trousers inside out to scrub them I think, Artémise. Each garment for me is a man for her" (102). If Adélaïde's job is washing the trousers of Artémise's clients, they might as well be in business together. This in turn is followed by a grudging compliment: "She must be made out of wrought iron"; and finally Adélaïde says: "She's protecting her business, I respect her, I can't do anything but respect her" (102).

Adélaïde, then, via an evolving identification with Artémise, redefines herself as a sexual subject who desires the outlaw Maho. This in itself constitutes a rejection of the Christian code of sexuality, but the identification has further implications for a more general western ideological construction of identity. The culmination of Adélaïde's movement toward Artémise is the idea, expressed in the last paragraph of the chapter, that she too might become a prostitute: "I'll go to the port to look for Artémise. If I can't find her, maybe I'll take her place" (104–5). This notion of women *taking each other's place* subverts the humanist conception of identity. It extends beyond this particular instance to include all three of the women in the chapter in a series of displacements and permutations: Adoline takes Adélaïde's place in Maho's house; Adélaïde takes Adoline's place with the nuns in the hospital; Artémise takes Adélaïde's place in the street: "See how in the street Artémise has replaced Adélaïde who had replaced madame Adoline in the hospital when madame Adoline replaced her in the overseer's house" (98–99); and, finally, Adélaïde envisages taking Artémise's place as a prostitute. This kind of circulation, in which Adélaïde can as easily assume a place working in the convent hospital as working on the docks as a prostitute, undermines the notion of the individual as possessing a singular identity.[43] It also redefines desire, since it takes place above all around Maho: the three women "replace" each other in taking food to him, in a "grand circulation" (102) in the woods. The women are not, ultimately, competing with each other for Maho but "relaying" each other in their common attempt to protect him from the police. Their desire for him, in other words, has no component of narcissism, and so reverses a certain set of Western humanist assumptions concerning individual subjecthood and desire. It also, more specifically, reverses the Lacanian schema whereby the *objects* of desire undergo a series of metonymic displacements; here we have a series of *subjects* of desire displacing (replacing) themselves in a circulation around a single object.[44]

There are other points in Adélaïde's narration where the opposition between subject and object actually blurs into indeterminacy, again in relation to desire, but also in relation to self-representation in general. Before Adoline agrees to move in with Maho, he spends all his spare time sitting on the veranda staring at the wall, as if he can see her on it. Meanwhile Artémise follows him about everywhere, without him seeing her. In other words, he sees the woman who is not there and does not see the woman who is. Commenting on this symmetrical paradox, Adélaïde says: "Maintenant il a deux femmes *pour courir après*, une sur la cloison, affichée comme une enveloppe de la poste, une qui court tous les chemins à peine ses tétés sont sortis" [Now he has two women to *run after* (him), one on the wall, stuck there like an envelope, one running all over the place with her tits hardly grown yet] (96, emphasis added). Is the grammatical subject of "courir après" Maho or the women? It is Maho who is metaphorically running after Adoline but Artémise who is literally running after Maho. But the syntax of the sentence annuls this difference, merging the two together in the infinitive phrase. The text thus exploits the nonstandard French of its narrator to construct Maho and the women as undifferentiated subjects-objects of desire.

Two pages later, a similar sentence structure brings together the same three people in the same indeterminate structure of subject-object relations. By this time Adoline has moved into the house, and Maho has seen Artémise with the other man. Adélaïde again comments: "Il a une femme *pour le servir,* une autre *pour la regarder coquer* quand il passe sur son mulet"[He has a woman to serve him, another to look at her screwing when he rides past on his mule] (98, emphasis added). In this case, the grammatical subject of "servir" is "a woman," that is, Adoline, but the subject of "regarder" is Maho, with Artémise as the object; but the parallelism of the two "*pour* + infinitive" constructions again works to neutralize the difference between subject and object.[45]

A third example concerns Adélaïde herself and her own representation (or lack of it) of herself as subaltern. It occurs in the context of her inability to speak—in this case to describe the incident of Maho's attack on Adoline: "Les gens demandent Adélaïde vous étiez là comment c'est arrivé toute cette tragédie? Je ne peux pas répondre, même si mon corps était là. Je suis femme réservée qui souvent *tombe en oubli*" [People ask Adélaïde you were there how did it all happen that awful tragedy? I cannot answer, even though my body was there. I am a quiet woman who often falls into forgetting/oblivion] (101, emphasis added). This in the first place literalizes the notion of the subaltern who cannot speak, whose "body" knows but is silent.[46] The reason Adélaïde gives for her speechlessness initially echoes the self-definition that opens the chapter ("Moi je suis femme réservée" [I am a quiet (literally, reserved) woman], 94), and that places her as a virtuous, nonsexual woman in the terms of the dominant Christian discourse. But it immediately switches to a much less clear-cut and assertive formulation: "qui souvent tombe en oubli" carries exactly the same ambiguity between subject and object as the two examples analyzed above. Here, however, it is to do with consciousness rather than desire. If the implied subject of the nominalized verb "oubli" is Adélaïde herself, then "qui souvent tombe en oubli" refers to a loss of consciousness of self: she "forgets" herself, "falls" into a kind of unconsciousness. It would thus be a parallel to "Je suis tombée en catalepsie" [I had a cataleptic fit] a few lines later. Alternatively, however, "souvent tombe en oubli" could equally well mean that *other people* forget her: she falls into oblivion, as in the more standard phrase "tomber dans l'oubli." In this case it implies the invisibility—evoked by Adélaïde herself elsewhere—and lack of presence of the subaltern to others. By as it were condensing "*en* catalepsie" and "dans l'*oubli*," the text makes it impossible to decide between these two alternatives, and in so doing positions Adélaïde as indeterminately subject and object of a "forgetting."

This blurring of any clear distinction between subject and object in relation to consciousness and sexual desire is completely alien to Western humanist representations of subjecthood, in which the polarity between subject and object subtends a number of other important distinctions and relationships. It is, therefore, a good example of the way in which the uncovering of subaltern subject-positions can, sometimes, exert an oblique kind of pressure on the dominant discourse.

Adélaïde is perhaps the most striking example of the representation of the subaltern in Glissant's fiction. Her observation that "La trace d'Adélaïde n'est pas tracée" [Adélaïde's path is not marked] (98) unites the Martinican sense of "path" with the standard French meaning of imprinting one's mark on the world and, perhaps, even the philosophical sense of the Derridean trace. The sentence as a whole encapsulates the paradoxical negativities inherent in the attempt to trace, precisely, the

"effaced itinerary" of subaltern consciousness. But the issue of subalternity has, as I have shown, a number of different kinds of relevance to
Glissant's writing: from the problems of political representation and
subaltern insurrection, to the fissuring, albeit marginal, of the hegemonic discourse and deconstructing of hegemonic representations of individual identity and desire.

4 The Other's Language

From Alienation to Madness

THE LANGUAGE of the white Other—*béké* or metropolitan French—is a constant and negative reference point in Glissant's theoretical writing and in his fiction. But, as the concept of counterpoetics and his analysis of Creole make clear, "white" language is not simply *opposed*: in fact, some of its most damaging effects derive from the way in which French and its cultural values are—partially and ambivalently—internalized by Martinicans. The French language becomes an object of desire and identification. This is less for practical reasons such as employment prospects than because the language is emblematic of white French civilization. The colonized subject, in other words, suffers a particular kind of alienation that involves imitating and identifying with the European Other and, hence, losing any autonomous perspective on reality. As Glissant formulates it: "The Martinican . . . sees through eyes that are not his own"; he goes on to quote the Creole saying: "Zié béké brilé zié nèg" [The white man's eyes have burned the black man's eyes] (*DA*, 289).

Glissant's term for this phenomenon is the *pulsion mimétique* [mimetic drive], and, in both his theoretical works and his fiction, he analyzes its psychological and social effects. In *Le discours antillais*, he argues that this "obsession with imitation" is impossible to live with, not only because the imitation can never succeed but because the obsession itself is unbearable: "The mimetic impulse is a kind of insidious violence" (*CD*, 18). Both *Le discours antillais* and the novels show how, in many cases, it leads to psychotic breakdown.[1]

Glissant emphasizes the importance of the mimetic drive's verbal dimension: to "be" the white Frenchman is above all to *speak* like he does, and Glissant explains "the desiring violence of speech" in Martinique as above all a desire to be other and to be elsewhere (*DA*, 292). Martinicans, he claims, are fascinated by eloquence, to the point where the substance of what is said matters less than its rhetorical style (*DA*, 380). Equally, the kinds of neurosis or mental breakdown that constitute the extreme form of this alienation are themselves predominantly to do with language, as he shows in a detailed analysis of what he calls "verbal delirium" (*DA*, 361–91). The mimetic drive, language, and delirium are thus inextricably linked.

Glissant's exploration of the mimetic drive is influenced by the earlier work of his fellow Martinican Frantz Fanon, whose *Peau noire masques blancs* [Black Skin, White Masks] (1952) and *Les damnés de la terre* [The Wretched of the Earth] (1961) had a great impact in France and beyond, and have become key texts in postcolonial theory. A comparison of these with the relevant sections of *Le discours antillais* illuminates both Glissant's theory and the representations of the mimetic drive in his fiction. Fanon was the first colonized intellectual to look in depth at the psychological effects of colonialism and to claim that the colonizing process per se created psychopathological conditions. This, he argues, can only be accounted for by positing a collective unconscious—not genetic, but created by social pressures.[2] The problem therefore can only be explained in psychoanalytic terms, but the psychoanalytic interpretation must itself be articulated with social and economic factors. Every kind of neurosis in the Caribbean, he states categorically, results from the cultural situation and the absence of a "black" vision of reality. This bringing together of psychoanalysis and socioeconomic analysis is central to Fanon's theory. In the introduction to *Black Skin, White Masks*, he formulates it as follows:

> I believe that only a psychoanalytical interpretation of the black problem can lay bare the anomalies that are responsible for the structure of the complex. . . . The analysis that I am undertaking is psychological. In spite of this it is apparent to me that the effective disalienation of the black man entails an immediate recognition of social and economic realities. If there is an inferiority complex, it is the outcome of a double process: primarily economic; subsequently, the internalization—or, better, the epidermalization—of this inferiority.

The psychoanalytic dimension means that theories of colonialism have to take into account the subjective experience of the colonized—as the chapter entitled "L'expérience vécue du Noir" (translated, rather misleadingly, as "The Fact of Blackness") implies—and this above all means *desire*: hence the famous opening question "What does the black man want?"[3]

The starting point for a possible answer to this question is Fanon's view of the colonial world as divided into two completely separate and incompatible zones, one white and one black, creating a Manichaean situation in which everything black is inferior and everything white is superior: "The colonial world is a Manichean world . . . [the colonizer turns the colonized into] a sort of quintessence of evil." The black man is defined by the more powerful white view of him, which he internalizes in an extension of slavery on the psychological level: "After having been the slave of the white man, he enslaves himself . . . a victim of white civilization" (192). He has no choice but to do this, Fanon argues in *Black Skin, White Masks,* because at least in the case of the French Caribbean (unlike North America, for instance), black people have not fought for their freedom and therefore have not *forced* whites to recognize them as *black*. In this situation there is no escape from the white view of reality, and the only way in which black people can escape from the white stereotype of them is to try to "become" white: "The black man wants to be like the white man. For the black man there is only one destiny. And it is white. Long ago the black man admitted the unarguable superiority of the white man, and all his efforts are aimed at achieving a white existence." This is Fanon's explanation for what Glissant calls the mimetic drive; Glissant's own explanation draws on it, as we shall see.[4]

Black Skin, White Masks as a whole is about the mimetic drive. On the one hand, Fanon sees this as the desire of every colonized people;[5] on the other hand, he devotes much of the text to the situation in Martinique, and here his comments are particularly trenchant: "It is in fact customary in Martinique, to dream of a form of salvation that consists of magically turning white." The desire to be white produces various forms of alienation. In the first place, it is alienating simply because it is a fantasy ("magically turning white"); later in the book Fanon claims that *all* perception of oneself and others is made unreal by being filtered through the ideal of whiteness: "in the Antilles perception always occurs on the level of the imaginary. It is in white terms that one perceives one's fellows . . . every Antillean expects all the others to perceive him in terms of the essence of the white man." Secondly, while the mimetic drive is in the first instance a tactic for escaping from the white man's stereotype of the black man, it also requires the black man, in his attempt to become white, to reject his own "black" view of black society, including his family.[6] Thirdly, desire in all human beings is closely bound up with identification; in Lacan's famous formula, desire is the desire of the Other. But when the Other is white, and the black subject's desire is to be desired as white—to become white by being desired by the Other— then all desire has to be channeled to this one, usually impossible, end: sexual partners and friends are chosen solely for their ability to confer the magic whiteness on the subject. Thus, Fanon writes of a mulatto woman loved by a white man: "She was no longer the woman who wanted to be white. She was white. She was joining the white world." In the chapter entitled "The Negro and Recognition," he uses Hegel's concept of desire for recognition to define the need for identification to be legitimized by the Other with whom one identifies: "Every one of the Antillean's actions is mediated through the Other . . . because it is the Other who confirms him in his need for valorization."[7]

Homi Bhabha makes extensive reference to Fanon's work throughout *The Location of Culture* and particularly in his second chapter, "Interrogating Identity." He theorizes the mechanism of identification, in its relation to desire and the construction of the ego, more fully than Fanon does, but from the same basic perception that "it is always in relation to the place of the Other that colonial desire is articulated." Colonial identification, he goes on to argue, always involves an acute form of *splitting:* "The demand of identification—that is, to be *for* another—entails the representation of the subject in the differentiating order of otherness. Identification . . . is always the return of an image of identity that bears the mark of splitting in the Other place from which it comes." In a subsequent chapter, "The Other Question," this is explained in terms of the fetishistic disavowal, which, as I discuss in chapter 1, Bhabha claims is at work in the mechanism of the racial stereotype. Produced by the colonizer, it is then also—as we have seen in Fanon's description—internalized by the colonized subject. Disavowal involves believing two contradictory things at the same time. It thus splits the colonized subject, obliged to hold two conflicting beliefs *about itself* at the same time: Bhabha refers to "the multiple beliefs and split subjects that constitute colonial discourse as a consequence of its process of disavowal."[8]

This notion of splitting is also prominent in Fanon's own writing. *Black Skin, White Masks* describes the Caribbean individual's illusion that Europe will confer a kind of plenitude on his or her being. In reality, however, the desire for Europe—the mimetic drive—itself has the opposite effect of splitting the ego, because the identification with whiteness, for all its desperate intensity, can by definition never be total. There are two reasons for this. First, black people can never, according to Fanon, free themselves totally from their acceptance of the white view of them as black and hence inferior: the more closely they identify with white values the more violently they reject their own, inevitably persisting, blackness: "There is no help for it: I am a white man. [So], unconsciously, I distrust what is black in me, that is the whole of my being." The Manichaean vision of colonialism aligns the opposition of good and evil with that of white and black, effectively splitting the black subject's identity: "Moral consciousness implies a kind of scission, a fracture of consciousness into a bright part and an opposing [dark] part. In order to achieve morality, it is essential that the black, the dark, the Negro vanish from consciousness. Hence, a Negro is forever in combat with his own image."[9]

The second reason for the impossibility of total identification with the white world is very different: it is the ambivalence at the root of the mimetic drive itself. In *The Wretched of the Earth* Fanon points out that envy and desire coexist with hatred of the white man and a desire for revenge. This ambivalence produces a "state of permanent tension" in which "taking the white man's place" is as much an act of aggression as of emulation: "We have seen that the native never ceases to dream of putting himself in the place of the settler. Not of becoming the settler but of substituting himself for the settler." Bhabha pursues the logic of this in terms of split identification: "the very place of identification . . . is a space of splitting. The fantasy of the native is precisely to occupy the master's place while keeping his place in the slave's *avenging* anger. 'Black skin, white masks' is not a neat division; it is a doubling, dissembling image of being in at least two places at once."[10]

The writing throughout *Black Skin, White Masks* is striking for its various images of splitting: scission, amputation, *fêlure* [crack], fissure, etc. All of these serve to underline the violence done to the colonized psyche by the mimetic drive. Fanon writes, for instance: "I shouted a greeting to the world and the world [*amputated* me from] my joy"; "From the moment the Negro accepts the *separation* [*clivage*] imposed by the European, he has no further respite"; "The Martinican is a man *crucified*. The environment that has shaped him (but that he has not shaped) has horribly *drawn and quartered* him"; and so on. Given this lexis of mutilation, it is not surprising that the mimetic drive tends toward the destruction of the ego's defenses. Fanon quotes Anna Freud on the healthy ego's capacity to withdraw into itself as a defense mechanism and contrasts this with the inability of the colonized ego to do so because it has no autonomous sense of interiority: "We understand now why the black man cannot take pleasure in his insularity. For him there is only one way out and it leads into the white world . . . it is from within that the Negro will seek admittance to the white sanctuary." Therefore, the ego may fragment: "when the Negro makes contact with the white world, a certain sensitizing action takes place. If his psychic structure is weak, one observes a collapse of the ego." Thus, the alienation caused by the mimetic drive often results in serious psychiatric disorders, including psychotic breakdown. The only cure, according to Fanon, is what in *Black Skin, White Masks* he calls "a restructuring of the world," which in *The Wretched of the Earth* becomes the less abstract project of revolutionary armed struggle.[11]

The psychological phenomena described in *Black Skin, White Masks* affect many different aspects of individual and social existence. But Fanon does accord "a basic importance" to language—the first chapter is "The Negro and Language"—because language for him is essentially concerned with existing for others and because of the close links between language and the cultural milieu: "To speak a language is to take on a world, a culture. The [Caribbean man] who wants to be white will be the whiter as he gains greater mastery of the cultural tool that language is."[12] This sensitivity to the social and cultural distinctions that language embodies has an effect on Fanon's own writing; it is unusually diverse for a theoretical discourse in that it constantly cites or mimics other people's language. There are a large number of referenced quotations, from literary as well as psychiatric and psychoanalytical texts. But he also incorporates fragments of language that are simply remembered, or perhaps invented, utterances from anecdotal, anonymous, but highly recognizable sources. These are invariably used ironically; the Other's language is parodied to reinforce the argument that Fanon is expressing in his own words. For instance: "Les Noirs, je les connais; il faut s'adresser à eux gentiment, leur parler de leurs pays; savoir leur parler, telle est la question" [Oh, I know all about black people; you have to be nice to them, and talk to them about their country; the thing is to know how to talk to them]; or the doctor addressing an Arab or black patient; or the exchange with the guard on the train. A more complex example parodies, not white speech, but the Cesairean discourse of Négritude (following an actual quotation from Aimé Césaire): "Eh! le tam-tam baragouine le message cosmique. Seul le nègre est capable de le transmettre, d'en déchiffrer le sens, la portée. A cheval sur le monde, les talons vigoureux contre les flancs du monde, je lustre l'encolure du monde" [Eh! the tom-tom gibbers out the cosmic message. Only the negro is capable of passing it on, deciphering its meaning, its impact. Astride the world, strong heels against the flanks of the world, I stroke the world's neck].[13] Although Fanon is here criticizing Négritude, he is also describing his own past involvement with it, so the passage contains a dimension of self-parody as well. His use of the Other's language thus makes possible a complex manipulation of different kinds of irony.

His theoretical stance on the role of language in the mimetic drive is, however, rather more simple. He sees it as a symptom of the larger problem, rather than as an issue in its own right. That is, French racists assume that black people cannot speak or understand standard French and therefore address them in their own idea of colonial pidgin or *petit nègre*. This is an important aspect of the stereotype and of its forcible imposition on the black man—a way of trapping him in it: "To make him talk pidgin is to fasten him to [his image], to snare him, to imprison him." The way out of the trap is simply to oblige the white man to recognize that the black man speaks standard French, exactly as he does, thus refuting the stereotype: "Nothing is more astonishing than to hear a black man express himself properly, for then [he really is taking on] the white world. . . . With him the game cannot be played, he is a complete replica of the white man." In other words, despite his insistence that a language carries with it its particular cultural world, Fanon sees no problem in the colonized subject's use of the dominant colonial language. He nowhere questions the subjective relationship *with* language that Glissant is centrally concerned with, and so he does not see any need, as Glissant does, for a "new" language.[14]

Looking at *Le discours antillais,* we can see how Glissant's view of the colonized subject's alienation is very close to Fanon's in its guiding principles, but Glissant develops and problematizes the role of language in far greater depth. In the article "Pôles et propositions" (*DA,* 284–93), he develops a version of Fanon's conception of a socially constructed collective unconscious, arguing that *in certain conditions* sociohistorical factors can act directly on the unconscious, as it were short-circuiting ideology, to form "a field of 'common' drives that one could therefore call the unconscious of a collectivity" (*DA,* 285). There are two such conditions, and both are present in the Martinican situation. The first— an alienated relation to the environment—results from the absence of any autonomous economic production and means that individuals cannot mediate their relation to the environment through "technical practice." The second is a lack of collective political action, which elsewhere, as we have seen in the discussion of the detour, Glissant explains as the result of the *covert* nature of political domination in Martinique. One could add a third condition, which he discusses elsewhere: the lack of any "real" (i.e., determined by its relation to economic production) class system in Martinique, so that the relations between social classes are obscured or artificial. In this situation, individual pathology results *directly* from social alienation and so can only be understood in the context of a social and cultural analysis (*DA,* 290). Psychosis here is a response to the social situation and thus, in a sense, a *choice*; Glissant refers to "the psychotic violence of radical choice in 'madness'" (*DA,* 292).

But, equally—and this too accords with Fanon's view of colonial society—behavior accepted as *normal* by the community is based on a misrecognition of its social situation, which is actually neurotic; "this misrecognition is compulsively subsumed by a sort of compensatory but unbalanced para-ideology" (*DA,* 289). For Fanon, such misrecognition can only be combatted by revolutionary action; Glissant, more pessimistically, sees it as the product of a situation in which revolutionary action is impossible because the enemy has become invisible in the "successful colonization" to which he refers at the beginning of *Le discours antillais*—the phrase itself echoing Fanon's sentence in *The Wretched of the Earth*: "There is thus during this calm period of successful colonization a regular and important mental pathology which is the direct product of oppression" (201).[15] The misrecognition in turn leads to the privileging of role over function (*DA,* 288): the importance attached to social status and image, corresponding to no real social function. The whole society is living with an acute but suppressed contradiction between appearance and reality.

This occultation of social relations has damaging psychological effects. Specifically, it underlies "verbal delirium" and accounts for its prevalence and its acceptance by the society as a kind of normality: "In the dramatic ambiguity of a colonial society *which no longer exhibits the extreme clear-cut forms of domination,* verbal delirium is not an 'illness' affecting some people, it is the temptation that affects everyone" (*DA,* 362). The section of *Le discours antillais* devoted to verbal delirium (361–92) is a central part of Glissant's critique of Martinican society. It makes the important and provocative claim that this is a society in which psychopathology is impossible to define. Sanity has become a kind of insanity and vice versa. "The analysis of what I call mental deprivation shows that its most obvious manifestations are not to be found

in the pathological or the delirious, but in the very texture of daily existence, through the lack of any reference to oneself" (*DA*, 212). European
distinctions between sanity and madness, normality and abnormality,
are untenable because the social situation as a whole is abnormal. Therefore the *individual*'s "abnormality" cannot be measured as deviance
from a social norm; the (statistical) norm itself is (psychologically) abnormal. Deviance is also a detour—an alienated way to find a way
around alienation.[16]

These contradictions, Glissant claims, are most evident in the area of
language use: "For if it is the situation itself that is likely to be 'abnormal,' then how could one use it as a basis for defining 'norms' in relation
to which a certain kind of verbal behaviour could be held to be 'delirious'?" (*DA*, 363). He constantly stresses the continuities between
"mad" and "sane" speech. The classic kind of verbal delirium is that of
the subaltern (who in this sense, too, cannot speak)—the mad ravings of
the homeless and unemployed, haranguing passersby in the streets
(362), which has been the object of much social-scientific comment in
the island and which would seem to have little in common with the over-
elaborate, controlled, but empty rhetoric of the elite. But Glissant argues
that they are both part of the same phenomenon.[17]

Verbal delirium, in other words, has both elite and subaltern forms,
and it is not necessarily pathological. Glissant in fact divides it into two
subcategories: "pathological verbal delirium," about which he has little
to say, and "routine verbal delirium" [*délire verbal coutumier*], which is
the main object of his analysis. But the fragility of the sanity/insanity
boundary is such that even this distinction becomes rather unstable in
the course of his analysis. Routine verbal delirium is a direct reaction to
the social situation: specifically, a symptom of the occultation of social
relations ("one of the signs of this crucial non-resolution of class relations," *DA*, 367) and is not perceived by the community as either abnormal (364) or socially dysfunctional (369), in the way that it would be in
Europe. And indeed it is socially functional insofar as it is also an alienated attempt to resolve, subjectively, the tensions caused by the misrecognition of social relations (364). It is different from pathological verbal
delirium in that it could be cured by collective political action, which
would remove the necessity for it; and also in that it is a form of social
participation, whereas pathological verbal delirium isolates the individual (369). Glissant sums up these differences in the formula that routine
verbal delirium is a *signifier* of the social situation, whereas the pathological version is a *refusal* of the situation (378).[18]

He then embarks on a more detailed analysis of routine verbal delirium, both on a stylistic (369–73) and an ideological level (373–74). The latter is articulated mainly around the concept of the mimetic drive and rejoins the main theses of *Black Skin, White Masks*. Thus, routine verbal delirium is determined by the interplay of "the view of the Other," in which the colonizing French Other is transcendent; and "the view of oneself," which is subordinated to the view of the Other; and "the view of the Other's view of oneself," that is, the demand for white recognition of oneself as white, usually masquerading as a universalizing humanism. To these Glissant adds a similarly mystified ideology of history, which represses the reality of the island's history and puts in its place "a reassuring pseudo-history" (374). He then distinguishes four subcategories of routine verbal delirium, differentiated along two axes. The first axis is simply elite versus subaltern. The second is the opposition between "de-propriating" and "reappropriating" types: "de-propriation" is the construction of an alienated pseudo-French identity, and "reappropriation" is the confused and largely unconscious attempt to express and come to terms with the social contradictions—it is a form of detour.[19] The four types of routine verbal delirium are representation, persuasion, communication, and dramatization [*théâtralisation*]. The first two are elite, and the second two are *populaire*; the first three are de-propriating, and only the last one is reappropriating. It is, however, this last one, the "dramatizing routine verbal delirium," that receives the most attention in *Le discours antillais* and that is in some ways the most significant. This is in the first place because *pathological* delirium is also reappropriating; so, among the routine types of delirium, the dramatizing one is the closest to madness: "It is insofar as dramatizing delirium, alone among the types of routine delirium, is also and above all an attempt at reappropriation that it possesses this characteristic of being perceived and accepted by 'the others' as a clear sign of madness, but a madness that one cannot but accept" (378).

Both pathological delirium and dramatizing routine delirium—because of their "madness," that is, their distance from the alienated social norm—possess a certain kind of lucidity and insight that is denied to the rest of the community. In particular, dramatizing delirium does not repress the problems of history but reappropriates and externalizes them, albeit in a violently confused fashion: "Dramatizing delirium is *the torment of history*, whereas the other routine deliriums are a sign of the absence or the refusal of history" (378). The boundaries between routine and pathological delirium become somewhat blurred here, but the advantage of dramatizing delirium is that it is able to communicate with and be accepted by the community. This in turn explains Martinicans' distinctively greater tolerance of "madness," compared with Europeans: the dramatizing delirium fulfills the function of a socially necessary *acting out* of collective unconscious conflicts: "A person with this type of delirium is 'dramatically' trying to reappropriate through the word. . . . This is why the community perceives him as mad (he forces the community to really look at itself), but as a spectacular and important madman (because it needs this look)" (378). *Le discours antillais* analyzes at some length a particular case of this form of delirium, with its strange mixture of spectacular delusion and acute perception, in "the Suffrin case" (381–89), the discourse of the founder of a mystical sect called Le Dogme de Cham. Evrard Suffrin was an agricultural worker from Le Lamentin who from the 1950s through the 1970s produced numerous pamphlets and preached his doctrines to crowds in public places. For Glissant he exemplifies the main characteristics of dramatizing delirium: "it has no elite form, it corresponds to an attempt at reappropriation, it manifests itself theatrically as a common aim acted out as spectacle by an individual or a homogeneous group" (381). Suffrin's characteristic style reappears in some of Glissant's fictional characters and is discussed later in this chapter.

The relationship between the mimetic drive and verbal delirium figures in much of Glissant's fiction but perhaps nowhere so prominently as in *Malemort*. In this novel, whose "central focus," Michael Dash argues, is "the verbal coding through which a collective neurosis manifests itself," almost all of the characters are affected by the impulse to "efface ourselves in the resemblance to the other" (*Mal*, 159).[20]

The mimetic drive, the desire to be (speak like) the Other, may be logically counterposed to the ideal of authenticity, the determination to "be oneself" and speak one's own language. But whereas the problem is often conceived as a simple opposition between authenticity and imitation—the true and the false—Glissant's texts present a more complex situation.[21] As we have seen, no available authentic language exists, and counterpoetics is a strategic response to this reality. A further complication, however, is the impossibility of *total* identification with the white Other theorized by Fanon and Bhabha, and outlined earlier in this chapter; this means that on the linguistic level also, mimesis can never be complete. The "fissures" and "ruptures" of split identification, which Fanon and Bhabha repeatedly stress, reappear in the actual speech of the characters of *Malemort*. There are few examples of straightforward, wholehearted imitation of metropolitan French; rather, *Malemort* presents the reader with a range of *split* discourses in which various relations to the other's language are materialized.[22] Some of them are self-destructive, but others are subversive (intentionally or unintentionally); that is, the imitation of European speech is attacked not by opposing it to pure authentic speech but by undermining it from within in a number of ways—all of which are so many "detours" around the Other. The *tactical* appropriation of certain features of the Other's speech can also in some cases be a more pragmatic form of indirect resistance or detour.

Bhabha's notion of "colonial mimicry" offers an illuminating perspective on certain forms of split discourse. In a short chapter in *The Location of Culture* entitled "Of Mimicry and Man," he argues that one of the major strategies of colonial power was the reproduction of its own values and attributes within a certain elite class of the colonized—native interpreters, civil servants, clergymen, etc.—thus producing a "reformed, recognizable Other": a copy of the white man who is almost the same, but not quite. But the strategy inevitably also produces effects that undermine the colonial authority it is meant to reinforce. The mimic can never be identical to the original, because the native Other cannot be allowed to be exactly the same, and also because the logic of colonialism requires some adjustment to the Western ideals of democracy: "to be effective, mimicry must continually produce its slippage, its excess, its difference." As a result, the mimicry reveals the ambivalence of colonial power (civilizing mission/racist oppression) and so irresistibly begins to look like caricature, or even parody. The slight difference or split between original and mimic becomes charged with the treacherous subjectivity of the colonized: "the look of surveillance returns as the displacing gaze of the disciplined." Mimicry thus fissures and menaces the authority of its original. The discourse of the mimic is itself *split* in the sense of being an *almost* identical doubling of its Western model.[23]

Glissant formulates these ambiguous relationships to the Other's speech through the concepts of the detour and counterpoetics, as well as in his study of verbal delirium. Thus, while the more self-destructive varieties are fictional examples of routine verbal delirium, the more subversive ones are more closely related to the counterpoetic strategy of simultaneously using and attacking the French language. Taken together, they represent a series of qualitatively distinct relationships to the other's discourse. Mikhail Bakhtin's definition of the novel as a "system of images of language" is relevant here insofar as these discourses constitute much of the substance of the text.[24] But rather than images of language per se, the novel gives a mise-en-scène of different subjective *attitudes toward* the dominant discourse—attitudes embodied in different practices of language. Thus, rather than *langue,* it is *langage,* in Glissant's sense of "the collective attitude toward the [*langue*] used" (*CD,* 121), that is represented in *Malemort*; that is, discourses that enact their speakers' diverse relations to the language of the European Other. These discourses do not include either outright militant opposition or unproblematic adherence, but they can be ironic, cynical, self-confident, self-destructive, neurotic, or psychotic. In the following paragraphs, I discuss six of them in more detail.

One whole chapter of *Malemort* (73–99) consists almost entirely of a monologue by Lesprit, the mayor's secretary, as he drinks and plays dominoes with his equally bourgeois friends. The doctor bets him that he will not be able to get the mayor elected again. Before accepting the challenge, Lesprit recounts the whole history of electoral fraud in the town—a history he himself is brazenly continuing. Lesprit exemplifies the mulatto class's aim to align itself with the whites against the blacks, and he has two special talents to help him: his mastery of French, and his skill at vote-rigging, which ensures him the prestige of political office. The three salient features in his mimetic drive are thus race, electoral fraud, and his "learned eloquence" (82). All three of these are disturbingly ambiguous.

As a mulatto, he distances himself from the black population and appears to have assumed a wholly and confidently "French" identity. Conscious that this can be confirmed only by the French themselves—and echoing Fanon's analysis of the struggle for white recognition—he says: "We don't intend to respect ourselves *from the inside.* What would be the point of that? We yearn for recognition from above. . . . Ah, our little country nestling snugly in the lap of the Great Fatherland" (87). And, as he is equally well aware, this in turn means total psychological, as well as political, dependence on the "fatherland": "We must be recognized, monsieur, we must . . . but in order to be recognized, we must also accept the eminence of Those Who Know. That is why we couldn't live without the fatherland" (87). As Fanon puts it, "then I will quite simply try to make myself white: that is, I will compel the white man to acknowledge that I am human."[25]

However, in order to become the *same* as the whites, the mulattoes had to start by *opposing* them; to gain an equal right of political representation, they had to beat the white candidates. The aggressive component in the desire to "take the white man's place," which according to Fanon underlies the ambivalence of the mimetic drive, becomes apparent here. Lesprit's pride in the victory of the first colored mayor is clear: "a man of color seated for the first time at the top of the municipal council, he founded the lineage of our councillors" (75). The mayor's achievement was that "defying humiliations and hatred, he raised our caste high up towards the scornful white man and far above the nigger rabble" (77). But although "up with the white man" is clearly where Lesprit wants to be, the fact that he describes the object of his desire as "scornful" [*méprisant*] introduces a slight reservation.[26] Curiously, this splitting in his identification with the white man is more sharply expressed in his description of the "nègres" he despises:

> Quel nègre? Qui est élu n'est pas un nègre. C'est un citoyen de la République, nous ne sommes pas des Africains. La plèbe peut noircir la nuit, elle est pour souffrir et élire. Mais est-ce parce que notre peau est nuancée d'un rien d'ombre . . . qu'il nous faudra encourir notre vie durant géhenne et malédiction? (79)

> [What nigger? He who is elected is not a nigger. He is a citizen of the Republic, we're not Africans you know. Let the plebeians blacken the night, their place is to suffer and to elect. But should the fact that our skin is tinged with a hint of shadow . . . mean that we must spend the whole of our lives confronting hell and malediction?]

He thus aligns himself with the white political class, against the blacks, and speaks from that position. So it is strange that the reason for dissociating himself from black people is explicitly stated as, not the black people's inferiority as one might expect, but their *suffering*—at the hands of the white man. Lesprit's cynicism results in a kind of honesty that is at odds with his belief in the values of European civilization and opens up the split, which the disavowal of colonialism tries to cover over.

As for his manipulation of the electoral process, at the beginning of the chapter an anonymous narrative voice states that vote-rigging is the one thing Martinicans do well (74). So one might conclude that, as practiced by Lesprit, it is a kind of colonial parody of European parliamentarianism. But the reader is surely expected to be aware that this—the famous corruption of developing societies—is a racist cliche, and that Western political practices are themselves often corrupt. The text gives no indication as to whether Lesprit's fraud is to be seen as a cynical *sub-*

version of Western democracy or as a cynical *imitation* of Western corruption. This colonial version mimics its model in a way that, through its own ambiguity, unsettles the self-assurance of the model itself, illustrating Bhabha's claim that "the effect of mimicry on the authority of colonial discourse is profound and disturbing. For in 'normalizing' the colonial state or subject, the dream of post-Enlightenment civility alienates its own language of liberty and produces another knowledge of its norms . . . the reforming, civilizing mission is threatened by the displacing gaze of its disciplinary double."[27]

Lesprit's mimicry is at its most elusive in his use of the French language. When he says, for instance, "Les dieux sont ainsi faits, il convient de les accepter tels. Leur caprice est notre loi. Ah! comme est longue la route de perfection. Combien d'embûches devant que de toucher au port. Mais le soleil n'est pas plus brillant que le midi de la réussite" [Such are the gods, we can but accept them as they are. Their whim is our law. Ah! how long is the road to perfection. How numerous the pitfalls before the ship comes home to port. But the sun is not more dazzling than the noonday of our success] (80), the extremely formal, old-fashioned syntax is so exaggerated that it tips over into parody. It can be read as a typical case of Glissant's "verbal delirium of representation," in which the intrinsically "parodic" culture of the colonized elite reaches a stage where it goes out of control (*DA*, 375). Lesprit's social and political position also fits well with Glissant's comment that this type of verbal delirium has to be seen in relation to the function and aspiration of the elites created by colonialism—created so that their supposed evolution can camouflage the exploitation of the rest of the colonized: it is thus a "delirium of *representation*" both in the sense of being about appearance and show rather than real social function, and in the sense in which it implicitly and misleadingly claims to be representative of the colonized as a whole (*DA*, 376). The way it is presented in the text could then be seen as adding another level of parody, in effect mocking those who suffer from it.

However, whether this is the author's parody, making his character appear ridiculous, or *Lesprit's* parody, making the French language appear ridiculous, is not at all clear. Sometimes sheer probability virtually forces us to read Lesprit's speech as *conscious* parody; especially since we have ample evidence of his down-to-earth intelligence from the success of his political manipulations. In fact it is when he is describing his fraudulent exploits, or those of his predecessors, that the exalted tone of his speech becomes so incongruous that we almost irresistibly read it as sarcasm—as, for instance, when he states: "Ce cycle recommencé d'héroïsmes, sur quoi trône Sa Majesté l'Urne. Cette brigade d'élus sur tout le pays. L'épopée. Les folies sublimes. Les sacrifices inépuisables" [This repeated cycle of heroic acts, over which His Majesty the Ballot Box reigns supreme. This brigade of the elected across the whole country. The epic grandeur. The acts of sublime madness. The never-ending sacrifices] (90). His praise of the first mayor (who miraculously never lost an election) is also one that in most contexts would be unambiguously ironic: "Sa vie fut un long triomphe sur le hasard électoral" [His life was one long triumph over the element of chance in elections] (77).

But this interpretation poses a very real problem, because it assumes a *criticism* that is in complete contradiction with Lesprit's whole position. He approves of the mayor's actions and sees himself as carrying on a proud tradition. So when he refers to this "chronique glorieuse" [glorious chronicle] (77), the phrase is too exaggerated not to be sarcastic, but equally it cannot be sarcastic because Lesprit is not in the least critical of its referent. If he is being ironic, then the phrase is not a *naive* imitation—and the irony goes beyond the referent (electoral corruption) to the words themselves, which are also parodied by being used of something so self-evidently inglorious. But if he is *not* being ironic, then the only alternative would seem to be that he is verbally identifying with the phrase "la chronique glorieuse"—and hence adhering sincerely to the mimetic drive's ideal of "high" French. The whole of his discourse hovers between these two poles. The logic of his moral and ideological position blocks the ironic reading, and the exaggerated, inflated quality of the discourse blocks the innocent reading.

Lesprit in effect takes Bhabha's notion of mimicry one stage further. Bhabha sees the "*menace* of mimicry" as an inherent consequence of the particular structure of colonial discourse: as the "*double* vision which in disclosing the ambivalence of colonial discourse also disrupts its authority." But here the "menacing" impact is accentuated by the colonized subject *actively exploiting* the doubleness of the vision. The "look of surveillance return[ing] as the displacing gaze" of the colonized here becomes a question of individual volition, in a sense not intended by Bhabha. The mimicry is threatening not just because its *unintentionally* caricatural quality "mocks" the European model, but because the mockery *may* be conscious and intentional—or it may not be. Lesprit's discourse occupies a borderline between naive imitation and parody, marking the unstable, undecidable moment at which one begins to turn into the other.[28]

The reader's difficulty with this has nothing to do with *obscurity,* because Lesprit's discourse is totally transparent; there is nothing hidden beneath its surface (as there is, of course, in the more classical kind of irony). Like Bhabha's mimicry, it "conceals no presence or identity behind its mask."[29] Lesprit's ambivalence is a kind of bravado: glorifying his own dishonesty *semi*-ironically and refusing to dissociate himself from a discourse that he nevertheless presents as ridiculously pompous and hypocritical. His particular kind of mimicry—imitation slipping into mockery and vice versa—transforms the usual function of language in the mimetic drive. The subject's relation to his speech is no longer a question of self-representation, as Glissant's theorization of "delirium of representation" implies, but rather a demonstration of mastery and manipulation. It involves, for instance, switching registers for comic effect, which he does without worrying whether it will dent his self-image; for instance, he describes his power behind the scenes as that of those "qui jamais n'aspirent à l'officialité, en sorte que leur race élue préféra une fois pour toutes l'âpre jouissance du pouvoir secret. Messieurs a-t-on vu un Maire réélu contre l'assentiment de son secrétaire? *Plutôt voir un manicou accoucher d'un phare de juva*" [who never aspire to officialdom: these chosen people opted once and for all for the grim pleasures of secret power. Gentlemen, has one ever seen a Mayor reelected against the wishes of his secretary? *You're more likely to see an opossum give birth to the headlight of a Juva*] (77, emphasis added). Instead of his speech giving him a self-image, he gives his audience a powerful verbal *performance*: Silacier decides "I'm voting for Monsieur Lesprit, his tongue has a ten horse-power engine" (96).

A later chapter of *Malemort* (151–71) is devoted to the schoolmasters: Lannec, Québec, and Bellem. They belong to the same social class as Lesprit and speak with a similar exaggerated eloquence. Québec, for instance, explains the importance of marrying his daughter to an educated man in caricaturally anachronistic and cliched but, despite the inserted Creole phrase, totally self-confident French:

> Voyons, vous connaissez ma fille Pétronise? Mademoiselle Pétronise Québec. Celle qui possède à fond son Littré. Je la viens de refuser à un jeune quidam. Entendez qu'il ne s'agissait point là de pignon sur rue, Pétronise ni toutt' lagen'ye, que non, que non, mon ami, c'est pure affaire de *bagage* intellectuel. (158–59)

[Let's see now, do you know my daughter Pétronise? Mademoiselle Pétronise Québec. The young lady who knows her dictionary backwards. I have just refused her hand to a certain young party. You must understand that it was not at all a question of his having a roof over his head, Pétronise has all the money she needs, no, no, my dear boy, it's purely a question of intellectual *substance*.]

Nevertheless, the schoolmasters have a significantly different relation to the European other's language from that of Lesprit. They constitute a more straightforward example of the delirium of representation insofar as the delight that they take in their "deliciously convoluted rhetoric" (158) is inseparable from their sense of self.[30] Their passion for the French language is the foundation upon which they construct an identity: "They who never for a moment doubted their grammar" are also "they who believed even beyond the point of madness that they were what they had been told they were . . . that they knew all the things that ought to be known about the world, that they belonged to that which deserved to last, the Empire the Union" (162, 170). Their very profession reinforces the equation between cultural knowledge and being that Glissant sees as characteristic of this type of delirium "in a period in which the intellectual congealed culture into strata of knowledge that equated with 'strata of being': there were superior beings corresponding to superior levels of knowledge" (*DA*, 379).[31]

They also ultimately reveal through their own mystified experience of it the *illusory* nature of identification with France. The Other upon whom they model themselves is nothing but their own fantasy, as they realize when they go to France; they have "pursued in a real elsewhere, like poor Lannec, the dream of the dreamed-of elsewhere" (*Mal*, 168). France, which was to have given them the "plenitude" of which Fanon speaks, by confirming their image of themselves as white, in fact makes it brutally clear to them that they are not white: "the Antillean who goes to France in order to convince himself that he is white will find his real face there." The "white gaze" insidiously "unravels" their subjectivity, "when the eye softly encounters the white expanse of a winter boulevard drenched in wind, where indeed they felt, from the prickling of their skin or the glance sliding over them, that they had no place" (*Mal*, 167)—an evocation strongly reminiscent, once again, of Fanon's traumatic moment of encounter in *Black Skin, White Masks* (also on a "white winter day") with the white vision of oneself as objectified and stereotyped black body. In Paris—"in this hole of night where it was Monsieur Lan-

nec's turn to go under . . . abandoned by the world and having already
gone beyond the outer limits of distress"—Lannec goes mad (*Mal,*
166–67). He ends up talking to himself deliriously in a subway station
(167); it is his speech, in other words, that disintegrates, and with it his
whole identity. The baroque eloquence of the delirium of representation
has broken down into pathological delirium, and "no one heard or pretended to hear this big black man going to pieces, still so elegant, of
whom one could still not have said with any certainty that he was losing
his mind" (167).[32]

The schoolmasters' vulnerability and dependence on the metropolitan
French ideal precludes the suspicion of mockery that attaches to Lesprit's discourse. Nevertheless, their discourse has its own kind of internal split. The schoolmasters' usual confident adherence to French
humanist values is occasionally and inexplicably disrupted by moments
of rebellion: "obscure resentments, a sudden need to disagree" (152).
When, for instance, an attractive female colleague asks to borrow Lannec's pen, speaking in exactly the same overblown gracious style that he
uses himself, "he turned around to her and shut her up with a resound-
ing *No!*" (155–56). This kind of lapsus suggests that their "deliciously"
elaborate, *excessive* discourse is not as spontaneous as it seems; that its
apparently smooth fabric is marked by small holes, which open onto a
much larger void underneath. We gradually realize that their relation to
language in fact signals a tense determination to cling to an identity that
they half recognize is ridiculous but that is the only possible way out of
the void: "as though convinced that they would have to live out their
caricature right to the end, if, pathetic as they were, they were to have
any hope of finally getting out of the hole of nothingness that they had
been stuck in" (152).

In *Le discours antillais* Glissant interprets this baroque discourse—
"the elaborate ornamentation imposed on the French language by our
desperate men of letters"—as the sign of a lack—"this kind of excess,
wrapped around a vacuum" (*CD,* 250). *Excess* is a sign of *lack,* and the
schoolmasters' discourse is punctuated, and punctured, by moments of
lack. Moreover, these breaks in their speech, the stumblings and silences,
reveal an unconscious desire for *truth*; their pupils learn to listen symp-
tomatically for "the nuance, the half-sigh, the lilt of the voice or the
rhythm of the silence that underlined . . . not madness or stupidity so
much as the appetite for truth that such madness or stupidity foretold"
(164–65). As Glissant writes in *Le discours antillais,* the elite "cries out
its anguish at not being what this elite thinks it is, and at the same time

its refusal to discover this, and at the same time its inability to stop *attempting* just such a discovery" (*DA*, 362).

If the lack—the "hole" in the discourse—is where truth is revealed, it is also the space that outlines the possibility of a different language. The baroque discourse itself, through its gaps, enables the next generation to begin to sense what its own counterpoetic discourse might be. When the masters stop talking, "we can hear around them . . . the future echo of the way of speaking that they would perhaps have wanted so much to know and against which they defended themselves so fiercely: our way of speaking, impossible and sought after" [*notre parler impossible et quêté*] (*Mal*, 153–54). Moreover, as this suggests, the schoolmasters themselves unconsciously and contradictorily *desire* the impossible authentic language. The very depth of their alienation—their delirious "depropriation"—harbors a secret opposition to the alienating other: "these excesses of perdition whereby a will to resist is revealed to itself" (161). Excess again reveals lack; it is precisely because the alienation is so total that it produces a feeling of loss, and lostness, which itself results in an intuition of change: "what they, through their manias and splendid uselessness, through their ridiculous speech and their spiritual death, began precisely to stammer out, which is that something is changing and that we must get it going in ourselves" (162).

Relatively little of this chapter of *Malemort* consists of actual reproduction of the schoolmasters' speech. It is above all the point of view of its listeners—the pupils—that we read: their responses, interpretations, and quotations of the masters' speech.[33] The repetition of "Eux" [They] and "Nous" [We] emphasizes the boys' effort to define themselves and their speech in relation to the masters. Although they are "emptier" than the masters (*Mal*, 154), they are a stage further in the struggle toward a new discourse (whose complexities and compromises are discussed in chapter 2). But the point is made very strongly that the masters are a necessary stage in this struggle, because, precisely through their caricatural eloquence, they "mark that moment when we suddenly feel that words can also be used to express, to express what?" (161). This obscure, supremely demanding turning point—"this moment, heavier to bear than any signal of discovery . . . with ahead the call of words which are not yet language"—is not accessible to "the scouts" who have brought it about: they relapse into the "gilding of the prescribed object; where, with simple confidence they decorate, they try to outdo each other: not daring to realize that these sanctioned words . . . are only the raw material with which to build another *langage*." But the next generation might be able to, "and it falls to us, the difficult descendants of these proud victims . . . to organize the wind-skimmed foam from which our language will emerge" (161).

"Our" language, in other words, cannot be created ex nihilo but only out of the conflictual relation to the Other that is materialized in the split discourse of the mimetic drive.[34] We also rejoin here Glissant's concept of detour, in that the Other's discourse is the obstacle to expression that must be "got around"—and only *by so doing,* via this detour, can we perhaps construct a new counterpoetic *langage.* What the unspoken dialogue between the schoolmasters and the pupils demonstrates is that the relation between mimetic and counterpoetic discourse is not a simple opposition; the condition of possibility of the latter is implicated in, in some sense internal to, the former.[35]

The third and fourth examples of split discourses are relationships to the "other language" of Christian discourse, and both are closer to popular culture, and popular delirium, than the preceding examples. The first of them is Madame Otoune's vision of an angel pointing to a place in her garden where he appears to be telling her that a treasure is buried; under the supervision of her husband, who is the local mayor, the garden is dug up, but no treasure is found. As this suggests, this part of the novel (the eighth chapter, 137–50) is more light-hearted in tone than much of the rest, but the comedy contributes to the critical treatment of Catholicism in *Malemort* as a whole.

Madame Otoune and her husband live in Trois Rivières; thus, they belong to the provincial bourgeoisie who remain closer to the people and are far less educated and sophisticated than Lesprit and the schoolmasters of Fort-de-France. Madame Otoune's relationship to "white" language is consequently much less direct; the other discourse that she is appropriating is the formal, biblical and liturgical discourse of the church, which, while it of course derives from and is marked by European culture (as demonstrated in Adélaïde's relation to the nuns' speech discussed in chapter 3), is also well-established in Martinican society. Thus, Madame Otoune is trying to appropriate, not white experience per se, but a mystical or saintly experience that offers a slightly different route to special status. In the Caribbean, Catholicism has been amalgamated with elements of African religions to produce the discourse of religious syncretism in which voodoo *loas* [spirits] are paired off with Catholic saints, and so on. A trace of this occurs in this chapter when Ragan l'Ether, the local specialist in finding buried treasure, gives his recipe for locating it, which mixes Christian images and practices ("blessed palm," "palma christi," "genuflection") with elements of voodoo (the four directions, the wooden post) into what is essentially a magic spell (144). But Madame Otoune's own version of split discourse is simply a mixture of the religious and the everyday. So, for instance, she alternates between the reverent and the colloquial, producing a fairly standard form of comic effect: "Parlez-moi ô mon archange. Car c'est un trésor sûr et certain. Seigneur tu m'as envoyé ta parole. Seigneur encore un pe-tit peu" [Speak to me O mine archangel. Because it is treasure, that's for sure. Lord thou hast sent me thy word. Lord just a little bit more] (137).

The hallucination itself, which opens the chapter, is an example of a *visual* "other discourse." It is not a figment of her own imagination but is taken from standard Christian iconography. In the text this is defamil-iarized by being described in free indirect discourse: that is, the text uses Madame Otoune's "own words" to describe a *private* vision, which is nevertheless largely *alien* to her; and her "own" words therefore also in-clude fragments of terminology that is not part of her normal speech ("trident," "glaive" [sword], "justaucorps" [jerkin]), mixed with vocab-ulary that is incongruous precisely because it is part of her normal speech (more homely phrases such as "Il pointait son trident comme une gaulette. Sa jupe plissée flottait" [He pointed his trident like a cattle prod. His pleated skirt billowed], 137). Any distinction between the su-pernatural and the natural is thus erased. She addresses the archangel as though he were her *social* superior within the same community rather than a celestial apparition: she calls him "mon archange," as one might say "mon Père" or "mon commandant," and puts him on the same level as her husband: "Non non l'archange est fâché monsieur le maire aussi" [No, no, the archangel is cross, so is Monsieur le Maire] (147). Ulti-mately, and despite her initial sense of awe, the apparition of the angel is not particularly surprising; and this is reinforced by Médellus's politely matter-of-fact reaction:

—Ah ah ah monsieur Médellus. Je viens d'avoir la visitation de Dieu ô Seigneur.
—De Dieu en personne madame Otoune?
—Non non, par l'intermédiaire de l'archange.
—L'archange Gabriel madame Otoune? (138)

["Ah there you are monsieur Médellus. I've just had a visitation from God oh Lord."

"From God in person Madame Otoune?"
"No, no, through the intermediary of the archangel."
"The archangel Gabriel Madame Otoune?"]

The vision of the angel leads to an out-of-body experience in which Madame Otoune's spirit flies out into the garden while her body remains petrified in the rocking chair. But this quintessentially mystical release of the spirit from its corporeal chains is achieved by the rather mechanical expedient of "pulling on her neck": "The angel's power paralyzed her. But by dint of pulling on her neck she detached her spirit from her body, she let her body fall weakly into the rocking chair like an old cloth and her spirit flew off toward the place that the angel had pointed to" (138). Here again the religious and the everyday are comically brought together; Fanon's theorization of the splitting of the ego under the pressure of alienating identification is parodied, rather than illustrated, in the splitting of Madame Otoune's mind and body.

It does, however, illustrate the serious problem of the connection between the mimetic impulse and madness. Both in the out-of-body experience and in her initial hallucination of the angel, Madame Otoune is having what could be clinically classified as a psychotic episode. The fact that it is not regarded as such, either by herself or by the rest of the village, demonstrates Glissant's belief that individual abnormality cannot be defined where there is no collective normality to measure it against; the generalized psychic dislocations of colonial society make the distinction between sanity and insanity extremely tenuous. In this particular case, Madame Otoune's "madness" is not perceived as such because it is legitimated by the religious beliefs of the community: not a uniquely colonial situation, but one that is facilitated and made more extreme by the Caribbean's greater tolerance of psychological instability—a tolerance that is itself a product of colonialism, as Glissant explains in *Le discours antillais*. From this point of view, Bhabha's concept of colonial mimicry once again becomes relevant: Madame Otoune's crudely literal version of a mystical experience caricatures its European model.

There is, of course, no inherent connection in orthodox Catholicism between archangels and buried treasure, and so another facet of the "split" quality of this episode is the combination of two different cultural aspirations: religious piety and fantastic wealth. This in turn means that Madame Otoune's efforts to produce correct forms of religious phraseology are motivated not simply by a concern for self-image but also by the more instrumental aim of pleasing the archangel and God so that they will tell her where the treasure is. In its pragmatic self-interest, this might seem a healthier, less alienated perspective than the usual form of mimetic identification; it perhaps counts as a kind of detour. But it does not alter the fact that the treasure itself is a fantasy and symptomatic of a slightly different, but related, form of alienation. The obsession with finding treasure is shared by the whole village: as the news spreads, the Otounes' garden fills with people wanting to help dig up the treasure and claiming to be experts in finding it. As well as being collectively sanctioned in this way, the fantasy also gives rise to a collective frenzy, in which, for instance, Epiphane's claim to expertise moves rapidly into full-blown verbal delirium: "You don't know about treasure. I'm telling you. There are the jars. . . . Sometimes at the bottom of the garden. But the garden is the forest. Sometimes in the entrance to houses. But the house has moved itself. The best of the jars are the chapels. All the priests do it. They smash in the base of the altar. They put the jar in upside down. So as not to desecrate the saint" (139).

The village's delirious obsession with finding buried treasure must be seen as one of the consequences of the absence of the technical knowledge and activity that can mediate the relationship to the environment—an absence which Glissant, as we have seen, gives as one of the reasons for the particular psychopathology of Martinique (*DA*, 285). When people have no sense of being in control of the physical environment through their own exploitation of it for rational and practical ends—such as food production, etc.—then they will be extremely vulnerable to the fantasy that the earth holds *hidden* wealth, in the form of gold coins, that is *immediately* accessible if only one possesses the *magic* formula that will locate it. Therefore, although Madame Otoune's "subversive" appropriation of religious discourse in the interests of material wealth preserves her from some of the self-destructive effects of the mimetic drive, ultimately she is merely exploiting one kind of alienation (religious) in the service of another equally alienated fantasy that is culturally different but derives from the same socioeconomic determinants of "the horrorless horror of a successful colonization" (*DA*, 15).

The other example of Christian discourse in *Malemort* concerns Dlan's founding of his own religious sect, "la Nativité du Dernier Temps" [the Nativity of the Last Hour] (187–92). This constitutes a further step away from orthodox forms of dominant culture: Dlan is working-class and uneducated, and his church is a breakaway from Catholicism. But this example of popular religion still produces a fractured discourse, incorporating fragments of biblical language and evangelical preaching into its idiosyncratic ideology, and so is not exempt from the pressures of the mimetic drive. As Glissant says in *Le discours antillais,* "the nature of popular belief in Martinique is that it still functions as if *the Other is listening*" (*CD*, 22). Thus, the names of the other sects—which Dlan, like a salesman denigrating rival products, cites in order to warn his audience against them—are made up of obvious biblical references combined with an odd kind of inventivity: "Matin de Joie" [Morning of Joy], "la Vierge Seule Bonté" [the Virgin Sole Source of Goodness], "l'Enfant Advenu" [the Child Come among Us], "Croyants du Lendemain" [Believers of the Next Day] (*Mal,* 188).

A particularly telling example of the ambivalent relationship to Catholicism, combining dependence with rivalry, is Dlan's behavior at funerals. He starts attending all the funerals he can find and ostentatiously joining the processions (188). "On the edge of the crowd, standing between two graves, visible to everyone, Dlan would reel off his silent words. . . . God will help them, he said. And, at the same time as the Catholic priest, he would bless the man or woman that was being put into the earth" (189). Thus, he literally mimics the priest performing the funeral service. Bhabha's notion of mimicry is here made particularly concrete. The "doubleness" that menaces the dominant power's ideology is in the split between Dlan reverently echoing the priest's actions while also setting himself up in competition with him and publicizing his own sect; but it is made all the more blatant by the fact that it occupies the same time and space as its original: Dlan's mimicking the priest's gestures *as the priest performs them* intensifies both the doubleness and the effect of mockery.

It is also, of course, the gesture of a madman. Dlan, here and in his preaching, acts out in exemplary fashion Glissant's delirium of dramatization—which, as we have seen, is the closest to the pathological of all the institutionalized forms of verbal delirium. Significantly, the opening page of *Malemort* refers to this part as "Dlan est tombé prêcheur" [Dlan falls preacher], as if becoming a preacher were comparable to *falling* ill or mad. The analysis in *Le discours antillais* of the "Suffrin case" as an example of "dramatized routine verbal delirium" is relevant here. Some of the stylistic features of Suffrin's discourse can also be found in a fictionalized version in Dlan's discourse. The high proportion of "learned terms," for instance (*DA*, 383), used in an approximate and incongruous fashion, reappear in Dlan's preaching: "Population de mes frères" [Population of my brothers] (*Mal,* 187, 191); "tu seras en félicité de rencontrer le frère Dlan" [thou shalt be in felicity to meet brother Dlan] (187), and so on. The phenomenon that Glissant calls "consecutiveness of exposition," which replaces logical progression with a kind of self-generating "proliferation" (*DA*, 371), can also be seen in the structure of repetition/variation in Dlan's speech:

> Population de mes frères, n'écoutez pas la parole des impies. . . . N'écoute pas plus qu'est-ce que quoi de discours de la Sainte Église que des Adventistes que des Témoins pas plus que du Septième Jour. . . . n'écoutez pas la parole de Belzébuth. *La Nativité du Dernier Temps* vous attend. Frère Dlan vous attend. Le Seigneur vous attend. (*Mal*, 187–88)

> [Population of my brothers, don't listen to the words of the wicked. . . . And don't listen either to the slightest thing of the Holy Church's speech or of the Adventists or of the Witnesses either of the Seventh Day . . . don't listen to the words of Beelzebub. *The Nativity of the Last Hour* awaits you. Brother Dlan awaits you. The Lord awaits you.]

The figure of the preacher as public *performer* is well-placed to fulfill the social function of dramatizing delirium—that is, to be the individual who, despite his "deviance," is not excluded from the community but who acts out for the community a shared delirium: "this individual is then an *actor on stage,* for the whole community which becomes simultaneously a spectator . . . and a participant (it attempts to realize itself through this actor)" (*DA*, 375). Discussing Suffrin in this context, Glissant reiterates the point that this form of delirium is an attempt to "reappropriate" cultural identity (381). In the case of Dlan, a similar anticolonial reappropriation can be seen in his appeal to the people not to emigrate to France: "Population of my brothers, stop running. Stop leaving" (*Mal*, 187). Moreover, urging the people to stay on the island where they were born leads him to invoke the non-Christian practice, taken from voodoo, of burying the placenta of a newborn baby and planting a tree over it: he goes on: "The lord will come and take you in the shade of the tree where your placenta is buried" (187). But he then immediately returns to Christian discourse, likening the *sin* of leaving Martinique to the conventional sin of gambling: "Betting on the races is an infernal sin. Leaving for distant parts is a purgatorial sin" (188).

In this sense Dlan's alienated religious delirium simultaneously acts as a vehicle for a *liberating* ideology combating the mainstream, superficially "normal" mimetic alienation of identifying with the metropolis. The point is made even more forcefully in the conclusion to this section of *Malemort,* when Dlan's preaching is "answered" (191–92) by another delirious performance that is, in contrast, completely dominated by the mimetic drive in its crudest and most deranged form. A man in the crowd screams that the metropolis has given them everything, and starts tearing his clothes off. The list of items that France provides rises to a crescendo, finishing:

> cravate c'est la métropole veston c'est la métropole (soudain il arrachait son slip avant que quiconque ait pu prévoir) et Son Eminence Petit Bateau pour coucher le gros coco c'est la métropole (il dansait frénétique en agitant tout son linge) c'est la métropole (il poursuivait sous l'ombrage de la nuit les jeunes femmes qui fuyaient en riant) c'est la métropole bafouillait-il en écumes, c'est la métropole. (191–92)

> [tie is the motherland jacket is the motherland (suddenly he tore off his underpants before anyone knew what was happening) and Son Eminence Petit Bateau[36] a nice little bed for the big fat cock it's the motherland (he danced around frantically waving his underclothes in the air) it's the motherland (he chased after the young women who ran away laughing in the shadow of the night) it's the motherland he spluttered foaming at the mouth, it's the motherland.]

It is as if Glissant is determined to relativize the eccentricity of popular religion by conversely stressing the more destructive insanity of total dependence on France—an attitude that usually passes for rational and normal but is, in his view, far more profoundly alienated.

The penultimate chapter of *Malemort* is devoted to Médellus's dream of land reform: his plan for a utopian community where he and a chosen group of acquaintances can start a new life protected from the increasing desolation around them. It is a completely unrealistic dream, because the land he is using has been bought by a development company, and he is eventually driven off it. Meanwhile visitors come to see him about the project, which has brought him local fame. The chapter consists mainly of his attempts to explain his project, and he does so in a language that, to the European at least, is close to real dementia. In the terms of Glissant's analysis of verbal delirium, however, Médellus is situated just this side of the problematic borderline that separates the routine from the pathological version. That is, his delirium is directly caused by the social situation, and it gives him a role in the community, for whom he deliriously externalizes its social contradictions. Médellus is in fact very similar to Suffrin, whom Glissant takes as an example of dramatizing routine delirium. The description of Suffrin's verbal style—"an orchestra of words or phrases, without any apparent link or any real syntax; they have a sort of self-evident but mysterious glow" (*DA*, 382)—is equally appropriate to, for instance, the "sacred text" that Médellus recites (*Mal*, 201).[37]

Dramatizing verbal delirium, alone among the routine versions, is *reappropriating*; this both brings it closer to pathological delirium and constitutes its value. It has, in part, gone beyond the mimetic impulse to a confused, "crazy" consciousness of the real problems. Thus, Médellus refers contemptuously to people who identify with white culture as "les blancs dans la tête" [white in the head] (211) and describes them as "those who remain there without bodies. You go through them as though they were rain. You turn them over like a little octopus. You beat them like conchmeat" (215). He also echoes Glissant's concern that the people have become alienated from their environment because they have lost the habit of working the land:

> Parce que tu as peur de la terre. Parce que pourquoi travailler?
> Souvenir depuis l'antan.
> La terre trop raide. Plonger la main.
> Tu préfères la main d'aumône.
> Mais prendre la houe par toi-même. (208–9).

> [Because you are afraid of the land. Because why work?
> Memory from the old days.
> The earth too hard. Thrust your hand into it.
> You prefer the hand that gives alms.
> But take hold of the hoe for yourself.]

(The Creole version of this, also given in the text, in fact demonstrates Médellus's delirious poetic *virtuosity*; it ends: "Lanmin plongé. Ou préféré lanmin longé. Mé longé lanmin'ou pou houé," 209.) Above all, his delirium is reappropriating simply because his aim is to reappropriate, in an entirely concrete fashion, the *land* taken over by the development company and thus to reverse the process of economic dispossession of the people. Here, too, he resembles Suffrin, of whom Glissant writes that he exemplifies dramatizing verbal delirium not so much because of his particular use of language as because "the constructions of the Dogma of Cham are a pathetic and irrepressible response to economic obliteration. Routine verbal delirium is a substitute for the economic power that has been reduced to nothing. It is startlingly true to say that Monsieur Suffrin's life is indistinguishable from his fight to make people recognize that *the land surrounding his house* does not belong to those who claim to be its owners, but to the Martinican community" (*DA*, 485).

But this reappropriating consciousness coexists with the alienated vision of self and of the Other that Glissant sees in all the forms of routine delirium. His analysis of Suffrin shows him to be split in precisely this way, between on the one hand "a real cultural demand, a call for originality and freedom of creation" (*DA*, 385) and an affirmation of black nationalism, and, on the other, a need to be recognized by the "great men" of white society and an imitative use, in his own speech and writing, of elevated and stereotyped French phrases. Thus, he sums up the contradictions of dramatizing delirium as "with oneself, against oneself" and "against the Other, through the Other" (*DA*, 386).

Médellus is split in exactly the same way. Like Suffrin, he writes letters to famous people all over the world, black and white: the Pope, the American president, the French president, Mohammed Ali, Mrs. Luther King, Brezhnev, and the Secretary of the United Nations (*Mal*, 213). And his own language retains the mimetic orientation to European discourse, albeit in a very fractured and "crazy" fashion. The chapter starts:

(il te parlait.)
"Réunir l'eau de terre à la communauté. L'eau de rivière, l'eau de source. L'écrevisse au manger du matin, le poisson noir pour le manger de vendredi. Nasses taillées pour la communauté. Le trou de bain. La Fontaine de résurrection." (200)

[(he talked to you.)
"Bring the earth water back to the community. The river water, the spring water. The crayfish for eating in the morning, the black fish for eating on Fridays. Nets cut out for the community. The bathing hole. The Fountain of Resurrection."]

That is, a series of entirely local concrete realities is interrupted by the abstract alien phrase "La Fontaine de résurrection." This is a water pipe, which happens to be on the piece of land on which he also builds, from scrap iron and planks of wood, "L'Assemblée générale des nations" [The World General Assembly] and a "Temple universel" [Universal Temple] (203). These names, taken from recognizable European discourses (political, mythical, religious) are woven into his own, combining very idiosyncratic obscure meanings with fragments of the Other's language.

Thus, we gather from the speech of the development company's engineer that Médellus tries to use the "alien" word "exterritorialité" to protect his land from them: "come on now be reasonable . . . you can't declare this road international territory what's that supposed to mean exterritoriality" (210).[38] The same mixture structures his "sacred text"—significantly, when he gives the Creole version of this, the abstract or commonplace phrases "peuples du monde" [peoples of the world], "l'élevation" [elevation], "la pensée universelle" [universal thought] remain in French, as though to mark their otherness (206). His delirium thus produces a bricolage of discourses rather than an entirely private asocial language, but the grandiose imported fragments are attached to private and movingly incongruous referents. Suffrin's double-edged "weapons" are also his: "the unending subversion of a *langue* that is not his own; the amazing unity of a *langage* that he himself has forged, and that is not reducible to anything known or analyzable" (*DA*, 485).

If Médellus is on the borderline between routine and pathological delirium, Silacier is definitely, by the end of the novel, in a psychotic state. Thus, unlike Médellus, who retains some degree of social participation and communication, Silacier becomes completely isolated and unable to communicate; for Glissant, this is the crucial difference between "routine" and "pathological" delirium. Indeed, here it is not a question of split discourse so much as of split ego. The splitting of the ego described by Fanon and Bhabha in Silacier's case takes a violently schizophrenic form. The ambivalence that is always latent within the mimetic drive— the ambivalence inherent in "taking the master's place," where the desire to be white coexists with the desire to drive out the white—reaches a point where it cannot be contained but turns into psychotic breakdown. This in turn means that, although the original cause of the splitting is still the ambivalent identification with the white Other, Silacier's madness has ultimately propelled him, so to speak, *beyond* the neurotic configuration of the mimetic drive: he no longer imitates "white" speech. This breakdown occurs in the course of the novel, and, in order to make sense of it, the reader has to juxtapose some of the incidents in the section already discussed here in connection with Lesprit, with the final chapter. It is precipitated by his suddenly remembering an incident that, although it is referred to only obliquely and never fully elucidated, is central to the whole novel.

In 1934 Lesprit appears to have arranged the murder of a rival election candidate named Nainfol. He was shot twice in the corridor of a house by someone, probably Odibert, who was then allowed to escape by the gendarmes on the square outside; Beautemps tried to chase after him but was prevented from doing so by Silacier himself, among others, who caught his arm and held him back. The first mention of the assassination in the text is the supposition that Beautemps may have remembered this as he killed himself to avoid being captured by the gendarmes (60–61). Later, in the chapter in which Silacier is listening to the conversation of Lesprit and his friends, Lesprit gives his version of the incident, again linking it to Beautemps. Someone—perhaps the doctor who has bet him that he will not be able to win the next election—asks "who killed Nainfol?"; Lesprit replies that no one knows and that the only person to accuse the authorities of complicity was the criminal Beautemps (93).[39]

But there has in fact been a previous and far more elliptical reference to the event earlier in this same chapter. Silacier is so hypnotized by Lesprit's eloquence that he almost forgets that he hates him (84). Almost, but not quite: the hatred, and the reasons for it, remain as dimly felt, angry, but inexpressible fragments of memory: "A murky vagueness stirred around inside him, an inarticulate cry, a gesture cut off, a little of the redness of midnight lit by torches" (84)—fragments whose full significance will emerge only in the final chapter of the novel. But it is already becoming clear that Silacier is occupying, in relation to his social superior and oppressor, two conflicting positions at once. While on the one hand he is the "dreamy echo of monsieur Lesprit," he is also immersed in his own history, that is, images of drowned and tortured slaves: "Silacier was moving, over depths of seaweed and blueish glints of chains [*de glauques reflets de chaînes*], over depths of bodies swallowed up by the sea, shackled in pairs, over depths of tortured bodies nailed to the yoke by their ears, their mouths gagged with pepper" (84). Bhabha's claim that "the very place of identification . . . is a place of splitting. The fantasy of the native is precisely to occupy the master's place while keeping his place in the slave's *avenging* anger" is exactly borne out here by the way in which Silacier identifies with Lesprit's version of reality while simultaneously holding on to an opposing identification with the victims of people like Lesprit. These, moreover, include Beautemps, because Silacier's "glauques reflets de chaînes" are another very elliptical reference back to Beautemps, whose fear of the sea was linked to *his* visions of slaves thrown overboard during the passage from Africa: "ce gouffre irrémédiable où un bel-air de noyés l'étoufferait dans une danse trop oubliée *glauque* rêvée de *chaînes* de boulets de feux brûlant sous les eaux" [this irreparable gulf in which the melody of the drowned would smother him in a dance now forgotten *blueish* dreamt of *chains* of iron balls of fires burning beneath the waters] (58, emphasis added).[40]

This is the beginning of Silacier's "split." After the mention of Nainfol's name (93), the content of the repressed memory becomes more detailed: "he forgot the corridor full of shadow and sunlight slanting in from the other side of the square solid with heat, the two walls corroded with darks and brights between which he had glimpsed something fall at the same moment that he had thought he heard gunshot, the running across the square, the policemen who had pretended to stop him, the stupefaction sealed in the blood near the flagstone, and Odibert's double or his zombie perhaps vanishing at the far end of the square" (94–95). But, even as he "forgets" all this, he knows that one day he will remember it again. Rather than repression proper, this is a kind of dissociation or disavowal in which one knows that what one has *decided* to forget can and will be retrieved, because it is being remembered in another part of oneself which is not unconscious but *split off*: the above passage continues, "Silacier forgot everything, suppressed everything in a corner of the wood that had sprung up deep inside him—*no, beside him, in a place where he knew he would be able to find it all again one day*" (95, emphasis added). Bhabha's articulation of the mechanism of disavowal and the splitting of the subject in colonial identification is strikingly illustrated by Silacier, who is going to vote for his enemy; even while he is "carried away convinced" by Lesprit, he "already knew without knowing it that one day he would search beside himself, that he would find all the things he was suppressing there" (95). Moreover, one of the items mentioned in the subsequent list gives a further reason for Silacier's ambivalence: "Beautemps whom he had grabbed hold of instead of lending him a hand" is the first indication that Silacier, at this crucial moment, actually helped the gendarmes to let Odibert escape. His guilt about this becomes more obvious later on.

The list ends with: "he would find it all again one day, and on the top of the pile, nicely sharpened, his machete" (95). This paragraph thus prefigures the section "The Machete," devoted to Silacier, which is the last chapter in the novel and which itself ends: "he was gently sharpening the blade of his machete" (232). The irremediable and despairing violence of *Malemort*'s world, and of Silacier himself, are thus underlined, but these two references to his machete also serve to link the last chapter with the earlier pages (93–96) on another level. His "transfiguration" (219) is comprehensible only in relation to the passage analyzed

above, which in essence predicts that the disavowed knowledge of Nainfol's death and Silacier's part in covering it up will resurface in his consciousness. It does so in the last chapter, and the effect on him is so explosive that, far from being able to resolve the ambivalence of
disavowal, his ego becomes split in a fully schizophrenic sense.

The present time of this last chapter is 1947—two years after Lesprit's
conversation over the game of dominoes and thirteen years after the killing of Nainfol. Both of these past events recur several times in the chapter as flashbacks. Silacier is watching a game of dice being played one
evening on the Place des Calebassiers when he has a sudden "vision" of
Odibert. It is triggered by hearing two drumbeats, sounding like the two
gunshots that killed Nainfol, but there are also other coincidental connections. For instance, the "torches" that he unconsciously associates
with the original event—as in his earlier confused memory of "a little of
the redness of midnight lit by torches" (84)—recur, as now we read: "He
turned his reddened eyes toward the hole of night beyond the torches.
He saw something move, his whole body shouted in his head: Odibert"
(219). Above all, one of the dice players is Néga, Lesprit's driver.

He goes home to get his machete and returns to the crowd on the
square. There are two more drumbeats from the marketplace, and "Silacier split open like dry ground. The two halves of Silacier went off in different directions. Straight away he was back to the sunlight and the heat
of that afternoon long ago when he saw Beautemps suddenly erupt after
a shadow which could surely only have been Odibert the steward, while
everyone rushed into the corridor where Nainfol had fallen. He was
holding on to Beautemps, he didn't know why" (220). In other words,
the impact of the disavowed, "split-off" memory returning into his consciousness is such that he cannot integrate it: *he* splits into two separate
parts, and for a while part of him remains in the past. The doctor's question "who killed Nainfol?" is repeated twice (220), and Silacier relives
his struggle with Beautemps ("Silacier was fighting to hold on to Beautemps") while simultaneously (in the next paragraph) "Silacier stood up,
he saw Néga, monsieur Lesprit's driver." For a moment the past is superimposed on the present, as Silacier grabs *Néga's* arm and shouts at him
"not to hold out his arm like that. Not to run like that in the corridor. To
slam his domino down in the middle of the table" (221). They start to
fight, and each wounds the other before they are separated and Silacier
runs off to hide his weapon.

The rest of the chapter consists, on one level, of Silacier going to the
hospital, meeting Ragan on the way and getting drunk with him, meet

ing Néga at the hospital where their wounds are treated, both being arrested, and Silacier ending up in a cell in the local gaol. But throughout,
only "part" of Silacier is involved in this; we are frequently told that the
other part of him is still on the square, caught in the moment when he
suddenly remembered seeing Odibert run away from the murder scene.
Initially this "other part" seems to be reenacting the scene as Silacier
would have wished it to be—that is, it helps Beautemps and chases
Odibert (222). But later it seems to *become* Odibert (the "zombie," 95):
"Silacier realized that the part of him that had stayed behind on the
square would never meet up with him again. It would be a new zombie
entering people's heads" (225). Then it vanishes: "Where are you, he
shouted at the part of him that had left him" (227). Finally, he wants to
lose the part of him that remains—"I want to lose the other half . . . go
away I'm telling you, I want to be without Silacier"—and has a terrifying hallucination of a huge snake entering the prison cell and "carrying
off the half of him that remained" (231).

The thirteen-year-long attempt to repress his knowledge of the truth
has broken down, in other words, and madness results. The truth is unbearable because it shows Silacier's complicity *with his social enemies*—
the mulatto middle-class—and the long suppression of the truth itself
compounds the complicity. The act of taking the oppressors' side, however accidentally, in corruption and crime, is emblematic of the self-destructive alienation that Jean-Paul Sartre, in his preface to *The Wretched
of the Earth,* attributes to the colonized subject who does not fight back:
"if he gives in, he degrades himself and he is no longer a man at all;
shame and fear will split up his character and make his inmost self fall to
pieces."[41]

Fanon himself diagnoses another consequence of the failure to fight
back against the colonial power: the accumulated but impotent violence
felt toward the master is displaced onto one's fellow colonized: "The
colonized man will first manifest this aggressiveness which has been
deposited in his bones against his own people."[42] Or as Silacier himself
says, "there's always a nigger who'll enslave or massacre another nigger" (*Mal,* 220). He is thinking of Odibert here, but as he realizes a little
later (224), the phenomenon is more general (it includes his own attack
on Néga, for instance). And, as he wonders why they are all so disu-
nited, it is once again the murder scene in "the corridor full of shadow
and sunlight" (94) that comes into his mind: "So he realized that everyone lived apart, if that's living. Apart from one another, defenseless.
. . . He Silacier who was looking for a *way through between the sun*

strokes drowned in freezing shadows. But he could not say exactly why. Everyone followed a path. All those paths didn't make up a road" (223, emphasis added).

Above all, however, Silacier's experience invokes the question of violence. Through the holes at the bottom of the cell door, he asks Célestin to bring him his machete; and the last words of the chapter—and hence of the novel—show him sticking his fingers through the holes and "gently sharpening the blade of his machete." Thus, of the three heroes of *Malemort*, Dlan ends up in the dramatizing delirium of popular religion and Médellus in that of a utopian scheme for land reform; only Silacier fails to find any kind of survival strategy through "routine verbal delirium" and is left in silent schizophrenic violence. Fanon's claim—in the chapter of *The Wretched of the Earth* entitled "Concerning Violence"— that violence is the only solution to the psychological damage caused by colonialism is clearly but ambiguously relevant here. When he writes, for instance that "the colonized man finds his freedom in and through violence. This rule of conduct enlightens the agent because it indicates to him the means and the end," he is thinking of the organized collective violence of armed struggle, which overcomes alienation and disunity in a "totalizing" praxis where "each individual forms a violent link in the great chain."[43] Silacier's violence, on the other hand, remains completely impotent because it isolates him from communication with others. Thus, he reacts to the traumatic anamnesis by becoming closed and hard, like a rock (*Mal*, 226) or a piece of wood (232); in a psychotic version of opacity, he withdraws from any communication: "No one would ever again force him to explain" (226); "Nobody would make him explain" (232).

Silacier differs sharply from the other characters of *Malemort* discussed in this chapter in that he does not *use* "white" language at all. His only relationship to the Other's language is a nonrelationship: a position of total refusal. But it is still relevant to the same problematic, for two reasons. In the first place it stems from the same split identification that, in less extreme cases, produces the kind of "split discourses" that characterize Lesprit, Lannec, Madame Otoune, Dlan, and Médellus. Secondly, it results in the refusal or inability to communicate with anyone at all. Silacier, in other words, serves as a negative demonstration of the profound and pervasive effects of the mimetic drive.

The fictional examples of split discourse discussed in this chapter span a variety of socially differentiated relationships to the Other's language. The first two belong to the elite and the "delirium of representation;"

the third—Madame Otoune—is halfway between elite and subaltern; the fourth and fifth are subaltern and illustrate the "delirium of dramatization"; the sixth is a case of subaltern pathological delirium. *Malemort* suggests that they have more in common than one might think: the schoolmasters, for instance, are "far away from Dlan Silacier Médellus, and yet so alike in their secret hammering" [*insoupçonné martèlement*] (151). But there are other important differences: between, for instance, the instrumental attitude to language of Lesprit and Madame Otoune and the obsessive verbal self-representation of the schoolmasters, or between Madame Otoune's alienated but pragmatic detour around orthodox Catholic discourse and the extravagant inventions of Dlan's popular religion. There is also a crude sense in which Lesprit is successful and Médellus and Silacier are failures. Médellus occupies an extreme position at the limits of what could be considered a strategic, or even simply viable, relation to the Other's language. He is arguably less alienated than Lannec, and does not suffer the latter's sudden mental breakdown, but exists permanently on the edge of a madness that is both a symptom of alienation and a desperate effort to escape from it. Silacier has gone over that edge, and *Malemort* ends with the despairing image of his violence and isolation. Later novels explore a rather different kind of "madness," as discussed in chapter 5.

5 Delirious Language

Living in the Unhomely World

WE HAVE seen how various forms of delirium and madness are rooted in the mimetic drive, that is, the ambivalent identification with the white Other's speech. Glissant's writing, like Fanon's, constantly stresses how destructive this is. But unlike Fanon, Glissant suggests in *Le discours antillais* that delirium can also be a kind of resistance—"delirium is a form of resistance to mental deprivation" (*DA*, 212)—and a survival strategy: "We know that delirious speech can be a survival technique" (*CD*, 129). Madness can be something that is *chosen*: "the psychotic violence of the radical choice of 'madness'" (*DA*, 292). The novels bear this out, in that we find in them examples of madness that seem, if somewhat ambivalently, to be a strategy for surviving in or on the margins of society. This kind of "madness" is less directly related to the white Other; it is not so much a consequence of the mimetic drive per se as a response to the dislocations and contradictions of present-day Martinican society and to the loss of history, which in Glissant's view is one of the main causes of this. As he repeatedly implies, the Martinican does not feel *at home* in Martinique or anywhere else. This condition is very similar to that which Bhabha calls "unhomeliness," and which he analyzes in "Unhomely Lives: The Literature of Recognition" in *The Location of Culture*.

This chapter is therefore concerned with two related concepts. The first is Glissant's notion of the "positive" functions of madness as a form of *detour*. This includes an awareness of how the borderline between psychic disintegration and psychic survival itself becomes highly ambiguous. Secondly, the extent to which this ambiguous strategy can be interpreted specifically as a reaction to *unhomeliness* is considered.

Bhabha defines unhomeliness as a state in which the boundaries normally separating private and public are erased, and as the anxiety this generates: "The recesses of the domestic space become sites for history's most intricate invasions. In that displacement, the borders between home and world become confused; and, uncannily, the private and the public become part of each other, forcing upon us a vision that is as divided as it is disorientating." The erasure occurs when individuals or communities lose their traditional, stable, homogeneous identities and ways of life (when they are thrown into what Glissant calls "errance"). The unhomely is the "estranging sense of relocation of home and world that is the condition of extra-territorial and cross-cultural initiations." Although it is not limited to postcolonial experience, it is especially characteristic of these communities, whether it results from colonization, decolonization, immigration, or the persisting aftereffects of transportation. With no secure "home" in either time or place, the individual becomes acutely vulnerable to the outside world. An echo of this in Glissant's fiction is Raphaël Targin's reference to "a new disease which had appeared . . . which was to be *affected by the world*" (*Mah*, 185–86). This situation demands a particular kind of response from the individual. Bhabha argues that "to live in the unhomely world" is a strategy that depends upon realizing a distinction between "control" and "accommodation": "we ought to concern ourselves with the understanding of human action and the social world as a moment when *something is beyond control, but it is not beyond accommodation*." "Accommodation" can be seen as Bhabha's version of Glissant's "detour" (and De Certeau's "tactic") but specifically in the context of individual anxiety and the threat of psychosis. It resonates particularly closely, therefore, with Glissant's more fully developed conception of delirium as a tactic for resistance and survival.[1]

All of Bhabha's literary examples of unhomely individuals are women. This is not surprising since women have traditionally been assigned to the domestic private space of the household—and it is exactly this space that is being penetrated by the public, political outside world. The title of the novel by Rabindranath Tagore to which Bhabha refers is, significantly, *The Home and the World*. If home and world can no longer be kept apart, women will experience and "dramatize" the collapse of the boundary more acutely, perhaps, than men. It is in any case true that, in Glissant's novels, unhomeliness is dramatized above all through a female figure, Marie Celat, to whom the latter part of this chapter is devoted.[2]

Bhabha's coinage "unhomely" refers back to Freud's notion of the *unheimlich*, usually translated as "the uncanny." Freud's paper, "The

'Uncanny,'" gives a number of different formulations of the concept. Bhabha bases his connection mainly on one of them, namely that the uncanny is "the name for everything that ought to have remained . . . secret and hidden but has come to light." The private, in other words, cannot remain private. Bhabha's unhomeliness is that form of the uncanny that results when "private and public, past and present, the psyche and the social develop an interstitial intimacy . . . that questions binary divisions."3

Freud's gloss on "ought to have remained . . . secret" is that it refers to repression. The uncanny is a return of the repressed: "among instances of frightening things there must be one class in which the frightening element can be shown to be something repressed which *recurs*. This class of frightening things would then constitute the uncanny." This in turn has two further implications, which Freud develops; one of them is reworked and extended by Bhabha, and the other he ignores, presumably because it conflicts with his notion of "unhomeliness."4

The first is that the return of the repressed has a *temporal* dynamic. For Freud, it is the return in adulthood of something that was "known" in childhood but subsequently repressed: "the uncanny is that class of the frightening which leads back to what is known of old." In other words, it invokes a relation with the past. Freud's examples are concerned with the past in the purely personal sense of childhood: castration anxiety in Hoffmann's story "The Sandman," for instance. Bhabha extends this to the collective, historical past that subtends the dislocations of postcolonial reality. In his discussion of Toni Morrison's *Beloved*, he cites "the unspoken, unrepresented pasts that haunt the historical present." In other words, the interpenetration of public and private is simultaneously that of past and present. Personal history cannot be separated from a collective history which is experienced as trauma and repression, and personal life in the present is inevitably lived in "an in-between temporality that takes the measure of dwelling at home, while producing an image of the world of history." In Bhabha's construction, then, "history" signifies both past and public. Equally, unhomeliness is the anxiety that accompanies *both* the repression of historical trauma and the "estranging relocation" of cross-cultural experience. One might object that these are two different things, which will not necessarily occur together. At least in Glissant's world, however, they do coincide: it is transportation that ultimately produces the loss or repression of the past.5

But Freud's analysis of the uncanny as the return of the repressed has a second implication, to which he in fact devotes greater attention. His paper opens with a discussion of the diverse meanings of *heimlich* and *unheimlich* in common German usage, in which he notes that these opposite terms are sometimes used synonymously. This paradox hinges on the senses of "homely" as *familiar* and as *secret*. It leads him to explore the idea that the *unheimlich* is simultaneously familiar and (because secret) unfamiliar. He explains this in terms of the mechanism of repression: what is repressed is something that was once, long ago, known and familiar. It appears unfamiliar only because it has been repressed. Thus, Freud formulates it as follows: "this uncanny is in reality nothing new or alien, but something which is familiar and old-established in the mind and which has become alienated from it only through the process of repression. This reference to the factor of repression enables us, furthermore, to understand . . . the uncanny as something which ought to have remained hidden but has come to light." Freud's emphasis on this idea of a secret, disguised familiarity recurs throughout the paper: "the uncanny is that class of the frightening which leads back to what is known of old *and long familiar*. How this is possible, in what circumstances the familiar can become uncanny and frightening, I shall show in what follows." Again, his final definition is "that the uncanny is something which is secretly familiar, which has undergone repression and then returned from it, and that everything that is uncanny fulfils this condition." In other words, many phenomena are frightening because they are strange and unfamiliar, but the *uncanny* is frightening because it is strange and secretly familiar. Bhabha does not make anything of this central characteristic of the uncanny, because it could not apply in the same way to his unhomely relationship to a collective, social past, as opposed to an individual's childhood, and because it is at odds with his more straightforward, less paradoxical emphasis on unhomeliness as the "estranging relocation" of cultural boundaries and the *invasion* of the private, familiar sphere of the domestic. In Glissant's fiction, however, the "secretly familiar" is an important element in some manifestations of the unhomely.[6]

La case du commandeur is, of all Glissant's novels, the one in which the unhomely is most strikingly present. There is a greater concentration here on *contemporary* life in Martinique, since the whole of the third and final section is set in the 1970s, and it shows the collective repression of a traumatic past on the part of "those of us who had come to terms with their numbness and who gallantly tried to lead their lives, stubbornly immersing themselves in duties so pressing that they allowed them not to think about the terrifying lacks and the evanescence" (180–81). But it is also in *La case du commandeur* that history is most explicitly represented as absent—as "this *hole* of time" (108, emphasis added). It was published in the same year as *Le discours antillais*, and there are a number of close connections between the two texts. In his interview with the journal *CARÉ*, Glissant juxtaposes *Le discours antillais* with *La case du commandeur* on the question of routine verbal delirium, which he defines as a form of cultural resistance, an "effort to clarify collective memory, its gaps and its permanence; to wrest from time the span [*la durée*] (the continuity of a history) that we deserved to be able to live." This link with collective memory and history, which, as we have seen, is a distinguishing feature of dramatizing delirium, is central to the novel as a whole. *La case du commandeur* is an attempt to remedy the loss of awareness of the past in the banalized, consumerist society that Glissant claims Martinique became in the 1970s. It traces the psychological effects that such a repression of history has on individuals and especially on two of its main characters: Marie Celat and her father, Pythagore.[7]

Pythagore is first introduced as a solitary deranged figure shouting at passersby at the crossroads (*CC*, 19), typical of the dramatizing delirium of "these wanderers [*errants*] who gesticulate at the crossroads, semaphoring the tragedy of our uprootings," and of whom Glissant writes: "We pretend to ignore them: we do not know that we speak the same language as them: the same impossible obsession with real production" (*DA*, 362). Pythagore shouts the incomprehensible word "Odono," which, we later discover, is the name of the mythical African ancestor transported to Martinique, and which also serves as a more general reference to the past and to the people's African origins. The only way in which history can be retrieved, it would seem, is in these confused, fragmentary visions ("The man, the mid-day sorcerer, glimpses things in patches" (19); "He sees in short bursts" (20)). But we learn that before reaching this stage, he had regularly "performed" before a more appreciative audience in the bar run by the overseer's wife—in other words, in the "case du commandeur" of the novel's title (26). Moreover, his speech revolves obsessively around the question of historical origins, in the form of a delirious evocation of Africa and a mythical, all-powerful "King of the Negroes" (26–27). A comment that Bhabha makes in the context of *literary* representation—"how the historical event is represented in a discourse that is *somehow beyond control*" (12)—applies here to the representations that Glissant sees as typical of dramatizing delirium in its social reality.[8]

This mythical king subsequently becomes identified in Pythagore's mind with the real figure of Béhanzin, king of Dahomey, who was deported by the French to Martinique in 1902, the year in which Pythagore was born. He tries, unsuccessfully, to find out more about the king's life in Martinique; and the motive for this reappropriation of history is to illuminate his own situation in the present: "to shed light on the dark area that moved within him" (37). But as his madness intensifies, he finds it impossible to distinguish between Africa and Martinique (39); far from gaining a sense of continuity with the African past, he loses any sense of belonging to Martinique—he has "passed over to the side of the wandering dreams [*des songes errants*], who cannot locate their landscape and are not anchored in any soil" (39). This condition of not being "at home" anywhere in the world, taken together with the spectral quality of the *songes errants* and with the impossibility of any settled, continuous relationship with the past, is strongly suggestive of Bhabha's concept of "unhomeliness."

The unhomeliness of the novel is, however, most clearly seen in the figure of Marie Celat, or Mycéa as she is known. She appears at least fleetingly in all of Glissant's novels, and, from the very first description of her in *La Lézarde,* her lack of individual solidity and almost pathological sensitivity to the exterior social-historical world are stressed: "It was as though her absent gaze veiled the disorders of a soul more sensitive than any other to the disturbances of the times, to the frenzied sloughing off of the skin of the old world, from which she suffered" (*L,* 27). In *La case du commandeur,* where she has her most prominent role, this impression is sustained. Even with her close friends, Mycéa always retains a kind of "apartness"; she is "opaque by nature" (146–47). The course of events reinforces this: after the election campaign, in which the group worked closely together, "we began to notice that Mycéa was imperceptibly leaving us" (148). This impression of absence makes her uncanny—familiar yet strange, she is there, and yet not there: "Marie Celat who we knew was existing there, close by, with the absent existence of those who have withdrawn themselves" (*CC,* 189). As her name suggests, she is a kind of human Marie Céleste: every detail of her person is present and correct, but at the same time, like the deserted ship, she is completely empty. (Freud, interestingly, cites "dolls and automata" as a classic case of the uncanny, since they raise "doubts whether an apparently animate being is really alive.")[9]

Mycéa's distance from other people is a form of intellectual courage. She is open to the unhomely condition and consciously tolerates its anxiety, whereas her friends repress it. Specifically, her courage allows her to venture further toward the edge of the void of the past: "Perhaps she was looking further into the gulf than any of us" (145). She refuses to conform to the collective amnesia of those around her, and as a result they find her uncomfortably odd and disturbing. Her strangeness slowly intensifies until at the end of the novel it becomes a far more obvious and spectacular madness; a madness which, therefore, is the exact correlate of the risk she takes in uncovering what has been collectively repressed. Her friends' vaguely uneasy sense that "something was missing" coincides with her mentally "going away" (178–79). Her madness constitutes a resistance to alienation not so much because it possesses as because it seeks a dangerous knowledge: it is the dangerous refusal *not* to know. People reject her because she strips away the "peel" that protects them from the anxiety of unhomeliness (181).

Mycéa's madness, then, is both a result of and a strategy for "living in the unhomely world." Her "absence" communicates with the absence of known history. This is expressed also through the textual play on "Celat." Critics have commented on the oddly neutral emptiness of this surname.[10] The novel itself, moreover, links this indeterminate presence with another "cela," which is, precisely, the repressed presence of history: "Going back into *that* which had been lost [*La remontée dans cela qui s'était perdu*]: how a population had been forged out of suffering shipfuls of Negroes seized and sold, . . . how coming from so many different places and landing up there (here) through the necessities of bargaining and profit, it had . . . endured; how it had secreted a language out of all the words torn from it or imposed on it; how the effort of forgetting so many offenses committed against it was wearing it out" (CC, 159).

The urgent desire to retrieve or re-create Martinique's history is, of course, a central theme in all Glissant's fiction, and its main exponent is Mathieu (particularly in *Le quatrième siècle* and *Mahagony*). But Mycéa's attitude is significantly different from that of Mathieu. In *Le quatrième siècle*, it is she who persuades him that what they need most is political action in the present rather than historical research (QS, 323). For her, politics in the unhomely world is exactly as Bhabha defines it: "the stressed necessity of everyday life."[11] Thus, we are told that "Mycéa, who had all at once gone beyond the poetic childishness born of their dizzying ignorance . . . made a deliberate point of emphasizing the discomforts of their life, the daily struggle, the prosaic necessity of eating and drinking" (*QS*, 313). This in turn involves an apparent rejection of the past: "she broke the thread, thrust the dazzling past far behind her" (314).

La case du commandeur similarly makes it clear that she is determined to live in the *banality*—the "platitude"—of the present: "They had to leave this period of the Plantations and Marie Celat was ready to plunge into irretrievable platitude, with no futile recriminations, while Mathieu Béluse was still clinging onto the dream of before" (*CC*, 161). This seems difficult to reconcile with her reiterated need to confront the "gulf" of the past, but the notion of unhomeliness allows us to see that what is at issue here is a different *relationship to* the past. Bhabha starts his section on "Unhomely lives" with a reference to Fanon's awareness of the importance "for subordinated peoples, of . . . retrieving their repressed histories."[12] But, he continues, Fanon also realizes the danger of this becoming just another version of the *fixing* of colonial identity in the stereotype and so is careful not to "recommend that 'roots' be struck in the celebratory romance of the past." This, arguably, is the trap into which Mathieu falls. In contrast, Mycéa's perversely deliberate banality can be seen as a way of consciously accepting the real emptiness of the past, rather than trying as Mathieu does to reconstruct it as a mythical plenitude. One rather cryptic sentence in the third part of the novel seems to express this idea. It includes a reference back to the last two sections of the second part, concerning, respectively, the female slave who kills her baby and the maroon leader tortured and burnt to death. Of Mycéa in the present, Glissant writes: "She *felt this hole* beyond which none could stretch his thought, yet where she had looked, even if she did not *fill it in* with a smothered child, with a mouth stuffed with burning coals" (162, emphasis added). The ability to experience the past as a "hole" without "filling it in" with horrifyingly colorful incidents is perhaps an aspect of what Bhabha in his opening paragraph calls "the negating activity," which inscribes division and difference rather than continuity and plenitude: it is, he says, "the intervention of the 'beyond' that establishes a boundary: a bridge, where 'presencing' begins because it captures something of . . . the unhomeliness . . . that is the condition of extra-territorial and cross-cultural initiations."[13]

Mycéa's banality is thus her way of assuming the unhomely condition. But it is more ambiguous than that. It is at the same time an artificially constructed defense *against* the madness and pain of unhomeliness, in which she takes refuge while never quite believing in it: "It was all of such exaggerated banality that at times she would stop, marvelling at such a completely successful realization of the genre. I'm perfect, it all looks so good on me, the little lawn, the metal Venetian blinds, the Lévitan dining room, the procession of men" (167). Even as she goes on trying to be "ordinary," the underlying anxiety keeps surfacing: "Marie Celat would weep for no known reason. Was there a curse of loneliness on her head? Something come from so far away (not in time but in the impression that one has of it and in the weakness that it brings) that there was no way of knowing it or warding it off? Then Marie Celat would laugh. I am an ordinary woman, she insisted; fabricating for herself this character, so difficult to sustain" (168). Moreover, what makes the ambiguity of the banality particularly complex is that ultimately both of its aspects have to do with the uncanny. Assuming the unhomely condition means accepting the uncanny. But equally, the anxiety that the banality in its other, defensive, function, serves to *repress*, can also be seen as uncanny. Freud's definition of the uncanny as the return of something secretly familiar, which seems strange and frightening *only* because it has been repressed, is exactly echoed in Mycéa's "curse": "something" which seems to come from "far away," but not objectively—not "in time"—but subjectively, in the "impression" that it creates and that makes you feel "weak." It feels distant because it has been repressed, in other words, and it is the nature of the repressed to be neither accessible to knowledge nor something that can be got rid of: "no way of knowing it or warding it off." We are forced to conclude that Mycéa's banality has two conflicting functions. It is both a brave, clear-sighted rejection of the "celebratory romance of the past," as Bhabha puts it, and hence an acceptance of the uncanny anxiety of the unhomely present, and a repression of the same uncanny anxiety. It is only at the end of the novel that the contradiction will be resolved.[14]

In order to understand this process we need to look more closely at the trajectory of Mycéa's developing madness. The sudden deaths of her two sons—Patrice killed on his motorcycle and Odono drowned in the sea—precipitate her breakdown; but, as we have seen, the madness begins before these events and is not simply caused by personal tragedy. Indeed, her reaction to seeing Patrice dying at the roadside conflates, with an extraordinary immediacy, personal loss and the abiding sense of collective historical loss: "She ran into the crowd, shouting let me through it's my son. He was there. Where do we come from, from what night swept with waves of steep astonishment? From what crazy memory, which keeps moving back out of our reach?" [*De quelle mémoire insen-*

sée, qui se retire à mesure?] (182). The unhomely interpenetration of private and public, domestic and historical, becomes almost shockingly acute. This state, in which "the borders between home and world become confused,"[15] is manifested again in the ambiguity of the name "Odono": both the mythical ancestor and her younger son. When, just after Patrice's death, she cries out "where is Odono?," one would assume she meant her son—except that we are told she is searching for "someone or something, she didn't yet know. It is a cry in her head, but which one?" The same ambiguity persists after Odono's death; she asks everyone, "Have you seen Odono?," but her close friends realize that she is referring not to the boy but to the distant ancestor (189).

It is this violent collision of the personal and the historical that consummates her separation from other people and leads to her forcible hospitalization. The indeterminate "cela" of historical lack resurfaces in the text as we are told "to feel her so vehemently hit by *that* [*cela*] which we assumed was not solely the loss of her sons . . . bewildered some people and enraged others" (191). She is taken to the mental hospital, which is in the forest. The shadow of the trees, stopping just short of the building, creates a boundary, separating "two worlds forever closed" (193); and it is this borderline between repressive social order and the mad but liberating wilderness of the forest that she crosses when, a few days later and with the help of Chérubin (an inmate who regularly runs away), she escapes at night from the hospital. Chérubin is another significant example of someone for whom pathological delirium functions as a strategy for survival and a certain kind of freedom. At this point *speech* becomes important again. Chérubin's delirious "hullabaloo" as they plunge through the dense forest together has a healing effect on Mycéa (194).[16] He describes her situation to her and tells her how to take control of it, and he tells her that she is not mad (197–98). Moreover, through listening to him she hears more clearly the "resonance" of the past: "Marie Celat went back in Chérubin's voice, toward all the things she had never known but which resonated more clearly than the word of the first day" (197); this is followed by the names of some of the ancestors who have figured in the earlier parts of the novel.

This episode, the climax of the novel, takes place in the "case du commandeur" [the overseer's hut]. That is, Chérubin has led her through the forest to the abandoned hut in which Euloge, her great-great-grandfather, had lived, and in which her father, Pythagore, had told delirious fantasies about Africa to his fellow drinkers. Here she experiences an obscure "awakening" that appears to restore her to sanity (198). The scene is full of fragmentary evocations of past events and previous generations, and it has generally been interpreted as a recovery of history: a healing and restorative filling in of the void of the past.[17] There is certainly evidence in the text to support this—in particular the sentence from page 197, quoted in the preceding paragraph, where Marie Celat "went back" toward her ancestors. But there are also some difficulties with this reading. We already know, for instance, that she is against the project of "recovering history" in Mathieu's sense. Tracing the sequence of her delirium, as she and Chérubin sit and talk in the darkness of the hut, one also notes that what immediately precedes and seems to trigger her recovery is not the identification with the ancestors on page 197, but her evocation of the "Table of the Islands" on page 198. At an earlier stage of her delirium she used to stand on the beach calling out to Dominica and Saint Lucia (181); now it is as if she suddenly sees how to situate herself and her community in relation to other, equally dislocated, collectives. This would suggest that it is less "filiation" than the "space" of Relation with the world in the present that cures her. Relation, in fact, is the project of a cure for unhomeliness.

But it is above all the peculiarity of the site that makes it difficult to read the episode as a simple case of Mycéa going back to her roots. Of all the homes that the novel could have chosen for this key moment, that of Euloge is the most ambivalent and the least *heimlich*. In contrast to the strong positive characters, such as Liberté, Augustus, or Adoline, Euloge is politically and morally dubious. He is also socially ambivalent: as an overseer, he occupies a place between master and slave, and he hates and despises his fellow workers (75). In addition, his hut was a shop and bar as well as a private home, and so exemplifies the unhomely "interstitial intimacy" of private and public, "question[ing] binary divisions." Bhabha's comments on the "unhomely homes" in *Beloved* and *My Son's Story* are relevant here: "What is just as important is the metaphoricity of the houses of racial memory that both Morrison and Gordimer construct—those subjects of the narrative that mutter or mumble like 124 Bluestone Road, or keep a still silence in a 'grey' Cape Town suburb." He suggests that "each 'unhomely' house marks a deeper historical displacement," because each is "half-way between" the two poles of a defined social opposition: neither black nor white, neither slave nor free. Euloge and his house embody exactly the same type of "in-between" condition.[18]

From this point of view, Mycéa's rediscovery of the "case du commandeur" is far from a straightforward homecoming. It can, in fact, even be read as a figuration of the *unheimlich* moment itself, but in a sense closer to Freud's original construction than Bhabha's version of it—a sense that hinges on the peculiar impact of the "secretly familiar." Following Chérubin through the forest, Mycéa does not know where they are going; the forest is unfamiliar, disorientating, and frightening; but then they suddenly come upon the hut where, when she was a child, her father used to drink with his friends. This reminiscence of childhood is paralleled by the reader's "distant" memory of the beginning of the novel, where the drinking scene is recounted. The text discreetly recalls the earlier passage; the "snake" and the "fireflies" on page 196 echo those mentioned on page 26, and the "tamarind bush" and "wooden table" on pages 29–30 recur as "they came out, Marie Celat and Chérubin, onto the clearing where the tamarind bush rose up in front of the hut. The table was outside, relieved of nearly all its planks but incomprehensibly still standing" (196). The hut is still there, but now abandoned and ghostly. Long forgotten, stumbled upon in the middle of nowhere and in the middle of the night, it exudes that combination of "strange but secretly familiar" that Freud attributes to the uncanny. It thus illustrates exactly the uncanny moment of recognition of the past. And, because of its associations with the troubling figure of Euloge, its unexpected rediscovery is equally "something that ought to have remained secret and hidden but has come to light."[19]

At the same time—and here we rejoin Bhabha's description of unhomeliness—what this means is that *history* is indeed present in the overseer's hut, but present as an unhomely disjunctive spectrality rather than a reassuring communion with one's ancestors. The ghosts of Euloge, his wife, and Adoline, which haunt the hut, are like Bhabha's "unspoken, unrepresented pasts that haunt the historical present." The strange song that comes back to Mycéa (197), in which we recognize the magic words her mother heard when she, as a little girl, was alone in the forest (65), and which Mycéa presumably heard her mother singing, produces a similar effect of uncanny recognition.[20] When she says to Chérubin, "Longoué was right when he told me, so long ago, that it wouldn't be under a guinep tree" (198–99), she is referring to Longoué's prophecy "that the lost girl would find herself in her night, but that it wouldn't be under a guinep tree" (162), which in turn is an allusion to Cinna Chimène, who as a child was literally found one night in the forest, "by the big guinep tree" (49). Thus, Mycéa also "finds herself" through a reconnection to her mother. This can be linked with the "curse of loneliness" (168), which, as we have seen, previously frightened her into suppressing her anxiety beneath an assumed banality. She had kept her distance from her parents out of a fear that she would "catch" their unhomely madness (153, 189). Now she has indeed gone mad, but she has emerged into the "other side" of madness (196) and has confronted and accepted the unhomeliness of her life. Her banality is therefore no longer ambivalent; it is no longer a defense against the uncanny but simply the resolution to live in the unhomely present. On the last page of the novel, she agrees with her daughter that "the time had come to live and let live, if they could."

Marie Celat reappears in *Mahagony* as narrator of the chapter bearing her name, and she seems once again to be delirious. The delirium now takes the form of a driving "rhythm" (*Mah,* 131) that takes her over: "when you have the rhythm fourteen fifteen sixteen / your head is a dance band living it up in front / you fly along behind more a humming-bird than the great wind" (132). She associates it with trees, a frightening image from which she cannot escape: "When I think in the rhythm, I'm always running in the woods, with the trees. I've run through the woods, I know you can't get out" (133). A little later, we realize that this is in fact an allusion to the climactic incident of the previous novel—the night spent in the forest in the overseer's hut: "I had not yet borne the weight of the night of the trees, where the overseer's hut was planted" (141). Thus, the key moment of unhomeliness has, in this subsequent novel, resulted in a kind of breakdown into a new form of delirious madness. Whatever the exact nature of the "awakening" that she experienced in the overseer's hut, she has not been able to sustain it. But she fights against this by trying to ward off the image of the trees (that "bring on" the delirious "rhythm") with an image of grass. That is, she sets up an opposition between trees and grass, in which she is on the side of the grass: "You'll plant your grass meadows, abandon these trees who think they're" (132). The "rhythm" threatens to drive away the grass— "I hope the rhythm doesn't come back into my head, or else I'll go off the subject. My subject is the grasses" (133)—but she persists. Grass, she says repeatedly, is the "subject" of this chapter, and she is determined to talk about it in a calm, sane manner. Sanity and homely grass will prevail over trees and unhomely delirium. She reassures the reader: "No, it's over, all that fussing about the big mahogany trees, I'm not going to bother you with that. I look at my little grass meadows, nicely *surrounding your houses*" (136, emphasis added).

Grass is thus a way of blocking out the dangerous memories of the night in the woods. Concentrating on it is a defense against the uncanny. It is also, however, a defense against the pain and madness resulting from the deaths of her sons. By preventing her from thinking about anything else, the grass screens out not only the symbolic trees but also the real human beings who have caused the pain, and who can be relegated to mere accessories of the grass. She states this twice, once at the beginning of the chapter (132–33) and once more explicitly at the end: "the only real subject is the grasses, enemies of the trees. Let the women the men the young boys of eighteen appear only in order to certify the grasses. I'm going to lock my head to stop me falling back into the rhythm" (142).

What motivates this "mad" choice of *grass* as a defense against madness? It is in fact a profoundly paradoxical choice, because it originates not in sane or happy associations but in the deaths of her sons. Its first connotations are those of violent grief and loss: Patrice lying on the grass by the roadside and Odono floating to the surface with "that sea-grass in his dead hair, the grass from the bottom of the sea that put him to sleep forever" (134). Marie Celat concludes "What I'm doing is harvesting the grasses that won't stop dying" (134). But it is precisely this tragic image that she transforms into a defense against pain. The grass even becomes an emblem of happiness, *both* in relation to her sons and to the unhomely "night in the woods"; she describes her life with the two boys as: "That time was a happy one, a lightness of grass meadows, well before the night in the woods. I grew up with Patrice, with Odono, we floated along together" (137). And, in an ultimate reversal, grass is transformed into a sign of life rather than of death. It proliferates "rhizomatically"— Deleuze and Guattari use grass and trees as key instances of "rhizome" and "root," respectively. Like Marie Celat, grass fights for survival in the city: "Those grasses make me cry, they're so obstinately determined to live" (143). It wages a guerilla warfare against the invading concrete: "The grass jumps across without you seeing it, it finds secret nooks and crannies that it can exploit" (143). The opposition between what Dash calls "the great trees of the past" and "the tenacious, anonymous and disorderly grass" thus acquires a further meaning, whereby the grass symbolizes the unheroic, multiple, *interstitial* resistance of the present day, in the city rather than in the forest. The grass literally fights and survives in the interstices of motorways and buildings: "I prefer the grasses sodden with cement water on the edges of town or the motorway" (143).[21]

Mahagony thus traces the trajectory of Marie Celat's attempts to live with unhomeliness through a further stage. Just as in the earlier part of *La case du commandeur,* she finds a strategy for repressing unhomely anxiety. But whereas then it was a "sane" tactic of immersing herself in banality and ordinariness, this time it is through a "mad" obsession with grass. This is, nevertheless, a "mad" way of *staying "sane."* Or, at least, it is a mad defense against madness. As such, it illustrates exactly the ambiguity of the borderline between sanity and madness, and of the detour through madness as a form of psychic survival. The grass is the first example of a survival tactic that is *undecidably* mad and sane; there will be others in Marie Celat's life later on.

The ambiguity of the grass, however, is not solely between madness and sanity. It is also to do with its relationship to grief. Initially, as we have seen, it signified the sons' death; and it was *for that reason* that Marie Celat desperately reversed it into a sign of happiness and life. It thus contains an unstable ambivalence, which makes the reader feel that it is not going to last as an effective defense and that Marie Celat will return to her dangerous exploration of the unhomely areas that other people repress. Indeed, Ida hints at this when, in the next chapter, she evokes her mother's urge to venture alone into forbidden and frightening territory: "What carried you so deep into the earth that you seemed an exile far from us" (159).

It is thus no surprise when Glissant's next novel introduces Marie Celat as: "She has known all misfortune and approached all truths, as though inspired" (*TM,* 13). *Tout-monde* shows the detour of "madness-as-survival" at its most ambiguous: a borderline strategy in which it becomes almost impossible to say what counts as survival and what as self-destruction. The novel stages her last conversation with Mathieu, the moment at which their relationship finally ends. Mathieu tries to keep her "here" with him, but in the end he has to let her "go away." She is mad again, we are told, and her distance from everyday reality is greater than ever. Moreover, the distance is created above all by her language: "At that moment when Marie Celat was falling into madness, and when she was forcing Mathieu Béluse toward that same transparency of language that distanced you from everything, was it possible really to relate, to hold together . . . our everyday problems and on the other hand that stream of startled words that the same Marie Celat brought here from so far away?" (345–46). She speaks, and hears, words that we cannot "approach" (358). It is, indeed, very difficult for the reader to make sense of what she says. But this is not because her speech is delirious in the usual sense of the word: it has none of the proliferating, wildly free-associating quality of Dlan or Chérubin, for instance. It is better described as cryptic and deliberately evasive: the text refers to "the Carib evasivenesses of Marie Celat" (346). There is also an oddly forced, histrionic quality to some of her declarations.[22] Thus, her madness seems to be an act of defiance and will, rather than a condition passively endured: "So much the worse for you if I'm the only one to look into the great depths. The only one to come from far away, like this wind! I show you the direction" (359). Similarly, we get a strong sense that she is controlling the situation. We are told, for instance: "But Marie Celat knew exactly what she had to sort out with Mathieu Béluse" (342); and "in her head she calculated the stretches of road she would be covering on her way, dragging Mathieu with her" (343). It is as if her madness consists not in being helplessly out of touch with reality, but rather in a calculated *positioning* of herself at a distance from reality: "Mycéa concentrating on her *wish* [*volonté*] not to *appear* living or involved in day-to-day quarrels: she *desired* only to float in a surroundings with no points of reference" (342, emphasis added).

The text does not give a full or rational answer as to why she is doing this. But it does offer some elliptical indications. The deaths of Patrice and Odono are still dominating her thoughts. Their names are still "running within her body," and she has decided that she must go on enduring this: "Mais voyez encore cette obligation de supporter mon corps et les noms qui courent dedans, au plus loin possible. Ah! Ne dis pas de calamité quand tu convoques l'éloignement. L'éloignement est noir et juste. Qu'est-ce qui s'éloigne n'est pas cela qui disparaît" [But see this obligation still to bear my body and the names which run within it, as far away as possible. Ah! Don't call it calamity when you summon up distance. Distance is black and right. What distances itself is not what disappears] (361). Distance is not the same as disappearance; this perhaps means that distancing (herself) is the only way she can keep the past from vanishing altogether. That is, it is only by being "au plus loin possible" (i.e., mad) that she can continue to remember the past without its being unbearable. Madness is the alternative to repression. Earlier in the conversation she has talked about how repressing one's suffering only makes it worse: "we have forgotten suffering, and that suffering exists. . . . But really suffering is not knowing how to suffer in suffering" (349).

The narrator's interventions in this section are often as cryptic as Marie Celat's own speech, but these too seem to be ambiguously evoking her desire not to "be there." For instance: "Pas un ne peut la faire paraître. Elle est là *où* elle ne veut pas, car pas un ne sait *ce qu*'elle veut. Elle paraît *ce qu*'elle n'est pas. Ho! Sommes-nous *où* nous paraissons?" [No one can make her appear. She is *where* she does not want, for no one knows *what* she wants. She appears *what* she is not. Ah! Are we *where* we appear?] (358, emphasis added). The play on the alternation of "où" [where] and "ce que" [what] makes the verb "paraître" ambiguous: to appear (somewhere) or to seem (something that one is not). She is both appearing somewhere she is not, like a ghostly "apparition," and seeming to be something she is not. But a further ambiguity surrounds what she *wants*: "Elle est là où elle ne veut pas" seems at first to mean "she is where she doesn't want to be." But this by implication contradicts the preceding sentence and leaves the subsequent "for . . . " unclear. If, however, we read it as "she exists in a place where she does not desire (anything), for no one can recognize her desire"—then it perhaps makes more sense, in the context of her "distancing" from reality: she places herself in a place where she has no desires, so the memory of her sons' deaths is no longer unbearable.

At end of this section she is at the very edge of reality—"at the limits. She is waiting to wait, right up to the end of this reality" (368). She is about to "go away" for good, in an absolute sense that is equated with *freedom*: "She is swept off and frees herself absolutely. What we call her madness is just that" (368). In this final parting moment—she does not appear in the novel again apart from a fleeting and silent appearance right at the end—she also says that she is a rock (like Silacier at the end of *Malemort*) that neither resists nor breaks.[23] She has made herself inanimate, passive but indestructible—another version, perhaps, of being there while not being there. If this is a survival tactic, it is one that involves a kind of playing dead in order to avoid pain. But it does not prevent her from pursuing her exploration of the void, because the "rock" is a projectile launched into it: "I am the rock which has thrown itself into the nothingness where you will never be put" (369). And in a further development of the image, she actually becomes the void, distancing herself from the fullness of the everyday despair and pleasures that others live for: "I am nothingness, for all those who will despair. For all the others who will get up, shout out their joy, plant and eat their fill, harvest rum and red sugar" (369).

Insofar as Marie Celat's madness in *Mahagony* and *Tout-monde* mutates, as I have tried to show, into a very tenuous strategy for living with the unhomely, the displacing void of the past—that is, for living with madness itself—it becomes a kind of *detour*. As in other forms of detour, the boundary between conscious control and unconscious compulsion is blurred. Equally, her madness is *both* an escape from the intolerable *and* a perilous exploration of the unthinkable. It inhabits such a subtle and perverse borderline between risk-taking and self-protection that it takes the indirectness of the detour to a further level of undecidability, in which madness is indeed a survival strategy but in which survival is not a question of escapism but a way of living with the unbearable truth.

6 Camouflaged Language

Detour and Ruse

WE HAVE seen in the previous chapter how the detour as an alienated, compromised strategy may be intimately linked with verbal delirium. But the other side of the detour's ambiguity means that it also manifests itself in less compulsive ways; it can also take the form of a conscious ruse. In this sense, language as detour is language that chooses to disguise its meanings by communicating *indirectly*: "Car nous sommes habitués au détour, où la chose dite se love. Nous effilons le sens comme coutelas sur la roche volcanique. Nous l'étirons jusqu'à ce menu filet d'eau qui lace nos songes. Quand vous nous écoutez, vous croyez la mangouste qui sous les cannes *cherche la traverse*" [For we are accustomed to the detour, in which what we say is coiled up. We sharpen the meaning like a machete on the volcanic rock. We stretch it out into the thin trickle of water that laces our dreams. When you listen to us, you think it's the mongoose trying to cut across under the cane plants] (*DA*, 19). Meaning winds in upon itself like a snake, it is slowly refined like a machete being sharpened, it has the meandering logic of a dream, or it advances sideways, like the mongoose zigzagging through the undergrowth. It emerges in cumulative, piecemeal, and oblique ways.

Glissant's novels are full of this kind of indirect language where the meaning is, as he says, "camouflaged." One example is the story of the "Senegal cattle ticks," which is told to the reader by Rigobert Massoul in *Tout-monde* (290–94). Massoul is fighting in the French army in Vietnam and Laos in the 1950s; he has a relationship with a Laotian woman and they have a child. He tells the reader: "Look, I'm going to explain my situation in this country, but I'll have to start a long way back in Guadeloupe, so that you'll get the point" (290). We know, therefore, that what follows is designed to help us understand his present situation in Savannakhet—and we are warned that it will take some time. He then says that "every species on earth is determined to pronounce its descent" [*prononcer la descendance*], starts to talk about Guadeloupe exporting food to Martinique, and says "why am I telling you this? You'll see, it's to express the power of descent" [*c'est pour exprimer la force de la descendance*].

From then on, cryptic references to "la descendance" punctuate the story, which is about a man from Martinique who went to live in Guadeloupe and bred oxen, then decided to return to Martinique with two pairs of oxen, one of which had two "Senegal ticks," called Il and Li, in its ear. Despite the ferocious scrubbing and dipping they are forced to undergo by the sanitary services in order to be allowed into Martinique, the two ticks manage to survive unharmed: "But Il and Li are clever, they've picked a corner where no brush can get them out. The rising steam suffocates them, but it's worth making the effort to hang on" (292). The man then sells two of the oxen, the ticks breed and spread all over the island, all of Martinique's oxen become diseased, but—this is the punch line—"pour Il et Li c'est man-fouté, ils ont mené la descendance" [Il and Li don't give a damn, they have carried on the descent] (293). At this point the reader still has no idea how all this is meant to shed light on Massoul's own predicament, but he tells us that it is the only way he can explain it: that is, he has to make us understand the strength of the drive that makes any species struggle to reproduce itself even in a new territory: "Because those good-for-nothing little insects, bringing catastrophe to all the livestock in the island, you've got to admire the way they survived, cheating death, not only that but breeding away, across the channel and then through two baths of chemicals that wipe out everything, to guarantee their continuation" (294). But, he says, the problem is that he does not have the same determination. In other words—and the moral of the story finally becomes clear—he is worried about what would happen if he took his Laotian woman and child home with him, and he finally decides to leave them behind.

So the subtext of a painful personal decision emerges only at the end of four pages of mock-heroic narrative about ticks and oxen. One of the features of "camouflaged language" is this deferral of meaning, where the detour takes the form of a delaying tactic: the *parole différée* [deferred speech], as Glissant call it, in which a piece of information is repeatedly withheld, or the story is full of irrelevant digressions, or folds back on itself in a series of loops rather than proceeding in a linear fashion. Alternatively, as here, the *point* of the narrative is sometimes not clear until the end. The reader may feel that he or she could perfectly well have understood Massoul's dilemma without all this; but the *kind* of concrete, situational understanding he wants requires that "I had to go through all that invisible stuff spreading infection throughout the herds, to explain to you my situation in that country" (294); and he is still far from sure that anyone will understand: "Anne wanted to come to France with me, but, you see, I was scared of taking the child. Can people understand that, is there anyone in the world who can understand that? I felt as though I would be pulling up a plant to plant it somewhere else. Is there anyone in the whole wide world who can understand that?" (295). We are thus put on our guard against a too rapid assumption that we have understood, and the opacity of his experience is restored through the detour of the *parole différée*. As Glissant comments: "We need those stubborn shadows where repetition leads to perpetual concealment, which is our form of resistance. . . . Thus, Caribbean discourse cannot readily be seized. But does not the world, in its exploded oneness, demand that each person be drawn to the recognized [opacity] of the other? This is one aspect of our [opacity]" (*CD,* 4).

The deferral of meaning is reinforced by repetitions of the key, but opaque, phrase "la descendance": "Alors vous comprenez la force de la descendance" [So you understand the power of descent] (290); "C'est là que vous voyez la force de la descendance" [That's where you can see the power of descent] (291); "Toutes les espèces sur terre sont acharnées à courir après la descendance" [Every species on earth is determined to run after its descent] (293); "Pour Il et Li c'est man-fouté, ils ont mené la descendance" [Il and Li don't give a damn, they have carried on the descent] (293). Another typical characteristic of camouflaged language is the avoidance of abstract or generalizing terms. Massoul explains his predicament in the concrete, figurative language of allegory. Not only are the two "Senegal ticks" made to convey the idea of the drive to reproduce the species, but they also acquire the metaphorical connotations of guerrilla freedom fighters (not unlike those Massoul himself is fighting in Vietnam, perhaps): "Il and Li who won this war and who went behind enemy lines" (292–93).

But this is not the poetic metaphoricalness in which we might expect a man to express his distress at leaving his lover and child; it is entirely lighthearted and rather silly. The combination of an apparently trivial or nonsensical discourse "camouflaging" a serious underlying meaning is also typical of the ruses of language as detour. Chapter 1 mentions this strategy—communicating meaning in the guise of apparently meaningless nonsense—which *Le discours antillais* defines as: "this form of nonsense that could conceal and reveal at the same time a *hidden* meaning" (*CD, 125*), and which works by exploiting for its own purposes the received image of black naiveté and stupidity. Elsewhere in Glissant's novels we find riddles and other kinds of word games used in the same way.[1]

The story of the Senegal ticks, therefore, illustrates three different kinds of detour characteristic of camouflaged language: the use of concrete images instead of abstract concepts; digression and repetition as a delaying tactic for deferring meaning; and apparent nonsense camouflaging a deeper meaning. Many examples of all three types, alone or in combination, occur throughout Glissant's novels, which show camouflaged language in a wide range of forms. Word games, such as riddles, are by definition camouflaged, and camouflage is also particularly characteristic of certain other forms of discourse, such as the *quimboiseur's* [sorcerer's] speech, or traditional folktales, which "strove to disguise with symbols, to say by not saying. This is what elsewhere I have called the practice of the detour" (*PR, 83*). But these techniques of disguise and indirectness pervade ordinary speech as well.

Camouflaged language is also an important issue in *Le discours antillais* and other theoretical texts, where Glissant gives an extensive analysis of its forms and functions. He is however for the most part referring specifically to Creole, which he claims is characterized by the features described above. These features, he argues, make Creole—as distinct from French—a language of detour, opacity, and ruse: "Camouflage. That is the context that facilitates [the Detour]. The Creole language was constituted around this strategy of trickery" (*CD, 21*). As seen in chapter 1, Glissant argues that Creole developed these features for practical historical reasons arising from the slaves' need to communicate without the master understanding what they were saying, but that the structures of Creole have been *permanently* shaped by the circumstances in which it came into existence. In other words, the camouflaging features may have outlived their original function, but they have become embedded in the language: "the Creole language in Martinique has gone beyond the process of being structured by the [Detour]. But it has been marked by it. It slips from pun to pun, from assonance to assonance, from misunderstanding to ambiguity" (*CD, 21*).

Moreover, the characteristic ambiguity of the detour ensures that it has more than one motivation: a practical strategy of deceiving the master on the one hand and, according to Glissant, a general rejection of the French language and French speakers on the other: "In the world of the plantations, Creole above all expressed a refusal. This might enable us to define a new mode of linguistic structuring which would be 'negative' or 'reactive,' different from the 'natural' structural evolution of traditional languages" (*DA,* 241). In other words, the language's very structure is a reaction against French. This means that the "opacity" of Creole is the result of a slightly different aspect of its historical genesis as well: not only practical camouflage, but also the subversive relationship to the dominant language (see chapter 1), which is less to do with deliberately excluding a particular listener in a particular situation than it is a by-product of the detour of the expression. From this point of view, the use of images rather than concepts, for instance, is a subversive detour "around" French: "But the Creole language, in addition, is marked by French . . . as an *internal* transcendence. . . . Thus, imagery, that is, the 'concrete' and all its metaphorical associations, is not, in the Creole language, an ordinary feature. It is a deliberate [detour]. It is not an implicit slyness but a deliberate craftiness" (*CD,* 126). Indeed, this is one of the reason's for the *lack* of Creole in its present state. Its function as a clandestine language is no longer relevant, but on the other hand it has not developed into a "normal" language, so that its present-day viability is undermined.[2]

Since Glissant's novels are written in French rather than Creole, his theoretical account of camouflaging in Creole might not seem relevant to camouflaged language in the novels. In fact, however, we find the same features occurring in both, and there are good reasons why this is so. Although the novels are texts written in a language that is recognizably French, the reader soon becomes aware of the extent to which Creole has infiltrated them. This is not just a question of particular words or phrases ("Creolisms") but, more importantly, of syntactic and rhetorical structures; Glissant defines these as a form of creolization and claims that it alone is a genuinely subversive action on the French language:

> Creolization in my view is not the same as Creolism: it is, for instance, the generation of a *langage* which weaves together the poetics—and they may conflict with each other—of the Creole and the French *langues.* What do I mean by poetics? The Creole storyteller uses techniques that are alien to the French *langue,* which even go in the opposite direction. . . . So much so that the French reader faced with such texts may say: "I can't understand any of it" and indeed he doesn't understand any of it because he literally cannot perceive those poetics whereas he can immediately perceive a Creolism. . . . But the poetics and the structure of the *lan-*

gage, the recasting of the structure of the *langages* will seem to him purely and simply obscure. (*IPD,* 121)

What the novels obviously cannot replicate are the different situational parameters of face-to-face spoken communication (described in *Le discours antillais,* 123–25); and one may suspect that these paralinguistic features—intonations, facial expressions, body language—assume a particular importance in the functional camouflaging of meaning. The "translation" of an essentially oral language such as Creole into a written text is not straightforward, as Glissant himself remarks. But even some purely oral features, such as the accelerated, staccato delivery typical of Creole, have their equivalents to some extent in the lack of punctuation and fractured style of passages of his writing.[3]

This form of coexistence of the two languages means that it is justifiable to refer to Glissant's analyses of Creole in connection with his fictional practice. The *relation between* Creole and French in fact constitutes a very general kind of opacity affecting the whole of Glissant's fictional writing. Certainly, as far as dialogue is concerned, most of the characters in his novels would "in real life" speak Creole and not French. Their speech in the novels is therefore (apart from a few phrases) *translated* by the author into French. However, the *narrative* discourse of the novels is also to a very large extent assumed by characters—either the amorphous collective voice of *Malemort* and *La case du commandeur,* or the individual narrators of *Mahagony* and *Tout-monde,* for instance.[4] Thus, no clear separation exists between the represented speech of characters and the narrative discourse: in both, we are in effect reading a French translation of a (nonexistent) original Creole text. Moreover, this is a deliberately imperfect translation, in which traces of Creole lexis and syntax remain perceptible even to a non-Creolophone reader. The presence of Creole makes itself felt behind the French words on the page, and this distances these words from their significations, creating the peculiar opacity that always inhabits a text that is obviously a translation. Creole casts its shadow, so to speak, on the text, unsettling its meanings so that we are not sure whether we have interpreted it correctly. The uncertainty that Glissant sees as characteristic of Creole per se—"one never knows if this speech, while delivering one meaning, is not at the same time being elaborated precisely in order to hide another one" (*DA,* 355)—is thus re-created in the way Creole impinges on French in the texts of his novels.[5]

In fact, Glissant has characterized translation in general as a form of detour: "it is the idea of the swerve or the trace which, contrary to the idea of the system, signals an uncertainty and a risk which converge and strengthen us." Thus, what translation produces is a new *langage* rather than a *langue*, an unpredictable relation between two languages: "the translator invents a necessary *langage* to link one *langue* to the other, a *langage* common to both of them, but somehow unpredictable on the basis of either of them" (*IPD*, 45). In the case of his novels, it is indeed true that the French language is to a significant extent *détournée* by the perceptible impact of Creole upon it. As Maximilien Laroche puts it, "When Glissant recommends the practice of the detour, he is suggesting that the writer becomes a trickster figure, that he 'maroons' [*marronne*, that is, both escapes and attacks] traditional writing and thereby makes us hear Creole speech within writing in the French language."[6]

What is at stake here is more than just the accidental opacity that arises from reading a translation—that is, from the virtual superimposition of any two languages in one text. It also has to do with *counterpoetics* as a deliberate strategy of subversion of French—the detour whereby the French language is turned against itself, becoming difficult to understand in the process—because this detour is accomplished by the use of *Creole* forms. Glissant defines "the poetics of Creole" as "a permanent exercise in the deviation [*détournement*] of the transcendence that is implicated in it: that of its French source" (*DA*, 32). The presence of Creole in the text is not just the residual trace of an imperfect translation but an active principle of disturbance and contestation. The reader is witnessing the counterpoetic struggle whereby a *langage* is constituted against the grain of the *langue*; in which the speaker must "force his way through the *langue* toward a *langage* that may not be part of the internal logic of this *langue*" (*DA*, 237).

A close analysis of the texts shows that the opacities and resistances of Glissant's writing do indeed derive to a considerable extent from the subversive presence of Creole and from precisely the features of camouflaged language that he himself identifies. The first page of the main text of *La case du commandeur* is a case in point:

> Pythagore Celat claironnait tout un bruit à propos de "nous", sans qu'un quelconque devine ce que cela voulait dire. *Nous* qui ne devions peut-être jamais jamais former, final de compte, ce corps unique par quoi nous commencerions d'entrer dans notre empan de terre ou dans la mer violette alentour (aujourd'hui défunte d'oiseaux, criblée d'une mitraille de goudron) ou dans ces prolongements qui pour nous trament l'au-loin du

monde; qui avions de si folles manières de paraître disséminés; qui roulions nos moi l'un contre l'autre sans jamais en venir à entabler dans cette
ceinture d'îles (ne disons pas dans cette-ci seulement dont la Saint-Martin
avait coché le jour de *découverte*—en Martinique—, comme si avant ce
jour n'avait flaqué à sa place de terre qu'un peu de cette mer Caraïbe dont
nous ne demandons jamais le pourquoi du nom) ne disons pas même une
ombre, comme d'une brousse qui aurait découpé dans l'air l'absence et la
nuit où elle dérive,—nous éprouvions pourtant que de ce nous le tas dé-
borderait, qu'une énergie sans fond le limerait, que les moi se noueraient
comme des cordes, aussi mal amarrées que les dernières cannes de fin de
jour, quand le soleil tombe dans l'exténuement du corps, mais aussi
raides et têtues que l'herbe-à-ver quand elle a passé par ta bouche. (17)

[Pythagore Celat used to shout out a whole lot of stuff about "us," without anyone being able to guess what it meant. *We,* who perhaps, when all
is said and done, would never ever make up that single body whereby we
might begin to enter into our portion of land or into the violet sea roundabout (today dead of birds, riddled with a hail of tar bullets) or into those
extensions that for us weave the far-away of the world; who had such
crazy ways of seeming to be scattered; who rolled our selves one against
the other without ever laying down foundations in this belt of islands
(let's not say in this one alone whose *discovery* had been notched up on
St. Martin's Day—Martinique—as though until that day nothing but a
bit of this Caribbean sea whose name we never question had puddled in
its land's place) let's not say even a shadow, as though of a piece of scrub-
land which had cut out in the air the absence and the night in which it
drifts—but we still felt that the heap of this us would spill over, that a
bottomless energy would file it down, that the selves would knot together
like cords, as badly tied as the last canes at the end of the day, when the
sun sets in the body's exhaustion, but as stiff and stubborn as worm-grass
when it goes through your mouth.]

The problem of understanding words is explicitly posed in the very
first sentence—no one knows what "nous" really means—and echoed
later in "cette mer Caraïbe dont nous ne demandons jamais le pourquoi
du nom." But it is also enacted by the text's own characteristic detours.
The whole page, for instance, consisting of one short and one very long
sentence, is structured by the repetition that Glissant claims is one of the
ruses of Creole: "*Nous* qui ne devions . . . qui avions . . . qui roulions
. . . nous éprouvions *que* de ce nous . . . *qu*'une énergie . . . le limerait,

que les moi se noueraient." And equally: "entrer *dans* notre empan de terre *ou dans* la mer violette . . . *ou dans* ces prolongements"; "ne disons pas" occurs twice; "aussi mal amarrées que" is echoed in "aussi raides et têtues que"; "terre" and "mer" are juxtaposed in "dans notre empan de terre ou dans la mer violette" and again in "à sa place de terre qu'un peu de cette mer." As a result, the text does not advance in a direct linear fashion, but—as in the "detour, where what we say is *coiled up*" (emphasis added)—keeps looping back on itself.

The opaque insistence of Creole in the text is perceptible in expressions that are not standard French—"final de compte," "cette-ci," "éprouver que"—but perhaps more significantly in the way a distinctively *oral* register is incorporated into a written text: "final de compte" again and the final address to the reader, "passé par ta bouche." Also, the repetition of "jamais jamais" is a good example of Glissant's point that the characteristic "doubling" of words in Creole is a faux-naïf exploitation of the oral "nonsense" stereotype.[7] The avoidance of abstract nouns is also very noticeable, creating the phrase "l'au-loin du monde," for instance, instead of "distance." Despite the fact that it is expressing *ideas* about the problems of collective identity, there are only four abstract nouns in the passage: "prolongements," "absence," "énergie," and "exténuement." Two of these, moreover, are combined with verbs referring to concrete actions: "ces prolongements qui . . . trament"; "une énergie . . . limerait." This figurative use of language is another major feature of the detour, and it occurs throughout this passage to convey, less directly but more effectively, abstract conceptions of identity, presence and absence, etc. Thus, the individual separate "selves" are like balls: "nous . . . qui roulions nos moi l'un contre l'autre." The images are taken from everyday life and are *contextually* specific: the selves are also compared to the local plant "l'herbe-à-ver" and to sugar canes that are badly tied into bundles because the workers are tired at the end of the day. The final reference to "ta bouche," as well as emphasizing sensation over abstract thought, serves to bring the reader into the context, implying a shared cultural experience. The fact that this whole string of images is introduced by the nonstandard "nous éprouvions que" rather than "sentions," for instance, also underlines the concrete, sensuous nature of the experience.

But perhaps the most opaque of these concrete images is: "ne disons pas même une ombre, comme d'une brousse qui aurait découpé dans l'air l'absence et la nuit où elle dérive"—which seems to be evoking an idea of the minimum degree possible of presence, via images of shadow, bush, air, and darkness. Unlike some of the other features of the passage, this is not in any sense a simple *imitation* of Creole usage. It is closer to devices more typical of poetic language—as are also the description of the sea as "défunte d'oiseaux" and the invented verb "flaquer." It illustrates, in other words, Glissant's strategy of creolization: constructing new kinds of indirect meaning, distinct from those existing in Creole but performing an equivalent role in the text in which they occur. Thus, the relationship between the detours of Creole and those of the literary text is itself not a straightforward one. It is, however, fundamental to the whole of Glissant's writing.

The above analysis of the first page of *La case du commandeur* also reveals a close connection between the features of language that Glissant ascribes to the Creole detour and the literary value of his own texts. Opacity—i.e., meaning that is not immediately obvious—and concrete imagery are characteristics that we associate with *poetic* language in general, and much of the poetic force of Glissant's writing derives from them, as it does also from his use of rhythm and repetition. His comment on the narrative techniques of Caribbean novels applies most specifically to his own: they "introduce . . . densities and breaks—like so many detours—into the material that they are using; putting into practice, just as the Plantation folktale did, techniques of doubling, of breathlessness, of parenthesis" (*PR*, 85). Thus, those qualities that can on the one hand be seen to relate specifically to the indirectness of the detour, with all the very particular determinations and connotations that this involves, are on the other hand also the qualities that to a large extent give the texts a more generally recognizable poetic value. As a result, Glissant's statements about the limitations, compromises, and difficulties of counterpoetics almost seem to be contradicted by the "poetic" eloquence of his own writing—even when he is making these statements. We are thus confronted once again with the ambiguity of the detour, where lack and constraint become indistinguishable from freedom and mastery.

These same questions, of the relationship between vernacular and literary language and of camouflaged language as *mastery,* are central to the work of the African-American Henry Louis Gates Jr., who argues that African-American literature grows out of the tradition of "signifyin(g)" in vernacular black speech in the United States (the parentheses around the final "g" mark the word's difference from standard white English). Moreover, signifyin(g) shares many of the features of Glissant's ruses of Creole; Gates calls it a "language of indirection." He differs from Glissant in stressing above all its *ludic* functions, as a free exercise of virtuoso verbal skills. In the first place, signifyin(g) is free of the repressions of white English—it "luxuriates in the inclusion of the free play of these associative rhetorical and semantic relations." Secondly, it has no practical function but exists as a playful, competitive demonstration of verbal mastery; it is "the ultimate triumph of self-consciously formal language use," and, as such, Gates argues, the basis of the African-American *literary* tradition. Signifyin(g), therefore, is play, mastery, and artistry. In some ways it has more in common with the dramatizing delirium of figures such as Chérubin in *La case du commandeur,* in his "crazy" *playing* with words, than it does with the deliberate ruses of camouflaged speech; but Chérubin, conversely, lacks the control that Gates also stresses.[8]

Although Glissant places less emphasis on play and mastery in his theoretical descriptions of Creole, he does point out that Creole continues to communicate indirectly even when the original situation that caused the necessity for concealment has ceased to exist, and one can assume that the camouflage acquires other functions that may have more to do with ludic competition and verbal mastery. It is certainly the case that these are amply illustrated in his fictional texts. For instance, signifyin(g) most often refers to games and rituals such as name-calling; to "signify upon" someone means to get the better of them verbally. It is a way of defending oneself against aggression and establishing one's mastery, and there are many examples of it in Glissant's novels. An exact equivalent of the ritual insults exchanged in front of an appreciative audience, which in African-American culture are called the dozens, appears at the end of *Le quatrième siècle* in the "dizzying oratorical tournaments" (*QS,* 321) between Charlequint and Bozambo—which consist in finding the most far-fetched, original, and hurtful ways of describing each other's lack of teeth. A different but equally ludic kind of virtuoso contest takes place in *Malemort,* again on a regular basis, between two characters of very different social status: Lannec and Médellus. Here, rather than insulting each other, each tries to express himself in the most elaborately obscure way possible, challenging the other to understand (*Mal,* 156); camouflage is thus absolutely central to the game.

Gates also cites a whole body of poems and folktales centering on the "Signifying Monkey," who pits his verbal skills against the physical strength of the lion and outwits him, and these equate with Glissant's emphasis on the role of the *conteur* [traditional storyteller]. But Gates argues that signifyin(g) is a very pervasive mode of language use (a *lan-*

gage, in Glissant's sense) that goes far beyond these specific games and folktales. Ultimately, it defines the African-American vernacular's tendency to use figurative and indirect modes of expression. He uses the formulation given by the sociolinguist Claudia Mitchell-Kernan to conclude that "the most important defining features of Signifyin(g) are 'indirect intent' and 'metaphorical reference,'" which, of course, are the equivalent of Glissant's detour and imagery.[9]

Such uses of camouflaged language are essentially pleasurable rather than defensive; the pleasure is derived from the comic skill with which the speaker avoids obvious or straightforward statements. In the novels, they extend beyond games and rituals, as Gates suggests, occurring also in less formalized contexts. For instance, at the beginning of *Malemort,* Dlan describes to Colentroc's little boy various "trades" they have found to make money; he then challenges Médellus and Silacier to describe another one: "So that's fine, now are you going to tell this child what you do *psi-psi-psi* and so do I every evening behind the mangroves? How are you going to tell him about that?" (*Mal,* 40). This eventually turns out to refer to the "trade" of catching crabs by urinating in their holes at night to make them come to the surface. Médellus accepts the challenge, evoking the process with a delicacy of innuendo that Dlan appreciates:

> —On peut donner la confidence, dit Médellus, que nous avalons le poids d'une demi-dame-jeanne d'eau, et dans les quatre heures nous déversons le trop dans les trous de crabe.
> —Ah, dit-il, c'est très bien raconté. Ah j'avais peur de l'inconvenance. Et voilà, c'est un autre métier. (40)

> ["One may say in confidence," said Medellus, "that we swallow the weight of a half-demi-john of water, and within four hours we pour out the excess into the crab holes."
> "Ah," he said, "that's very well put. I was afraid of some impropriety. And there you are, there's another trade."]

Dlan himself then elaborates on the description, avoiding the verb "pisser" with an equally skillful obliqueness which lends the process a kind of comic professional dignity:

> Parce que pour avaler autant d'eau il faut appeler la soif et pour retenir il faut s'efforcer et pour distribuer dans au moins six trous de crabe il faut doser. Mais quand les crabes montent dans le trou vous admirez ce que tu peux faire avec une demi-dame-jeanne d'eau.

— Six crabes pour un demi-franc, dit Médellus. (40)

[Because to swallow so much water you must work up a thirst and to
hold it in you must make a real effort and to distribute it between at least
six crab holes you must measure it out. But when the crabs come up the
holes you admire what you can do with a half-demi-john of water.
"Six crabs for half a franc," said Medellus.]

The humor that characterizes these kinds of speech is prominent
throughout the novels, and Gates provides an analytical interpretation
of it that is not developed very fully in *Le discours antillais*.[10]

There are several other striking similarities between Glissant's camouflaged language and Gates's signifyin(g). Just as Glissant's detour turns
to its own ends the white stereotyped image of Creole as nonsense, so
the figure of the Signifying Monkey is "the ironic reversal of a received
racist image of the black as simianlike . . . he who dwells at the margins
of discourse, ever punning, ever troping, ever embodying the ambiguities
of language." And like counterpoetics, signifyin(g) is a "guerrilla action" that subverts and reappropriates English into a distinct black vernacular. In Glissant's terminology, it forges its own *langage* out of the
tension with which it inhabits the *langue* of white English. Unlike counterpoetics, however, it does this through a reflection on meaning (signifying) itself and on the rhetorical procedures whereby it institutes meaning. Thus, Gates writes: "The language of blackness encodes and names
its sense of independence through a rhetorical process that we might
think of as the Signifyin(g) black difference." It does this by parodying
white English. More fundamentally, however, signifyin(g) reworks the
language by changing the very relation between signified and signifier
that constitutes meaning: for Gates, its figurative nature liberates it from
fixed meanings and opens it up to the infinite chains of associative meanings that Lacan has identified with the unconscious: "Signifyin(g), in Lacan's sense, is the Other of discourse; but it also constitutes the black
Other's discourse as its rhetoric." Although Glissant does not formulate
it in the same way, or nearly so explicitly, there is an equivalent sense in
"Poetics and the unconscious" of counterpoetics' greater closeness to
the unconscious, as the "unconscious rhythm" (*CD*, 163) of everyday
speech.[11]

Given these similarities between camouflaged language and signi-
fyin(g), it is surprising to find that Gates's account of the *origin* of the
practices is in complete opposition to Glissant's. For Glissant, camou-

flaged language arose from the slaves' lack of a common language, independent of French, and which excluded the white master; it was a strategy invented in and for the particular conditions of plantation slavery. For Gates, however, signifyin(g) is the continuation into present-day America of an African rhetorical tradition. He traces the American figure of the Signifyin(g) Monkey back through its association in Yoruba and Fon poetry and legend with the god Esu-Elegbara. The Yoruba god—who becomes Legba in Haiti and Echu-Elegua in Cuba—is "the divine trickster figure" who acts as mediator, interpreter, and rhetorician; "Esu is the Yoruba figure of the meta-level of formal language use, of the ontological and epistemological status of figurative language and its interpretation."[12]

Signifyin(g) therefore represents *continuity* with the African past, whereas Glissant's hypothesis stresses the consequences of the break with African culture and the need to develop new strategies in the context of slavery. Gates is in fact vehemently opposed to those who, like Glissant, claim that transportation constituted a radical separation from Africa and obliterated all but very fragmentary traces of African culture. The opening pages of his book argue that: "The notion that the Middle Passage was so traumatic that it functioned to create in the African a tabula rasa of consciousness is as odd as it is a fiction, a fiction that has served several economic orders and their attendant ideologies. The full erasure of traces of cultures as splendid, as ancient, and as shared by the slave traveler would have been extraordinarily difficult." From an empirical point of view, the degree to which African cultures have survived in the Americas clearly depends upon a whole range of historical, demographic, and economic factors and varies greatly between different black communities; it is, therefore, not the case that if Gates is right, Glissant must simply be wrong and vice versa. Similarly, Gates's oddly positive view of slavery as a beneficent force for multicultural enrichment—the above extract continues: "Slavery in the New World, a veritable seething cauldron of cross-cultural contact, however, did serve to create a dynamic of exchange and revision among numerous previously isolated Black African cultures"—has a certain empirical validity.[13]

But on a theoretical level, Gates's valorization of the continuing African heritage is a strategy of empowerment that differs radically from Glissant's view of the Caribbean relation to history and, on the basis of this, the concept of *identity*. As discussed in chapter 1, Glissant rejects the "root-identity," which bases identity on filiation, and the equation of a singular identity with a single language. Gates, on the other hand, is essentially concerned with establishing the roots, precisely, of African-American identity in its continuity with African cultural traditions; and this more traditional conception of identity also makes him lean heavily on the idea that signifyin(g) creates and promotes a distinctive black identity in speech. For example, he interprets the adolescent signifying games as a kind of training that the black community gives its young generation to ensure the transmission of a cultural identity, and he says of the Monkey tales: "The black person's capacity to create this rich poetry and to derive from these rituals a complex attitude toward attempts at domination, which can be transcended in and through language, is a sign of their originality, of their extreme consciousness of the metaphysical."[14]

These theoretical differences impact on the actual characterizations of signifyin(g)/camouflaged language; as we have seen, Glissant analyzes a compromised response to an imposed situation while Gates interprets signifyin(g) as an entirely free exercise of rhetorical agility and poetic verve. There is, nevertheless, one further aspect of Gates's theorization of signifyin(g) that is extremely relevant to the representations of *langage* in Glissant's novels, although here again it is not one that Glissant comments on in any detail in his own theoretical writing. It concerns the very general question of how meaning itself is conceptualized. In both writers, we find, with varying degrees of explicitness, an attitude toward meaning—its production and reception—that is significantly different from that of classical Western humanism. Gates quotes, in support of his definition of signifyin(g), Mitchell-Kernan's definition of "indirection": "the correct semantic (referential) interpretation or signification of the utterance cannot be arrived at by a consideration of the dictionary meaning of the lexical items involved and the syntactic rules for their combination alone. The apparent significance of the message differs from its real significance. The apparent meaning of the sentence signifies its actual meaning." In a very similar fashion, understanding the detours of all Glissant's kinds of camouflaged language presupposes a particular attitude to meaning as such. Because meaning is never literal, there is no straightforward, discrete relation between signifier and signified. Instead, understanding an utterance involves two less direct orientations: relating it to its *context,* and relating to it as a *whole* rather than as a string of separate words each with a fixed meaning. It also often relies upon intuition rather than referential logic.[15]

This mode of understanding is almost always used by the characters in the novels. For them, individual words are unimportant; in fact, one of the most inventive detours of language occurs when Mycéa and Papa Longoué simply change the meanings of a whole series of unfamiliar words that do not belong in the Caribbean context:

> se trompant mais avec la justesse et la précision du malfini au ras des vagues: pensant *la glace* c'est quand l'eau accouche une roche qui laboure ta chair, et *le vin* c'est quand la messe est à midi en plein soleil et te rend fou, et *l'été* c'est quand tu as tellement froid que ta peau fait des flammes . . . et *un rhinocéros* c'est Belzébuth qui fait le tremblement à pattes, et *un Anglais* c'est de l'autre côté du canal de Sainte-Lucie. (*CC,* 67–68)

> [making mistakes but with the accuracy and precision of the seahawk skimming the waves: thinking *ice* that's when the water gives birth to a rock that ploughs your flesh, and *wine* that's when mass is at midday in the full heat of the sun and makes you mad, and *summer* that's when you're so cold that your skin gives off flames . . . and *a rhinoceros* that's Beelzebub making a trembling on his paws, and *an Englishman* that's the other side of the Saint Lucia channel.]

In particular, the *effectiveness* of words has little or nothing to do with their literal meaning; the Latin phrases of the catechism are *détournées* [deflected] and are used by the children as magic spells to catch fish (63).

Conversely, the people in Glissant's novels can intuitively understand meaning without understanding the words. Louise, in *Le quatrième siècle,* is surprised to find herself listening intently to Longoué's "impenetrable" African speech (105); and when Mycéa asks her father what he can possibly understand of the French political speeches on the television that he spends all day watching, he replies that "he had his own way of understanding and that, for instance, from the *color* of the words he could see that that man was lying" (*CC,* 201). An extreme case of intuitive, "holistic" understanding is the reception of the *quimboiseur*'s magic discourse. Magic institutes a different relation with the listener, in that ordinary verbal transmission is superseded by the communication of a "vision," which erases the normal boundaries between speaker and listener. Mathieu, listening to Papa Longoué's evocation of the past, "sees" the eighteenth-century slave ship and "hears" the slavers' voices: "Suddenly he saw the narrow cabin, with its strong smell. . . . He saw the new rum on the chest, the six men huddled over grubby tin mugs, and he heard the words, not even knowing if Papa Longoué was repeating them for his benefit or if it was the wind" (*QS,* 46–47). Sometimes this goes even further: Mathieu not only "sees" the first Longoué being taken ashore in a rowing boat off the slave ship but actually *becomes* him in a delirious interior monologue:

> ô gabarre moi gabarre et il moi sur le ventre la poudre moi bateau et cogne sur le dos le courant et l'eau chaque pied moi corde glisser pour et mourir la rade pays et si loin au loin et rien moi rien rien pour finir tomber l'eau salée salée salée sur le dos et sang et poissons et manger ô pays le pays. (*QS*, 40)

> [oh rowing boat me rowing boat and him me on the belly the powder me boat and hit on the back the current and the water each foot me rope slide for and die the harbor country and so far away in the distance and nothing me nothing nothing to end up falling the water salty salty salty on his back and blood and fish and eat oh country the country.]

The critique of understanding (or at least the humanist conception of understanding) as an aggressive appropriation of the other, which Glissant mounts in *Poétique de la relation* (see chapter 1), is relevant here, insofar as camouflaged language can *only* be understood in a way that respects its opacity—which traces it through the detours of its context rather than trying to reduce it to transparency: "One cannot elucidate the obscure, there is no possible recipe, but one can bring it back to what one knows round about" (*TM*, 257).

Camouflaged language, then, demands an attitude toward meaning as both contextual and holistic; as in the comments by Mitchell-Kernan quoted above, the "signification of the utterance cannot be arrived at by a consideration of the dictionary meaning of the lexical items involved . . . alone." It is ultimately less a question of understanding the words than of understanding *through* the words—that is, understanding the detour: Papa Longoué speaks "this inestimable *langage,* all mannerisms and repetitions, which nevertheless moved steadily forward toward *a knowledge, beyond words*" (*QS*, 17, emphasis added).[16]

One particular, and perhaps the most important, instance of meaning being dependent on a specific cultural *context* concerns the use of imagery. Imagery, as we have seen, is central to various different kinds of camouflage. Whether it is the quasi-allegorical detour of the folktale—to which Massoul's story of Il and Li is related—or a less elaborate kind of figurative language, the difference between expressing an idea through abstract concepts and through concrete imagery has a number of implications: "Now imagery, in what we call expressions of collective wisdom, is deceptive. . . . All languages that depend on images (so-called concrete languages) indicate that they have implicitly conceptualized the idea and quietly refused to explain it . . . imaginative expression is secreted in the obscure world of the group unconscious" (*CD*, 126). One of the most important of these implications is the closeness of the image to the cultural situation in which it emerges. It is not a question of using a folksy, proverbial style to add a certain local color, but of producing an expression that has to be deciphered *contextually*. An abstract concept is independent of any specific social, regional, or cultural context; but to "read" an image, we have to know the particular background in which it is based. The men betting on the motor race in *Malemort,* alternately depressed and elated, are described as: "Deader than the black of night on the Vauclin mountain. More frenzied suddenly than Monsieur Thérèse's cockfighting pit every Wednesday Saturday and Sunday at three o'clock" (174–75). Both of these images draw on purely local realities, but whereas the first one is a fairly conventional equation of darkness and death that does not actually depend upon our knowledge of the Vauclin mountain, the second makes a point of stressing its particularity and so achieves a comic precision that serves both to deflate and to defamiliarize its referent.

A more complex example of the determining force of context in figurative language is the recurrent metaphor of the "right-hand half of the brain" in *Le quatrième siècle*. This is far odder and more opaque than the two images just discussed, and it plays a more important role in the text as a whole. It occurs for the first time after Papa Longoué has been lamenting Martinicans' inability to remember: "For where has all that gone, everything that rises up to your brain, burns in your head without you knowing what the fire is, although you suffer the burning?" (201). Memory, in other words, figures as a "burning" in the brain, and he goes on to say that its disappearance is a different form of deprivation from material poverty ("It's not poverty, you don't have to go looking for that," 201). He then talks about the way the slaves were punished by having parts of their bodies amputated. These two elements come together in the idea that *memory* has also been amputated by the plantation owners: the right side of the brain (which is the hemisphere responsible for intuitive, creative, emotionally charged thought) has been cut off, so that they are separated from their sense of the past:

On croirait qu'à force de couper le bras droit, et puis la jambe droite, ils ont fini par amputer tout un côté du corps: un poumon, un testicule, un œil, une oreille. Et voilà peut-être ce qu'il faut chercher dans l'entassement: cette partie de toi où la brûlure sillonne comme un éclair, et qui pourtant est restée loin de toi dans les bois ou sur la mer ou dans le pays là-bas: la moitié droite du cerveau. (201)

[You would think that with cutting off the right arm, and then the right leg, they ended up amputating one whole side of the body: one lung, one testicle, one eye, one ear. And perhaps that's what we have to look for in the heap: that part of you where the burning leaves a furrow of lightning, and yet which remains far away from you in the woods or on the sea or in the land over there: the right-hand half of the brain.]

The image is thus rooted in the sociohistorical culture of slavery and can only be interpreted within that context. But we also see how this kind of contextualizing understanding is an ongoing process, which continues to operate within the space of the text itself, as different characters pick up the image and rework it. The first occurrence of the image occupies a prominent position at the end of a chapter; and when, fifteen pages later, it is repeated in a far more elliptical form, we can make sense of it only by recalling the original context of physical mutilation juxtaposed with suppression of memory: "ce qui lancinait dans cette moitié du cerveau après laquelle il courait depuis si longtemps" [what was throbbing away in that half of the brain that he had been running after for so long] (218). The image has moved, also, from Papa Longoué's speech to the narrative discourse. The third time it appears it is spoken by Mathieu, after a much longer gap of nearly eighty pages. He picks up several elements of Papa Longoué's original formulation: "Ah! papa, ce n'est pas la misère, non, non. La misère vient avec, mais c'est d'abord la moitié du cerveau, le bras coupé, la jambe qui nous manque depuis si longtemps. Et c'est enterré si loin dans la terre, papa" [Ah! papa, it's not the poverty. Poverty comes along with it, but first of all it's the half of the brain, the arm cut off, the leg that has been missing for so long. And it's buried so far away in the earth, papa] (308); but the phrase "la moitié du cerveau" would nevertheless remain completely unintelligible without our *memory* (which is exactly what is at stake in the image itself) of its first occurrence. From the point of view of the reader, this has a further implication: the initial cultural context is relayed and supplemented by a *textual* context in which understanding depends upon making links between different parts of the text.

It is the *reader's* reaction to camouflaged language that we now need to examine. As we have seen, the characters in the novels intuitively understand it because it is part of their culture. But what is the position of the reader confronting these disguised, indirect meanings in the text of the novel? In the first place, the experience of not understanding is an important part of the overall experience of reading Glissant's novels. To make us aware of opacity not just as a phenomenon analyzed by the author but as opacity *for us*—opacity as an unmediated effect of reading—is obviously one of the writing's main strategies of resistance. Secondly, though, we gradually realize that we are being invited to understand in a different way: that the unintelligibility can itself be meaningful, but also that the text "teaches" us strategies and detours that help us to read it.[17]

The kinds of camouflaged language that the reader is faced with include everything that has been discussed so far in the represented speech of characters—their jokes, riddles, stories, etc., obviously have to be interpreted by the reader as well as by their fictional interlocutors. But since the novels do not merely illustrate the theories of Creole ruses and camouflage, there are other detours and opacities that, while not unrelated, are specific to the reading experience. Central among these is the question of contextualized imagery. We have seen how concrete imagery can be understood only through an understanding of the cultural context from which it is drawn—as in the example of the "moitié droite du cerveau" above. The reader, of course, often lacks this cultural knowledge. But, as the above example also illustrates, the text compensates for this by building its *own* context through the *repetition* of a given image, with variations and refigurations, so that the reader accumulates and links together different partial aspects of the image, and its meaning becomes progressively clearer. In this way the novels construct a distinct but functionally equivalent process of indirect, deferred understanding.

A typical example occurs in *La case du commandeur*. Toward the end of this novel we are given a clear indication that understanding is a gradual process, always deferred and never a finished whole: in Glissant's terms, it is a "trace." As Mycéa says: "No no, there is no end, don't say that you understand, say that you have called out all along the Path" [*tout au long de la Trace*] (198). For the reader, too, opacity means that the text can never be grasped as a whole—that is, as a wholly known and therefore circumscribed entity. Instead, the areas that remain opaque mean that its borders are left undefined and open. Reading thus becomes similar to "errance" (see chapter 1), in the sense that "the wanderer [*l'errant*] . . . seeks to know the totality of the world and knows already that he will never accomplish this—and that herein resides the en-

dangered beauty of the world. . . . He dives into the opacities of that
share of the world to which he has access" (*PR*, 33).

Understanding, then, works by the reader creating links within the
text rather than referential connections with anything outside it. These
textual links typically operate at long distance; there are often many
pages in between the repetitions of an image. An example of this can be
seen in the evolutions of one particularly opaque phrase in *La case du
commandeur*: "casser la surface des eaux" [break the surface of the
water]. A version of this occurs for the first time at the end of Augustus's
long, very cryptic declaration of love for Adoline: "La surface des eaux
va pour s'ouvrir et déboucher la couche. Nous sommes détombés ici, et
nous avons cassé le plat des eaux. Vous et moi mademoiselle dans la rivière" [The surface of the waters is going to open and bring up its bed.
We have fallen here, and we have broken the flat plane of the waters.
You and I mademoiselle in the river] (79).

In order to make sense of this, we have to start by working back
through the text, and then work forward again from page 79 to almost
the end of the novel. In so doing the reader follows several different interwoven strands of imagery; the process is by its very nature difficult to
describe clearly, but it does illuminate the way in which the whole novel
creates meanings through detours and deferrals.

The sentence just before the fragment quoted above includes the
phrase: "like a boat is at the same time a fish and at the same time a
room." This is a reference to the story of the *poisson-chambre* [fish-
room], which Ozonzo tells to the child Cinna Chimène (56–60). It is a
version of a folktale that Ozonzo "adapts" for her (56) and is told in the
traditional way with repetitions, nonsense words, and the usual formu-
las of storytelling. It is about a huge magic fish that swallows people up;
it contains a room for counting money; and underneath this, in the fish's
gut, are "all those who are marked for deportation" (57). The fish, in
other words, is a slave ship, transporting Africans to the Caribbean; but
this is not stated and in fact the people are said to come from Haiti
rather than Africa (58). Its captives include two brothers and the woman
that they fought over; one brother had betrayed the other to the *poisson-
chambre* in order to have the woman to himself but then had been captured as well (58); and now no one knows which brother is which (59).
When Cinna Chimène has heard the story, the text asks: "Did the listener guess what actual history was taking shape beneath this story? Of
course she couldn't" (60). In the first place, then, the story is an example

of the use of apparent nonsense to both conceal and reveal another meaning. But it is also the starting point for a number of further developments. In subsequent pages there are several brief references to it (64, 69, 71), linking it to the magic language of the *quimboiseur,* which Cinna Chimène therefore defines as "words of Haiti" (69). But, later, when she marries Pythagore, he tells her that "Ozonzo's story was a more ancient story in disguise": the people did not originally come from Haiti but from Africa—"Guinea the Congo" (71).

The next reference to the *poisson-chambre* is Augustus's declaration to Adoline in the following chapter, cited above. It is prefaced by the information that Adoline, the daughter of Euloge, lives in a district known as "Grand Congo," which is by a river, whereas Augustus lives in "Petite Guinée," which only has a few stagnant ponds (76, 78). In the course of his declaration, Augustus refers to the innocent brother of the *poisson-chambre* story as Odono and says he has "drunk the water of the pond" (79). Thus, the distinction between still and flowing water is associated with Africa (Guinea and the Congo) and with the two brothers; and the phrase "casser le plat des eaux" (79) is juxtaposed with the story of the slave ship and the arrival of Odono and his brother.

A few pages later, in a completely different context, Euloge is fascinated by the wealth and urban sophistication of the mulattoes, particularly by one house that has a large mirror. His wife (who always speaks in the past tense) says that "chaque glace *avait été la surface des eaux,* et que cette glace-ci *avait été* la plus profonde" [every mirror *had been the surface of the waters,* and this mirror *had been* the deepest] (84, emphasis added). This equation of the "surface of the waters" with a mirror is repeated when the mirror miraculously survives a cyclone intact, flying through the air wedged between two mattresses: Euloge's wife says, "Vous aviez sorti la glace de la couche. La surface des eaux n'était pas cassée" [You had taken the mirror out of the bed. The surface of the waters was not broken] (87). Adoline repeats her words, and this time it is also linked to the opposition between pond [*mare*] and river [*rivière*], as the paragraph continues: "Adoline . . . avait vu trop de vent dans trop d'eau. Elle ne supporta plus de vivre à la Petite Guinée: croyant à tout moment entendre enfler cette mare et déborder cette rivière qui avaient borné sa vie" [Adoline . . . had seen too much wind in too much water [i.e., the cyclone]. She could no longer bear to live in Petite Guinée: thinking each moment that she could hear the swelling of the pond and the overflowing of the river that had bounded her life]. Five pages later, Augustus identifies himself with the river: "Il disait, je suis un seul passage et une seule rivière. Ma vie est décidée pour ça" [He would say, I am a single passage and a single river. My life has been decided for that] (91)—just before he is drowned while crossing a river during a flood. His death is interpreted as a return to Africa, "de l'autre côté des eaux" [on the other side of the water]; and while the connection is strengthened in his case by the previous association of the river with Africa, this equation of water, Africa, and death is already inherent in voodoo ritual.[18] In her delirious mourning, Adoline formulates it in terms of breaking the surface of the water, which now seems to mean *drowning*—but hence death as an escape from slavery and return to Africa, led by the traditional magic figure of "tonton Riffin" [Uncle Riffin]. Speaking in "the manner of the old storytellers" (92), she asks:

> Quel était le pays où *la surface des eaux avait été brisée* . . . où la mort tombait tellement qu'on en faisait du guano pour la Plantation . . . voyez-vous *[tonton Riffin] est entré là-bas dans la surface des eaux il l'a cassée* en combien de petits morceaux il a traîné la fièvre les bêtes-longues la foule des Nègres jusqu'à *l'autre côté*. (92, emphasis added)

> [What was the country where *the surface of the waters had been broken* . . . where so much death fell that they made it into fertilizer for the Plantation . . . you see *[uncle Riffin] entered the surface of the waters over there he broke it* into so many little pieces he dragged the fever the snakes the whole crowd of negroes over to *the other side*.]

She also asks herself, "les yeux tout portés sur cette mare et cette rivière, 'Odono, ki Odono?'" [her eyes riveted on that pond and that river, "Odono, who's Odono?"] (93).

The next chapter, continuing the movement back in time, gives us the preceding generation's versions. Anatolie's famous story, parts of which he tells to all the different women he makes love to, but which the reader never hears, is written down by the planter's wife, and her uncertain and fragmentary account contains a sentence that could be seen as a distortion of the water as a mirror (*eau* and *glace*) equation: "Il entra dans l'eau glacée de la (*illisible*)" [he entered the icy water of the (*illegible*)] (98). There are also vague references to two brothers (99). But then Liberté Longoué gives her version of Eudoxie's version (Eudoxie was Odono's daughter) of the *poisson-chambre* story, which we first came across told by Ozonzo, Liberté's grandson. This repeats the idea that Odono was one of the brothers but that no one knows which one; but it also draws together more clearly than previously the elements of the *poisson-chambre* itself, transportation, drowning, water as a mirror, and the phrase "casser la surface des eaux." Liberté lists what she has learned, and these items include:

> la capture, la grande pirogue qui était devenu monstre, poisson naviguant sur les hautes eaux, avec sa chambre de comptes et les enfers en-dessous; *l'eau à l'infini comme une glace qu'il faut casser pour contempler ton image*; le fond des eaux où les boulets t'ont ensouché. (107, emphasis added)

> [the capture, the big canoe that had become a monster, a fish navigating the high seas, with its counting room and the hell beneath; *the water stretching to infinity like a mirror that you have to break in order to see your reflection*; the bottom of the sea where the balls and chains have planted you.]

Drowning is thus contextualized here as the deaths of the slaves thrown overboard on the voyage, weighted down with "boulets" (a recurrent image in Glissant's writing); and the expansion of the original phrase suggests that it is only by drowning—that is, perhaps, by returning to Africa (as with Augustus, above)—that one can truly "see" oneself, as though in a mirror.[19] The "mirror" has to be broken before one can see one's image.

Liberté's version of the story is an important moment in the "trace" of the phrase's meaning, because it gives a single context for most of the previous fragmentary associations: all of these, in other words, can now be placed as *quotations* from Eudoxie's story, which itself, in its original form, remains out of the reader's reach. What is missing from the contextualization on page 107 is the reference to still and running water and their connection with Africa; but even this is supplied a few pages later as we read that Liberté, in a kind of catatonic trance that precedes her death, "avait choisi de chavirer du côté de cette mare où Odono s'était baigné, ou dans cette eau débordée qui avait emporté Augustus" [had chosen to go under by the pond that Odono had bathed in, or in that overflowing water that had carried Augustus away] (113). This is the end of the first section of the book.

But the following of the "trace" continues, although less prominently, in the second and third sections. The episode of the capture of the maroon Aa ("Actes de guerre") includes Aa's version—given as he is being burnt alive—of the Odono story. Here the link between Odono and the "pond," first mentioned by Augustus in his declaration to Adoline (79), is expanded and clarified: "That the song had begun beside that pond where they washed, in the country over there, when two young men, one a shepherd the other a warrior, met a young girl" (141). He stresses the idea that no one knows which is the treacherous and which the innocent brother, because, he explains, they were *both* called Odono (141); and, finally, reveals that he, Aa, is one of them—but even at the moment of his death by torture will not say which one: "and that at the moment of that oven none could tell which of them was thus feeding the production of smoke with his flesh. That he would not tell them and that he would only consent to recognize that it was Odono who was dying there" (141).

Then, in the third section of the book, Marie Celat's son, also called Odono but known as Donou, drowns. The resonance of this tragic incident is deepened by the way in which it reconnects us to the original Odono story in some of the fragmentary forms in which it has appeared in the text. After Patrice has been killed in the motorcycle accident, Donou's obsession with deep-sea diving seems to be a way of finding his dead brother: "Perhaps in the blue of the sea he multiplied time, went back down in time to join his brother or some unforgotten knowledge" (188). When he himself is discovered drowned, it is again as though he has acquired some secret *knowledge* from having "casser la surface des eaux": "he seemed . . . to be waiting for us all, to show us perhaps what he had discovered or guessed at there in the depths, that we had not been able to make out" (188). Marie Celat's delirious mumbling is perfectly comprehensible to the reader *because* of the textual context that has by now been created for it: "People say . . . that she stammered something about the surface of the waters, the surface of the deep waters" (188)—not only echoing Adoline's delirium when Augustus was drowned: "What was the country where the surface of the waters had been broken" (92, see above), but also *all* the previous versions of the phrase.

The meaning of "casser la surface des eaux" is then cumulative and contextual rather than definitive. It is gradually clarified through its juxtapositions with other images until it draws together a complex of ideas about death, self-knowledge, transportation, and Africa. Its basic opacity remains intact, however, in the sense that, even at the end of the novel, it is not possible to give a simple paraphrase or translation of it; but the reader, I think, has nevertheless acquired a sense of its meaningfulness.

The same process of following this "trace" through the text has also answered another question, posed far more explicitly at the beginning:

what does "Odono" mean? At first there seems to be no connection between the two opaque phrases; but Liberté's story brings them together and, in integrating the various fragments into a single narrative, also tells us that the answer to the question "Who or what is Odono?" is not a *referent* (the ancestor) so much as the *story* itself, with all its variations. The impossibility of telling the brothers apart is emblematic of a larger indeterminacy, in which no one version of the narrative is ever adequate. Pythagore's comment that "Ozonzo's story was a more ancient story in disguise" (71) is reiterated when Liberté tells Anatolie that "Eudoxie's story was double" (107), and again when Papa Longoué tells Marie Celat that "every story has a meaning that twists away behind like a winding lane, that Odono has his meaning that comes round to the front again like the procession round a church" (149).

There are other similar examples in the novel—and in Glissant's other novels—of this kind of network of repeated and varying phrases running through the entire text, often with many pages in between two adjacent occurrences. The reader's understanding of the text depends upon an awareness of its internal structuring—the way the "networks" are gradually woven together—more than upon relating any one occurrence of the image to a reality outside the text. The meaning of "casser la surface des eaux" is the product of its juxtapositions with other phrases—in other words, its evolving contextualization within and by the text as a whole.

This, of course, profoundly affects the reader's relationship to the fictional reality of the novel. I have argued that the textual context acts as a compensation for the European reader's lack of cultural context by providing a kind of artificial equivalent of the experience of contextual meaning. But it also has another, more negative and perhaps more significant effect. It means that our natural reaction to bring our own experience to bear on the novel is to a large extent frustrated; we cannot "translate" the fiction into our own terms. As Glissant writes in "Transparence et opacité," "the written text counters everything that within the reader might have led him to formulate the author's intention differently, *while at the same time he can only just make out the contours of that intention*" (PR, 129, emphasis added). Thus, opacity turns out to be a structural issue as well as one of the immediate difficulty of some of the language; the text is opaque above all because it is structured in such a way as to make us realize that we can understand it only by following the "paths" that it sets up within itself. It blocks our attempts to read it in direct relation to our own experience and, in so doing, protects the opacity of its otherness. We cannot enter the other's world, but we can, perhaps, through the ruses of indirection, be made to *suspend* our own world by entering into a text that, as it were, disqualifies it by making it irrelevant. This detour, which turns the reader away from his or her own lived experience by offering a different kind of reading experience, is one of the most intransigent but also one of the most generous of Glissant's strategies of resistance.

The analysis I have given above of *La case du commandeur* features the transmission of a story from one speaker to another: Eudoxie, Anatolie, Liberté, Augustus, Ozonzo, Aa, etc. This structure of repetition provides a framework for recontextualization; but it also makes the point that no single version is ever "the full story" and that all stories, therefore, have a multiplicity of authors, not all of whom can ever be known. This idea of narrative as a collective production, "relayed" from one speaker to the next, is explored in the next chapter.

7 Relayed Language

The Weave of the Text

"LA RELATION relie (relaie), relate" [Relation links (relays), relates], Glissant writes in *Poétique de la relation* (187). Relation is, among other things, a principle of narration: what is "related" is what is *told*. And it is also what is *relayed* from one person to another, forming a chain or network of narrative "relations." Relayed language is a strategy of diversity that operates within discourse generally but especially as a principle of narrative; it resists the oppressively singular authority of what Mikhail Bakhtin calls the "monologic text," putting in its place a plural text made up of a number of different contributions or versions, in which no one person has control of the whole story.[1] Relayed language is also a strategy of resistance against the language-identity equation—the notion that individual subjects are the origin of their language, which forms an inherent and essential part of their identity; language both expresses and is *authenticated* by a unique, stable identity. Relayed language implies, in contrast, that language is passed around a number of subjects and also that there are "relays" intervening between subject and language. It thus works toward a more strategic, counterpoetic relationship with a number of different discourses.

The relay, in other words, has a double significance: a nonhierarchical diversity of narrative structure and a break or spacing in the relation between subject and language. Moreover, the two are closely linked; the authority of monologic discourse is not impersonal but derives from its authentication by the figure of the author in the language-identity equation. It depends upon the perception that the subject *owns* his or her language. Derrida makes this point in *Le monolinguisme de l'autre,* where he argues that, while language is in reality not the property of any of its speakers, a certain kind of "terror" can be exercised by imposing the belief that the oppressor does indeed own the dominant language, and that this happens typically in the colonial situation:

> Because the master does not possess exclusively, *naturally*, that which he nevertheless calls his language . . . because he cannot substantiate or state this appropriation except through an unnatural process of politico-phantasmatic constructions . . . for that very reason he can historically, by means of a violating cultural usurpation, in other words always colonial in its essence, pretend to appropriate it for himself in order to impose it as "his own." That is his belief, he aims to make others share it by force or by ruse, he aims to make others believe in it, as though it were a miracle, by his use of rhetoric, schooling or the army. (45)

Monologic authority and the language-identity equation reinforce each other, and relayed language works against both of them. In this it is similar to Spivak's characterization of "rumor" as an anonymous plural discourse that cannot be identified with any single consciousness and that is also "unauthorized" in the sense of being unofficial and unreliable; I return to this subject later.[2]

The nonhierarchical diversity of relayed language is a central feature of *Mahagony*. *Malemort* and *La case du commandeur* both employ a collective "nous" as narrator in an attempt to overcome the singularity of the individual voice. But this remains undifferentiated; it is only with *Mahagony* that Glissant divides the narrative between a number of separate voices.[3] Unlike the previous novels, its chapters are attributed to different individual narrators, and the story is gradually pieced together on the basis of the relations between the various sections, without ever becoming an integrated whole. Each of the ten narrators tells his or her part of it and then hands over to another, in a relay that becomes an increasingly explicit formula as the novel progresses. Marie Celat, for instance, realizes that "I am not the right sort of person to know Mani's story: it's the young people's business. That's why what follows can only be studied by my daughter Ida" (144). But Ida, in the following section, is equally aware of her limitations compared to her mother, to whom she dedicates her section—"Marie-Celat, my mother, it is to you that I dedicate it. Because *you have concentrated inside your head everything that we have scattered* carelessly with our hands" (158–59, emphasis added)—in words that partially echo, as a kind of textual homage to her mother, Marie Celat's own remark: "In other words, we are just as *scattered*, we never *concentrate inside our heads*" (137, emphasis added).

Then, nearer the end of her section, Ida raises other questions that she cannot answer and so passes the text on to her father—"I feel that what follows can only be told by my father Mathieu" (162)—who in turn relinquishes his control over "what follows" to the author, ending the next section with: "What follows can only be my author's commentary. I am letting him take my place" (174). Within individual sections, also, a kind of relay operates whereby the main narrator, instead of telling the story in his or her own words, presents the reported speech of another character: Ida, for instance, reproduces the accounts she received of Mani's disappearance from "the sailors' child" (148–50), the soldier Félicité Bienvenu (150–51), Annie-Marie (152–56), and the fisherman, Maître Palto (156–57).

Thus, the narrators hand over to each other; they are all of equal status, and none of their versions is definitive. Moreover, one of the narrators is the author. He has no privileged position with regard to the others; he exists on the same diegetic level, and some of them are as aware of him as he is of them, so that he, in effect, becomes a *character* in his own book, variously referred to as "the chronicler"(15), "he who comments" (175), "this friend [who] has written all along my story" (134), etc. This decentering of the author ensures that the text cannot be seen as either his property or his responsibility. But the process of "unauthorization" goes further: Mathieu, who narrates the first chapter as well as several of the others, describes how he was previously merely a character in the author's novels but has now "escaped" from the author's control (22); he will now produce his own representation of the fictional events (20), some of which have already occurred in the previous novels.

The mise-en-scène of the author as character is a fairly familiar device in antirepresentational fiction, where it serves to highlight the conventionality of realism by transgressing diegetic levels. But *Mahagony* hints that this is not its purpose here and that it is in fact a textual ruse of a rather different kind, whose motivation extends beyond *Mahagony* to the whole corpus of Glissant's novels and the intertextual relations that exist between them: the overlapping of characters and events from one novel to another. What the ruse enables the text of *Mahagony* to do is to "relativize" (to use another Bakhtinian term) all the previous novels, in which Mathieu was merely a character, by getting Mathieu, in his new position as narrator, to comment on the inadequacies of their (that is, "Glissant's") representations of events. For instance, *Le quatrième siècle* had failed to mention the existence of Gani at the same time and in the same places as Liberté Longoué; *La case du commandeur* omitted the fact that Odono Celat had a friend called Mani who committed murder in 1978 (*Mah,* 27–28). But perhaps the most developed example of this reworking and enlarging of the intertextual narrative concerns Maho, whose story was central to *Malemort.* The repeated rhetorical question "Who thinks of the woman?" (*Mal,* 55, 58) is given an answer in *Mahagony,* through the narrative of Adélaïde, who gives her different perspective on Maho and includes far more material on Adoline; and also through Papa Longoué's relation to Adoline and his therefore equally different version of the events. Through these and similar revisions, not only the earlier novels but *Mahagony* itself are revealed as incomplete, open-ended parts of an expanding matrix of relayed narratives.

The process continues, moreover, in *Tout-monde,* which contains an explicit challenge to Mathieu's version of the stories of the three heroes of *Mahagony.* The chapter entitled "Bezaudin" brings together two characters from *Mahagony,* Artémise and Marie-Annie, and stages a confrontation between them and Mathieu. This serves to challenge the narrative of *Mahagony* in several ways. In the first place, they tell Mathieu's "story" to him: that is, they tell him how when he was a baby his mother brought him down from Bezaudin in the hills to Le Lamentin (167–73). None of the previous novels mention this, and the reader has assumed that Mathieu was born in Le Lamentin. The women also retell the stories of Gani, Maho, and Mani, and although they were directly involved in some of the events, *Tout-monde* stresses their role as participants in an uncertain, disoriginated series of relays: "Memory failed them . . . they chased those names (Mani, Maho, Lomé, Gani) that had accompanied the crazy stories they had traveled through—they got mixed up as to which was which" (163). But, equally, they provide a *different* perspective and give a different version of events: "And so they also relived our stories, in ways that we had probably not had the chance to live them" (163). And they mount a vigorous challenge to Mathieu's version ("You have cut up *our* time like a cassava!," 181): they do not believe that Gani's open resistance to his masters would have been possible (181), or that Maho used the same tracks and hiding places as Gani (182). In particular, they accuse Mathieu of marginalizing Mani by presenting him merely as a double of the famous Marny, rather than as the man Marie-Annie was in love with: "'But look at Marie-Annie, he wasn't a double for her, her Mani-Mani, . . . he was the throbbing of her life and the shining of her light.' 'Yes yes,' said Marie-Annie" (182–83).

As a result of these intertextual revisions, each text remains connected to the others without being bound by their versions of the story.

Through the device of Mathieu's "escape" and assumption of the role of a new, different narrator, *Mahagony* can *move on*, escaping from or divesting itself of the determinations that the common intertextual universe of Glissant's fiction had previously put in place. Rather than a vertical structure of diegetic levels, the Mathieu-author relation is thus better seen as inaugurating a *horizontal* movement forward: a strategy whereby the text can differentiate itself from its previous representations. One consequence of this is that the occasional factual inconsistencies—for instance, in *Le quatrième siècle* it is Anne Béluse who buries the knife under the ebony trees, in *Mahagony* it is Gani; in *Le quatrième siècle* the *barrique* [cask] is handed on to Mathieu, in *Tout-monde* it is given to Mycéa; the Annie-Marie of *Mahagony* becomes Marie-Annie in *Tout-monde*—do not matter. More importantly, the text can demonstrate, rather than merely proclaim, the importance of relayed narration by showing that a single narrator is inevitably insufficient.

The plurality of discourses is crucial to Glissant's promotion of diversity against the domination of a single universalizing truth—it ensures that "the rigidity of elucidating history gives way to the pleasure of stories" (*Mah*, 176). No one discourse can possess the truth, but *a* truth, of a kind, emerges from the intertext as a whole: "a truth swells in the mass of events, recounted or transcribed, without being solicited by any declaimer or chronicler." This quotation continues: "As a song or as a slogan, the depths of time return to the surface" (176); and it is important to recognize that the recovery of the past—as *histoires* [stories] rather than *histoire* [history]—is not a finite activity, and that this is not just because the past is not totally knowable. It is also because no single "order" can account for it; the past continually *interrupts* the present, disrupting it with its discontinuous, "incommensurable" fragments: "But the ordering, too, exhausts itself and disappears. We can never have done with our excessive ancestors, comic paladins, lost in the fields where we forget them. The present is constantly expanding with their deactivated words. Your head is cluttered up with them. You fall into the maelstrom" (192). This is reminiscent of Bhabha's questions: "How does one encounter the past as an anteriority that continually introduces an otherness or alterity into the present? How does one then narrate the present as a form of contemporaneity that is neither punctual nor synchronous?"[4]

Relays between narrators do not, however, exist solely on the level of their narration. A different kind of relay is also implicated in the construction of a model of subjectivity that erodes the notion of individual identity—and hence also, as we will see, the relation between identity and language. This, in other words, is the role that the relay plays in dismantling the language-identity equation. The narrators are telling the life stories of Gani, Maho, and Mani, and recounting the experiences of many other people: Longoué talks about Adoline, Adélaïde talks about Artémise, and so on. But they are also linked to the other characters in ways that go beyond narration and description; they participate in each others' experiences and literally take each others' place.[5] A series of intersubjective relays breaks down the separation between their individual identities, so that these become extremely labile. Subjectivity, in other words, is not seen here as a self-contained autonomous unit but more as a constant circulation of overlapping positions.

For instance, Gani, Maho, and Mani each have a dream (in 1831, 1936, and 1978, respectively) about the mahogany tree being attacked by three magic animals—a hairless ox, a dog with horns, and a snake. It is almost the same dream, shared between them. But even more striking is the fact that it is relayed to us by three separate narrators, none of whom simply report it, but who have in varying degrees made it their own. Annie-Marie says to Ida after Mani's death, "Everything's still in my head, it's Mani's dream, I don't know how many times he told it to me, if I pass it on to you perhaps it'll relieve my brain" (155). But Maho's dream is literally *dreamt* by Marie Celat—who could not in any case have known about it in any other way: "But how am I dreaming with the head of the overseer, tell me, how come I'm dreaming? Who did he tell it to that has told it to me?" (132); "I dream the overseer's dream. Fate has made this dream for the two of us, with no beginning and no end. That's where I've met him" (143–44). Finally, Mathieu's account of Gani's "original" version of the dream (which comes last in the novel) generalizes the process, emphasizing the number of intersubjective relays it went through before reaching him: "Gani entrusts his dream to Tani who reports it to Eudoxie who tells it to the mourners" (164), and implying that they all share in it: "Is it Gani's dream, or does it belong just as much to the procession of undoubting storytellers who relayed it from one to the other to save it from oblivion?" (164).

This web of intersubjective connections can extend even across novels and across diegetic levels. In *Tout-monde,* for instance, the section entitled "Mycéa c'est moi" is in fact not narrated by Mycéa but by Anastasie, who has never met Mycéa but has read about her in the books written by "the author." Anastasie comes to see him, to talk to him about Mycéa and herself. What she has in common with Mycéa is apparently only the fact that both were rejected by men whom they loved; otherwise, her life has been completely different, involving a poverty and humiliation that Mycéa has never experienced. Nevertheless, she says: "Mycéa is me. Yes, you could say that she is me" (*TM*, 195); and she speaks of "this story which is mine as much as it is Marie Celat's" (195). Her identification is based, not on the events of their lives, but on what she perceives as their common way of enduring suffering: as a *secret invisibility*. When she attends her lover's wedding, people look at her but do not realize that they cannot "see" her: "I'm standing there like Marie Celat, monsieur, but I am invisible in the ceremony. People think that they can see me, but in reality it's their shade. Marie Celat is invisible, you can't see her body even once in the whole country. We listen, she and I, to the noise that the shade makes on the foliage where you place those scraps of debris" (211). The "author" tentatively sums up this shared attitude as "the same manner as she had, silent, proud, indomitable" (212). But the reader cannot trust his interpretation, because Anastasie has already told him several times that he does not understand Mycéa. Men cannot understand women: "Allow me to say this, monsieur, I know you have tried to understand. But which of you can understand?" (196). He is a dupe of the secret invisibility; like the guests at the wedding looking at Anastasie, he takes Marie Celat's "shade" for her self: "with Marie Celat's shade, you are that shade, monsieur, and the scraps of debris you place on the foliage are the books that you write, all that" (211).

Anastasie's speech suggests that another thing the two women have in common is delirium; Anastasie's secret invisibility is reminiscent of Marie Celat's determination, also expressed most strongly in *Tout-monde*, to place herself out of reach of other people. Both are fantasies, but both also contain the kind of truth that Bhabha has in mind when he writes: "By disrupting the stability of the ego, expressed in the equivalence between image and identity, the secret art of invisibleness of which the migrant poet speaks changes the very terms of our recognition of the person."[6] But the notion that other people cannot see one is also shared by another subaltern woman, Adélaïde, who says: "No one looks at me, even without a word, without a start. Adélaïde's path is unmarked" [*La trace d'Adélaïde n'est pas tracée*] (*Mah*, 98)—echoed in turn by Anastasie here: "I left . . . without jewels or clothes or memories, or a path that had been marked" [*ni trace qu'on a tracée*] (208). (Adélaïde, too, ends her story with the implication that men cannot understand women. See chapter 3.)

But Anastasie's only contact with Mycéa is through the author's representation—a representation that she claims is incomplete and flawed.
Her relationship with the author parallels that of Mathieu in *Mahagony,*
in its mixing of diegetic levels and its challenging of the author's authority: "I will tell you Mycéa's secret, if she hasn't told you. Yes, it's quite
true, you're the one who knew her, you're the one who's telling her story,
but I have been where she has been, my eyes have seen what she has
seen. What can you do? You can only listen to the person who laughs in
the sunshine or weeps in the shade. Forgive me, I don't mean to offend
you. But there are truths that you cannot find, or even guess at, it's impossible" (202). But a significant difference is that while Anastasie
claims to know things about Mycéa that the author does not know, her
knowledge (unlike Mathieu's) is based entirely on what the author has
written about Mycéa. She identifies with her—"I have been where she
has been, my eyes have seen what she has seen"—on the basis of a male
author's inadequate representation of her. Spivak argues that representing the subjectivity of the subaltern woman is possible only, if at all,
through the silences and breaks in the text (see chapter 3). Anastasie
adds a further twist to this: as a subaltern woman, her own "effaced itinerary" is traceable only through her *reading* of the negative traces
("what the work cannot say") in a male intellectual's representation of a
female intellectual's life.[7]

Anastasie is perhaps an extreme case of the fragile and tortuous relays
that constitute identity in Glissant's characters. But the "rhizomatic"
conception of identity developed in *Poétique de la relation* informs the
whole of *Mahagony* and *Tout-monde.* Within Relation, identity is no
longer a permanence or "root" but a "capacity of variation, yes, a variable, controlled or frenzied" (*PR,* 156) in which the elements are constantly changing. One of the elements of creolization, equally, is the
principle that "what supports us is not simply the definition of our identities, but also their relation to the whole set of possibilities: the mutual
mutations generated by this play of relations" (103). The subject is constituted within this fluid and multiple, "relayed" circulation of identifications.

The relationship between identity and *language* cannot, therefore, remain stable either. If identity is not singular, it cannot be bound to a single language, and the language-identity equation cannot be sustained. In
Introduction à une poétique du divers Glissant states this very clearly;
and in his recent fiction the characters have neither a fixed personal identity *nor* a "natural," intimate connection with the language they use.[8] In

Tout-monde the "Bezaudin" section to which I have already referred is prefaced with an extract from Mathieu's "Traité du tout-monde," which defines "authentic" speech (that is, the language-identity equation) as a trap that the oppressed must avoid falling into: "We observe how many ex-masters, and especially intellectual masters, adore listening to the words of their ex-oppressed, when these words stoutly close in on themselves and resound with allegedly primordial authenticity" (*TM*, 158). It recommends instead a strategic, "calculated" relationship to a plurality of languages and a plurality of identities: "So argue, no less stoutly, that you calculate your being. . . . Go on! Blow up that rock. Pick up its pieces and spread them out all around. Our identities relay each other, and for that sole reason those hidden hierarchies, those hierarchies which surreptitiously insist on preserving themselves under cover of praise, collapse in futile pretensions" (158).

This program for liberation is, however, most strikingly carried out by the narrators of *Mahagony*. We have seen how the diverse narratives of the novel distance themselves from and disown previous representations of the same events, but the narrators also *dis-own,* in one way or another, the *discourse* of their narratives. That is, they distance themselves from their own use of language by criticizing their "style." Hégésippe, for instance, writes: "In the night . . . I deliberate that my way of giving the story has neither goodness nor rightness. It is too pretty as I tell it" (*Mah*, 33). Marie Celat oscillates between her delirious "speaking in rhythm" and the calm rational style she at times succeeds in adopting instead: "Now then, I'm going to be calm, tell it from beginning to end, like a historian" (132); "You notice how I'm telling this nice and calmly. Don't go saying that I'm off again with my gobbledygook, if I want to I can really put on airs with words" (134). She also distances herself from her language through gentle mockery: "'Well, well' thought Marie Celat, who never missed an opportunity to make fun of herself: 'It's over now—the rhythm, the special words. Looks like I'm going home'" (182).

Mathieu goes through two stages of self-correction in the course of the novel. His first idea is to "correct in a more measured style . . . the tumultuous obscurities" (28) of the style he had previously shared with the author and to replace it with a more "scientific" discourse that, he feels, will be more effective in uncovering the truth behind all the stories. It becomes increasingly difficult to sustain, but he perseveres throughout part I of the novel:

J'éprouvais parfois quelque gêne à imaginer mon tumultueux auteur rigolant à grosse voix de ma plongée incontrôlée: moi qui avais prétendu lui opposer des leçons de clarté. Aussi m'exerçais-je, répertoriant les cosses du passé, à une tranquillité d'écriture qui garantissait à mes yeux la seule liberté vraie par rapport à tout auteur possible. Ma prétention à l'objectivité s'évertuait dans ce tohu-bohu. (61)

[I would occasionally feel some embarrassment as I imagined my tumultuous author's loud guffaws at my plunging out of control: I who had claimed to confront him with lessons in clarity. I therefore trained myself, itemizing the husks of the past, to write with a calmness that alone in my view guaranteed true freedom in relation to any possible author. My claim to objectivity strove to fulfill itself amidst this commotion.]

The trouble with this new style of discourse is that, as can be seen from the above passage, his attempt at calm objectivity in fact results merely in an over-solemn and distinctly pompous style: this section begins, for instance, with:

Ma déconvenue fut réelle de constater que les personnes . . . Je parle des personnes qui ne m'étaient pas proches, n'ayant aucune raison même discrète de partager mes préoccupations. . . . Il arrivait à ces personnes ainsi décontenancées de justifier leurs craintes en se prévalant de celle-ci que j'aurais pu encourir: la détresse de l'avenir. (59–60)

[How real was my discomfiture in observing that certain persons . . . I am speaking of persons who were not close to me, lacking any reason, even discreet, to share my preoccupations. . . . These persons would from time to time, when thus disconcerted, justify their fears by exploiting something which I too might have incurred: distress at the future.]

By part II Mathieu has realized that this was the "wrong" style; the effect of the other narrators on him has made it impossible to continue to assert such superb independence from the maelstrom (and this is of course relevant to Glissant's critique of transparence): "The time of sonorous phrases, majestic parables and solemn reprimands is over. Eudoxie, Adélaïde, the *quimboiseur*: they had broken my voice. I still wanted to make out what was stirring beneath the surface, but I no longer applied to it what is called an appropriate style" (110).

Several of the narrators thus display an acute consciousness of their discourse as "style"—as hesitating between different possible styles or as momentarily adopting someone else's style. This can be ironic, as when Ida says, "Mathieu would say, *in his sighing tones* [*dans son langage soupiré*] that the wrappings of happiness are fragile, that the dead cannot enter" (147, emphasis added). Or it can be sincere: Ida again, describing the "country" style of her fiancé's family, says "straight away, different words, a different way of speaking, came into my head. Every word was a ceremony, time passed between each sentence, I was getting into the *langage* of the place"—and going on to adopt, ironically this time, the "other" style of yet another character to comment on *this* "other" style: "Do you realize, as Annie-Marie would have put it, there are still people who talk flowery" [*parlent fleuri*] (160). Marie Celat, on the other hand, tries to find a style that will differentiate her from others, deliberately writing in an "ordinary," nonliterary way that will be unlike Mathieu's and that he will not approve of (140). But—such is the flexibility of the subject's use of discourse—she realizes that in fact Mathieu is able to appropriate, by his approval, any style that she tries out; her discourse cannot escape from his: "he is quite capable of applauding my unclothed words, of assuring me that it's a way of entering directly into everyone's voice. I can hear him already. When he wants to, he can prove to you that you are the stuff of legend. Or quite simply that you are crap" (140–41).

   This could perhaps be seen as a different, less alienated version of the appropriation of the Other's language discussed in chapter 4, the others in this case being friends and equals rather than social superiors or oppressors. It is yet another way in which discourse has become strategic, rather than unproblematically spontaneous, and is therefore related to the notion of counterpoetics. Mathieu reflects upon Hégésippe's "counterpoetic" use of French, making it clear that it involves working on the language, "bending" it to serve his own ends—"if he had had that other kind of genius, paraphrasing the *langage* of those who considered themselves his masters, miraculously reforming it and bending it to the merciful relation of Gani's childhoods"—and that this is one instance of the much larger work of "variation of the *langues* that we make use of, their vertiginous transmutation into a relevant *langage*" (61). The narrators, in other words, are engaged in a search for a possible discourse—a discourse that will "work"—rather than being solidly installed in a given discourse that is assumed as their own.[9]

   All of these phenomena reveal a gap or break—as when Mathieu says "they had broken my voice" (110)—between the subject and his or her language. Language is not unmediated expressivity but provides a kind of temporary, tactical construct of identity: a "personnage," in the sense that Mathieu uses the term when explaining his stylistic project in the opening section:

> Qu'estimait à travers moi ce personnage que *j'avais été* mais que je ne voulais plus *avoisiner* . . . écrire une préface au récit où *il s'était vu* grandir, et corriger d'un style mesuré—intervenu en tête de tout l'ouvrage—les tumultueuses obscurités d'où avaient germé . . . son langage de convention, ou de littérature. . . . En tête de l'ouvrage, c'est-à-dire au fondement de l'entreprise dont *il* était la créature et qu'*il* investissait à son tour en créateur tout-puissant. Et *j'étais* cette créature, et *je* devenais ce créateur. (28, emphasis added)

> [What did this character that *I had been* but that I no longer wished to *frequent* think through me . . . to write a preface to the narrative in which *he had seen himself* grow, and correct with a measured style—intervening at the start of the whole work—the tumultuous obscurities which had nourished . . . his conventional language, or his literary language. . . . At the start of the work, that is to say at the founding moment of the enterprise of which *he* was the creature and to which *he* in turn was committed as all-powerful creator. And *I* was that creature, and *I* was becoming that creator.]

That is, it is the "personnage" who wants to "correct with a measured style," etc.; the "personnage" here, in other words, does not simply equate with the "créature" but is *both* character and author, and as author is adopting a particular style—but, even as author, is ambiguously distinct from Mathieu as subject [*je*]. The slippage in the pronouns, from "je" to "il" and vice versa, multiplies the ambiguity already attaching to Mathieu's double identity as character and author, as both cause and effect of the text he is "in."

Through continually disowning its discourse, the subject is placed in yet another kind of *relay*—"passed on" through a succession of different mediations, temporary stylistic constructs that serve a strategic purpose rather than being the expressive incarnation of a permanent individual identity. Language is always as it were sliding away from the subject; the gap is always opening up again. Conversely, the subject is constantly sliding through language via a series of relays, leaving its "own words" behind, like a snake shedding its skin. At the same time, since the subject has no fixed identity independent of language, it is itself caught up in the gaps and sliding relays of the discourses that it so ambivalently adopts.

The various discourses that make up the text of *Mahagony* are thus disowned and disoriginated.

The process is compounded by the way in which the relay works over time, so that the origins of individual utterances are lost: no one knows if the reported words are in fact the individual's "own words" or not. Thus, a piece of direct speech attributed to Gani is followed by the qualification: "No one knows for sure if he said it like this: the text we have here is the final link in a chain that has long been trailing through the grasses of time" (64). Even the text of one of the narrators is "contaminated" by the same uncertainty: did Hégésippe write in Creole or in French? And if in Creole, then at what point was it translated into French? (61). Eudoxie assumes it is French: "Hégésippe croit il est bel esprit, pour broder francé comme pas un" [Hégésippe thinks he's a smart fellow, writing French like nobody's business] (49). But this raises another problem, which the text does not comment on but of which the reader is presumably meant to be aware: Eudoxie's own narration is a *prayer*—how did this essentially private discourse ever get handed on to anyone else? And since she cannot write, why is her text misspelled (*francé* for *français*) as if she were writing it? Mathieu eventually realizes the futility of asking this kind of question. The result of this persistent obliteration of origins is again that the notion of authenticity becomes irrelevant; the link between utterance and individual subject is dissolved.

It is here that Spivak's analysis of rumor becomes relevant. It occurs as part of her discussion of the work of the Subaltern Studies group on insurgency.[10] The group emphasizes the difference between official, authoritative, written communication and spoken rumor—and Glissant makes exactly the same distinction in *Mahagony* where the antagonism between the collective, often anonymous nature of speech and the monologic basis of the written, authored text is a recurrent theme.[11] But for Spivak rumor is characterized above all by the features of Derridean "writing": it is spoken but anonymous and plural, not attributable to an individual. It cannot therefore signify the immediacy of a particular consciousness; it is not phonocentric, in other words. Spivak argues that, paradoxically, writing in the monologic sense is phonocentric, whereas rumor is like writing in the deconstructive sense. It is rumor's "non-belonging to any one voice-consciousness" that makes it subversive and transgressive, a subaltern weapon against the dominant enemy. It is "primordially (originarily) errant, always in circulation with no assignable source. This illegitimacy makes it accessible to insurgency." It is not necessarily false, but nor is it verifiably accurate; no one is in control of it; it changes as it circulates, generating different versions of itself; and yet it always appears to be referring back to something else: "Rumor is a relay of something always assumed to be pre-existent."[12]

Rumor thus shares with relayed language the double resistance to both monologic authority and fixed individual identity. But it also has the additional implication of being a proliferating, "rhizomatic" *force*, extending across time and space. There is another image in *Mahagony* that brings together all three of these connotations. It first occurs at the beginning of the novel and becomes one of its key concepts. This is the *trame* [web], introduced as:

> La chronique avait enroulé le premier fil de l'histoire sans pour autant suffire à la *trame*: d'autres paroles devaient y concourir. Elles se soutiennent de temps à temps, elles fouillent plus dru, elles tissent plus serré. *Le même disant, changé par ce qu'il dit,* revient au même endroit de ce même pays, et voilà que l'endroit lui aussi a changé, comme a changé la perception qu'il en eut naguère, ou la chronologie établie de ce qui s'y est passé. Les arbres qui vivent longtemps *changent toujours, en demeurant.* (15–16, emphasis added).

> [The chronicle had wound the first thread of the story but still could not cover the whole *web*: other words had to join in the work. They support each other through time, they dig down more deeply, they weave more closely. *The same sayer, changed by what he says,* comes back to the same place in this same country, and finds the place has changed as well, and so has the view of it that he had before, or the established chronology of what happened. Trees that live a long time *are always changing, while still remaining.*]

The *trame* is constantly "changing" the subject, who moves around in it, and it is itself, like the mahogany tree, always changing. This helps to elucidate the notion of the subject's "sliding" position in language, discussed earlier; the *trame* forms a kind of matrix within which, as in Relation, the subject circulates.[13] Identity is "given in the chaotic *trame* of Relation" (*PR*, 158). Thus, Mathieu describes the characters in the novel as being supported by, strung out along as it were, the relays of the text: "Les personnages que nous sommes à nous-mêmes descendent au long de la parole" [The characters that we are for ourselves descend along the words] (124). *Trame* normally means web, or weft, or network; the etymology of "text" is similarly to do with weaving ("elles tissent plus serré"). As this suggests, the *trame* is a production in language:

a collective intertext—"the violent and skillfully stretched out *trame* of our intertextuality" (*PR*, 134)—based on an infinite number of relays. Each subject actively participates in the production of a collective, but differentiated, "relayed" text that *also* becomes the environment in which the subject circulates and is thereby continuously changed. It is the result of all the individual speakers or writers who have contributed to it; but in so doing, they lose their individual identities. What counts is the collective matrix of the *trame* itself: the "weave" of relayed and transformed utterances, proliferating like Deleuze and Guattari's rhizomes. Thus, *Poétique de la relation* speaks of opaque discourses "weaving cloths that can be truly understood only in terms of the texture of the weave and not the nature of the component parts" (204).

The *trame* thus also works to resist the closure of the text. There is no limit to the number of different discourses that will enter the intertext or to the period of time over which it will operate. Near the end of *Mahagony*, Mathieu adds Raphaël's *discours* to it—"The speech which was going to come would probably meet the *trame* that I had claimed to untangle. A speech is a *trame*, and vice versa" (185)—and the *trame* itself is also expanding and meeting up to combine with other *intertexts*: "Raphaël Targin, who had been in at the tiny beginning of my story, happened to be there for us at that moment when every story dilates in the air of the world, perhaps to be diluted in it, sometimes to reinforce another *trame* which has appeared far off in the distance" (186). It is process rather than entity and a process that is in principle boundless: "L'ici-là est la trame, qui ne trame pas frontières" [The here-and-there is the web, and it does not weave frontiers] (*PR*, 204). It brings together the two effects that we have already seen at work jointly in the relay: that is, both *trame* and relay erase the boundaries of both textual closure and authorial identity. It creates an opening and releases an energy that will continue to characterize Glissant's later, more optimistic writing.

8 Language as Strategy of Resistance

GLISSANT'S WORK in the 1990s displays a strong sense that the monolithic hegemony of "sameness," while remaining the principal enemy, is no longer as powerful as it used to be. The various concepts that dominate his recent texts, such as chaos, creolization, the rhizome, archipélisation, and of course *tout-monde* itself, all convey the exhilaration of this breakup of the old, singular system of domination and its replacement by a world view based on diversity and unpredictability. In his most recent publication, *Traité du tout-monde,* Glissant expresses this in the almost untranslatable formula "Ma proposition est qu'aujourd'hui le monde entier s'archipélise et se créolise" [What I am proposing is that today the whole world is becoming archipelagized and creolized] (194). He does not mean, of course, that oppression and the struggles against it have ceased, but they have become more localized. The advantage of the "chaotic" world is that unexpected victories can sometimes occur; he cites the trajectory of Nelson Mandela, from prisoner to president, as an example. Above all, he believes that the globalization of mass media has meant that local struggles are no longer carried on without the knowledge of the rest of the world. It is significant that the first section of the *Traité* is entitled "Le Cri du monde"; in other words, "the struggle with no witnesses" described in *Le discours antillais* has given way to a situation in which "the cry of the world" can always be heard. Contact between cultures has irreversibly put an end to the isolation that was such a dominant feature in the Martinique of his youth. "For the first time, the semi-totality of human cultures are wholly and simultaneously placed in contact and in effervescent reaction with each other" (*TTM,* 23).

A major manifestation of this interactive plurality of relations has, as we have seen, been the development of a more explicit critique of the notion of identity. Identity is a psychological concept, of course, but it is also a political and ethical one, and it is these dimensions that are central to the critique. Glissant's increasing emphasis on the political dangers of the "root-identity," as opposed to the plural, relational "rhizomatic" identity, continues throughout the *Traité*. This is both a new development and a continuation of his previous constant questioning of the social construction of identity, particularly in its relation to language.

In fact, one way to define the whole evolution of Glissant's thinking, from the 1950s to the present day, is to trace his changing articulations of what I have called the language-identity equation. These revolve around the Martinican subject's perception of *lack* that formed the starting point for my analysis. The lack of language is experienced as a lack of being; in other words, not having a language that adequately, immediately, and fully expresses what one wishes to say about the world and, perhaps particularly, about oneself, becomes equated with not having a fully realized self. The fact that French is to a significant extent perceived as a foreign language, and Creole as a limited and inadequate compromise, leads in turn to a feeling of existential inferiority. This generates a desire for an unproblematic "full" language that will hopefully convey a full and unproblematic subjectivity, and in Glissant's early work—*La Lézarde* and *Le quatrième siècle*—this desire is endorsed by the texts as the only solution to the problem. In the second stage, which is the one I have been most concerned with, exactly the same sense of lack produces a different projected solution: the (social and literary) construction of a strategic counterpoetic *langage* that is not a straightforward component of one's personal identity but a position from which a kind of guerilla warfare can be waged against the dominant language and dominant culture. This, as I have tried to show, is the position underlying *Le discours antillais* and the novels *Malemort, La case du commandeur,* and, in part, *Mahagony*.

The third and final stage retains this conception of a use of language that is not tied to a singular identity, that simultaneously inhabits and subverts an existing dominant language and culture. Now, however, the conception is both *generalized* and *pluralized,* and as a result loses the original sense of lack. Thus, although many of *Tout-monde*'s individual episodes are powerful representations of situations of social inequality and suffering, *language* is no longer seen as being implicated in the problem; the language of the text is a "chaotic," liberated multiplicity of free-floating idioms, and Glissant believes—rather optimistically, perhaps—that this is increasingly the case in the world as well. So, from *Mahagony* onward, the kind of subjective relation to language that originally arose from the *specific* social situation that, out of oppression, necessity, and constraint, produced the counterpoetic *langage,* is now seen as characteristic of a far more *general* change in worldwide culture in which language and identity are *everywhere* seen as mobile and plural constructs, and as so completely dissociated from each other that the notion of lack becomes redundant. Thus, in the *Traité du tout-monde,* we read, as a statement of fact, "Language is no longer the mirror of any being" (85).

In this context we may return to the question I posed in the introduction to this book. How does the colonized subject relate to a language initially imposed by the colonizer but subsequently, *to some extent,* subverted and reappropriated, and what part can fiction play in this process? I have tried to show how, for Glissant, language can operate as a mode of cultural resistance, and how this resistance is both an everyday activity that is represented in his novels and a literary activity that is exemplified by his novels. The particular forms that the resistance takes are obviously determined by the nature of what is being resisted: the dominant characteristics of French colonial power in the Caribbean are, according to Glissant, less those of economic exploitation than of a cultural policy of assimilation to the supposedly universal values of Western—and particularly French—civilization. Resistance, therefore, is primarily a matter of defending cultural difference. The Caribbean archipelago—a collection of islands that are very diverse but also intimately linked to each other—has in Glissant's recent work become a prominent image of this movement against universality. In *Traité du tout-monde,* for instance, he writes that "the relation between the components of the Carib reality is not simply rational or logical but above all subliminal . . . in a state of permanent transformation" (76). And he goes on to imply that language—specifically the relation between *langue* and *langage*—is the key issue here: "To express this multilingual reality that we share, it is *langage* that is important, as it bends the limits of the *langues* in use" (76). Resistance is also necessarily *indirect*: in a situation where open political struggle is virtually bound to be ineffective, it adopts tactics of evasion and camouflage. Glissant makes a connection between the idea of the archipelago [*la pensée archipélique*] and that of the detour: "Archipelagic thought is well suited to the ways of our worlds. It adopts their ambiguity, their fragility, their diversion [*dérivé*]. It accords with the practice of the detour, which is not the same as flight or resignation" (*TTM,* 31).

As a strategy of resistance, then, language asserts diversity—it evades reduction to the sameness of Western assimilation—and it operates deviously, replacing the clarity of the French classical ideal with a counter-poetics of detour and opacity. In the course of this book I have looked at various manifestations of this. First, there is the way in which the very inadequacies of a certain use of language can be turned into opaque weapons of defense against cultural oppression. Then I have analyzed the detours of representation, which can reveal the traces of the subaltern subject-position in language and its occasional ability to fracture the dominant discourse. The relation to the speech of the white Other is traced through a number of versions of "split discourse," ranging from ambiguously cynical manipulation to the uncontrolled, compulsive, but equally ambiguous detour of verbal delirium. Other "mad" forms of language are unconscious strategies for assuming the unhomely anxiety of cultural dislocation and historical trauma. Alternatively, the detour of language can be more conscious, and even playful, in its use of rhetorical techniques derived from Creole and the oral culture of the plantation folktales, to disorientate and reposition the Western listener or reader. And, finally, the narrative and discursive "relays" that structure Glissant's more recent fiction put into literary practice the idea of relation in diversity that has always been central to his thought.

The conclusion that emerges from this is that a strategic relation to one's language always involves placing it in relation to something other than itself. This may simply be other languages: "We write in the presence of all the world's languages" (*TTM*, 85). Or it may be the difficult conflictual relation to a dominant language that itself refuses to recognize the presence of others and that one's own language tries to counter while still being dependent on it. Or it may be the harmonious and exuberant relation of the "relay." But in all cases, one's language can no longer be experienced as that naively and unreflectively *single* all-encompassing environment connoted by the expression "mother tongue."

In other words, if language is to resist sociocultural domination, it must be constructed and deployed strategically. Such a positioning of language has far-reaching implications for the subject's relationship to it. Within the humanist Marxist and Sartrean framework that was most influential in the 1950s and 1960s (in Fanon's work, for instance), the colonized subject is seen as *alienated* from metropolitan culture and language. But the concept of alienation may not ultimately be the most helpful way of defining the problem, insofar as it implies as its logical opposite the notion of an "own" language that would belong to and be an integral part of the subject's consciousness. We have seen how Glissant moves steadily away from the belief that alienation can be over-come by promoting an ideal of authentic self-expression, and toward the idea that it is only by breaking the link between language and identity, which this ideal involves, that some kind of liberation can be achieved. The subject's relation to language has to be a strategic one, in the various senses described above, if resistance is to stand a chance of being effective. Rather than seeking a solution to the problem as defined by the dominant culture, it changes the terms of that definition—twisting the parameters of the subject's situation in such a way as to turn lack, negativity, and otherness themselves into a means of resistance and self-representation. Both the theoretical importance and the poetic and emotional force of Glissant's work derive from this remarkable achievement.

Notes

Introduction

1. The Front Antillo-Guyanais led to Glissant and Niger (whose real name was Albert Béville) being banned by De Gaulle from the Caribbean *départements d'outre mer* in 1959; Glissant returned only in 1965. Niger was killed in a plane crash over Guadeloupe in 1962.

2. Benítez-Rojo, *Repeating Island,* 2.

3. It has also been argued, more generally, that these features of the Caribbean colonial situation have led to a more highly developed level of postcolonial theory being produced in the Caribbean than in other Third World countries. See Ashcroft, Griffiths, and Tiffin, *Empire Writes Back,* 117, 145–54.

4. Lamming, "Occasion for Speaking," 34, 35; see Brathwaite, *History of the Voice.*

5. Brathwaite, *History of the Voice;* Lamming, "Occasion for Speaking," 44. More recent analyses of the English-speaking Caribbean have, however, put more emphasis on the necessarily strategic and subversive relationship to the standard language, as Glissant does. Thus, Ashcroft, Griffiths, and Tiffin, referring to an unpublished Ph.D. thesis by the Jamaican Cliff Lashley ("Towards a Critical Framework for Jamaican Literature: A Reading of the Fiction of Victor Stafford Reid and Other Jamaican Writers," University of the West Indies, 1984), write: "Lashley and other critics prefer to see a relationship of subversion being invoked here. . . . Such subversion, they argue, has been characteristic of much West Indian literature and culture. These subversive strategies not only have historical and social antecedents, but provide the only possible means of linguistic assertion where there is no alternative language in which to reject the language (and hence the vision) of the colonizers" (*Empire Writes Back,* 48).

6. Tiffin, "Post-Colonial Literatures," quoted in Ashcroft, Griffiths, and Tiffin, *Post-Colonial Studies Reader,* 95–96.

7. See, for instance, Bhabha, "Interrogating Identity" and "The Other Question" (a modified version of "The Other Question" appears as chapter 3 of *The Location of Culture*).

8. Bhabha, "The Other Question," 150, 154 (emphasis added).

9. The second edition of Benítez-Rojo's *Repeating Island* cites Glissant's name in its acknowledgments (xi).

10. Glissant has also published one play: *Monsieur Toussaint* (Paris: Éditions du Seuil, 1961).

11. Crosta, for example, writes: "The optimism or the hope of seeing some meaningful changes improve the Caribbean situation fades away in his third novel, *Malemort* . . . [the novel] gives us a tragic glimpse of the psychological alienation of its characters, as they live through contemporary versions of 'malendure' or 'malemort' [these are old French words for 'suffering' and 'cruel death']" (*Le marronnage créateur*, 28). In a similar vein, Cailler writes "the element of despair in *Malemort* is immense; compared with the earlier texts, alienation and uprooting have never seemed more harrowing" (*Conquérants*, 108).

12. Glissant's concept of the Other contains echoes of both Jean-Paul Sartre and Emmanuel Lévinas. A cogent and subtle analysis of the difference between Lévinas's ethical position and Glissant's politically grounded *poétique* can be found in Gallagher, "La poétique de la diversité."

1 Concepts of Resistance

1. "One could never say that each particular culture constitutes a prime element among all those that are put in play in Relation, since the latter defines the elements in play at the same time as it sets them in motion (changes them); nor state that each culture is straightforwardly knowable in its particularity, since one cannot discern its boundary in Relation" (*PR*, 183).

2. Glissant's discussion of Western ethnography is often close to Edward Said's analysis of "Orientalism." In the first chapter of his book, Said cites the former British prime minister Arthur Balfour's assumption that British *knowledge* of Egypt, rather than military or economic power, justifies occupation of the country, so that knowledge itself becomes a primary form of power: "Knowledge to Balfour means surveying a civilization from its origins to its prime to its decline—and of course, it means *being able to do that*. . . . The object of such knowledge is inherently vulnerable to scrutiny. . . . To have such knowledge of such a thing is to dominate it, to have authority over it. And authority here means for 'us' to deny autonomy to 'it'—the Oriental country—since we know it and it exists, in a sense, *as* we know it" (*Orientalism*, 32).

3. The same idea is a central thesis of Ashcroft, Griffiths, and Tiffin, *Empire Writes Back*: "Paradoxically, however, imperial expansion has had a radically destabilizing effect on its own preoccupations and power. In pushing the colonial world to the margins of experience the 'centre' pushed consciousness beyond the point at which monocentrism in all spheres of thought could be accepted without question. In other words the alienating process which initially served to relegate the post-colonial world to the 'margin' turned upon itself and acted to push that world through a kind of mental barrier into a position from which all expe-

rience could be viewed as uncentred, pluralistic and multifarious" (12).

4. In giving his analysis of metaphor in Western philosophy the title "La mythologie blanche," Derrida makes precisely this point by linking and playing on the two senses of *blanche:* ethnic whiteness and the "blankness" of a philosophical system that erases the specificity of its own history. On the one hand we have "metaphysics—the white mythology that draws together and reflects the culture of the West: the white man takes his own, Indo-European, mythology, his *logos,* that is to say the *mythos* of his own language, to be the universal form of what he is still obliged to wish to call Reason"; on the other hand: "White mythology—metaphysics has erased within itself the fabulous scene which produced it and which nevertheless remains active, moving, inscribed in invisible [literally, white] ink, an invisible drawing covered over in the palimpsest" (*Marges de la philosophie,* 254). Indeed, metaphor itself is a process of reduction to "the same": "What could one find *other* than this return of the same when one is looking for metaphor? that is to say, resemblance" (317–18).

5. "You cannot become Trinidadian or Quebecois, if you are not; but it is from now on true that if Trinidad and Quebec did not exist as accepted components of Diversity, something would be missing from the body of world culture—that today we would feel that loss" (*CD,* 98).

6. "The fact is that the trajectories (from their European starting point to elsewhere) end up . . . destroying what had originally given rise to them in the first place: the linear projection of one sensibility across the horizons of the world, the vectorization of the world into colonial powers and colonies" (*PR,* 44).

7. Deleuze and Guattari, *Mille plateaux.* The rhizome's first two "principles" are those "of connection and of heterogeneity: any point on a rhizome can and must be connected with any other" (13). The third one is the "principle of multiplicity: it is only when the multiple is effectively treated as a noun, multiplicity, that it no longer has any relation with the One as subject or as object, as natural or spiritual reality, as image and as world" (14). In *Poétique de la relation,* Glissant says that "the rhizomatic way of thinking is at the center of what I call a poetics of Relation" and adds: "the notion of the rhizome thus maintains the fact of rootedness, but rejects the idea of a totalitarian root" (23). *Le discours antillais* already refers to the rhizome but in less unreservedly positive terms; here, while acknowledging its similarities with Relation, Glissant also criticizes it for ignoring the importance of otherness and for being over-abstract (196–97).

8. Benítez-Rojo, *Repeating Island,* 3, 4.

Benítez-Rojo, claims, for instance, that "there's no center or circumference, but there are common dynamics that express themselves in a more or less regular way" (ibid., 24). In the first chapter, he compares different interpretations of Caribbean reality from the point of view of their differing stress on unity and diversity, and sees his "reading of Chaos" as bringing both together: "where we detect dynamic regularities—not results—within the (dis)order that exists beyond the world of predictable pathways" (ibid., 36).

9. This view is not shared by Henry Louis Gates Jr., who argues in *The Signifying Monkey* for the continuity of African cultural patterns in black culture of the New World. This difference is discussed in chapter 6.

10. Even in Africa itself, however, Glissant notes that the great epics such as the Zulu *Chaka* are not concerned with the founding moment of a people—as are the Iliad, the Old Testament, etc.—but with a moment of "entering into Relation": the encounter with a conquering people from the north (*CD*, 134). "They are the memories of [Relation], which are put together collectively by a people before being dispersed by colonization" (*CD*, 135).

11. Ashcroft, Griffiths, and Tiffin, *Empire Writes Back,* 34.

12. Glissant, "La vocation de comprendre l'autre," 33.

13. Benítez-Rojo, *Repeating Island,* 9.

14. Glissant, "Conférence inaugurale," in *Antilla,* 8; Bhabha, *Location of Culture,* 2.

  Glissant contrasts his concept of creolization with that of *créolité* (as propounded in *Éloge de la créolité,* by Chamoiseau, Confiant, and Bernabé), which, he says, remains a form of essentialism—"une visée à l'être" [directed toward being]—whereas: "we are not offering essence, or models of humanity" (*PR,* 103). In an interview given in *Le Nouvel Observateur* (2 Dec. 1993) and reprinted in *Antilla,* he makes the further distinction that *créolité* is specific to the Caribbean, whereas creolization is a worldwide process. In an implicit criticism of the residual essentialism of *créolité,* he adds: "Unfortunately, the Caribbean islands carried out their decolonization with that same model of identity in the name of which the West had colonized them. It is therefore absolutely necessary to invent another path instead of the demand for identity" [*inventer une autre trace que la revendication identitaire*] (Interview by Gilles Anquetil, *Antilla* 563, 10 Dec. 1993: 35–37). Michael Dash, in this connection, comments that *créolité* "lacks the ironic self-scrutiny, the insistence on process . . . that is characteristic of Glissant's thought. Indeed, despite its avowed debt to Glissant, *Éloge de la créolité* risks undoing the epistemological break with essentialist thinking that he has always striven to conceptualise" (*Edouard Glissant,* 23).

15. See, for instance, the discussion of "that one presupposition of deconstruction which problematizes the positionality of the subject of investigation." Spivak, *Post-Colonial Critic,* 121.

16. See Spivak, *In Other Worlds,* 92 ("The dissimulation of political economy is in and by ideology. What is at work and can be used in that operation is at least the ideology of nation-states, nationalism, national liberation, ethnicity and religion.").

17. Stating this idea in more general terms, Glissant writes: "we will change nothing in the situation of the peoples of the world unless we change that set of images, unless we change the idea that identity must be a single root, fixed and intolerant" (*IPD,* 66).

18. Spivak, *Post-Colonial Critic,* 38; Derrida, *Le monolinguisme de l'autre,* 61.

19. "Thinking in terms of opacity moves me away from the absolute truths which I might otherwise believe that I possess. Far from confining me to useless inactivity, opacity relativizes in me the possibilities of all action, by sensitizing me to the limitations of all methods" (*PR*, 206).

20. Benítez-Rojo, *Repeating Island*, 2.

21. Derrida, in "La mythologie blanche," makes a strikingly similar analysis of the metaphorical basis of the *concept:* "the concept of the concept cannot but retain . . . the schema of the gesture of mastery, taking-keeping, comprehending and grasping the thing as an object" (267). Moreover, he points out, the same etymology is at work in Germanic languages: "begreifen" means to seize or grasp, and he quotes Hegel's remark that "when for example we must take 'be-greifen' in the spiritual sense, it never occurs to us to think of sensory apprehension *with the hand*" (268, emphasis added) (compare with Glissant's "There is in this verb 'comprendre' the movement of hands taking hold of the surrounding world and bringing it back for oneself," *PR*, 206).

22. Spivak, *In Other Worlds*, 209; Spivak, "Can the Subaltern Speak?," 283.

23. One example is in Spivak's analysis of "Draupadi," a short story by Mahasweta Devi, in *In Other Worlds*, 179–86.

24. Macherey, *Theory of Literary Production*, quoted in Spivak, "Can the Subaltern Speak?," 286.

25. "Human behavior is by nature fractal; to become aware of this, to give up trying to reduce it to the transparently obvious, is perhaps to help lessen the burden it places on any individual, as soon as he begins not to 'com-prehend' his own motives, to dismantle himself in this way" (*PR*, 207).

26. Richard Burton's "Le thème du regard dans la littérature antillaise" develops this idea in relation to a number of Caribbean writers, including Glissant.

27. Fanon, *Wretched of the Earth*, 42; Toumson, *La transgression des couleurs*, 467.

28. This idea that the relationship between master and slave includes a dimension of desire and fear is central to the work of Fanon and Bhabha. The same argument is made within the Afro-Caribbean context by Jacques André in *Caraïbales* and Fritz Gracchus in *Les lieux de la mère dans les sociétés afro-américaines*. In *The Location of Culture* Bhabha uses Fanon's writing to illuminate the interconnectedness of the colonial subject's racial and sexual identifications. This view is supported by Jacques André, who comments, in the context of a discussion of Glissant's novels, that "one of Fanon's fundamental merits in *Black Skin, White Masks*—although his continuing dependence upon a philosophy of the subject meant that he himself was not capable of developing all its implications—is to have shown that the racial question is from start to finish a sexual question" ("Le renversement de Senglis," 45–46). Fritz Gracchus's book analyzes the structure of the Caribbean family in terms of a phantasmatic "white Father."

Freud, *Instincts and their Vicissitudes*. See also Laplanche and Pontalis,

"Renversement dans le contraire," in *Vocabulaire de la psychanalyse,* 407–8.
Bhabha, "Other Question," 171.

29. Bhabha, "Other Question," 162, 148–49, 164, 166. See also Gracchus, "Race/énoncé raciste."

Freud's analysis of the fetish ("Fetishism") links it with castration anxiety. The woman's lack of a penis becomes an intolerable sign of the possibility of castration; the woman's sexual organs appear to be mutilated; and the fetish is constructed to play the role of a substitute penis, thus masking the absence of the real one and transforming the female genitals from a terrifying to a desirable object. The subject thus both knows that women do not have penises and denies or disavows this knowledge. Disavowal, for Freud, operates primarily in relation to knowledge of sexual difference; Bhabha extends the same mechanism to knowledge of racial difference, which he argues is equally threatening.

Gracchus argues in similar terms that racism is simply one manifestation of a fetishistic disavowal of difference that superimposes racial difference on sexual difference: "Cathexis of the signifiers nigger, Jew, Arab, young, woman occurs after the libidinal processes of refusal of difference which originate in the phantasmatic relation to the mother and culminate in the disavowal of sexual difference" ("Race/énoncé raciste," 24).

30. Ménil, *Tracées,* 24; Bhabha, "Other Question," 165–66; Fanon, *Black Skin, White Masks,* 110.

31. The same process operated in the Anglophone Caribbean: "the transplanted Africans found that psychic survival depended on their facility for a kind of *double entendre.* They were forced to develop the skill of being able to say one thing in front of 'massa' and have it interpreted differently by their fellow slaves. This skill involved a radical subversion of the meanings of the master's tongue" (Ashcroft, Griffiths, and Tiffin, *Empire Writes Back,* 146).

32. This is, of course, a very particular and controversial analysis. Raphaël Confiant, in his review of *Le discours antillais,* objects strongly to the implication that Creole is not as straightforwardly "authentic" as any other language, writing that "creole is absolutely not a 'detour', as Glissant asserts, a slave's ruse or whatever" (37).

33. Spivak, *In Other Worlds,* 253; Glissant, "Assimilation ou antillanité?," 46.

34. Rosello, *Littérature,* 15–16.

35. See de Certeau, *L'invention du quotidien*; Rosello, *Littérature,* 36, quoting de Certeau.

36. Rosello, *Littérature,* 32, 36.

37. Ibid., 37, 39; Glissant, "Entretien avec le *CARÉ,*" 10, 22 ("I've tried to show that [the Caribbean woman] possesses *a knowledge of camouflaged reality* which the Caribbean man is unable to master in its full extent"); Cailler, "Edouard Glissant" (discusses the development of this critique of male heroism).

38. Benítez-Rojo, *Repeating Island,* 10, 11, 311. Thus, it gives the Caribbean

peoples "something remote that . . . carries the desire to sublimate apocalypse and violence," and the culture as a whole is characterized by "the attempt to move an audience into a realm where the tensions that lead to confrontation are inoperative" (ibid., 16, 20).

39. Roger Toumson takes this idea even further in defining the psychological significance of Creole as a "pseudo-mother tongue"—a false substitute for a lost *African* mother tongue that is itself a fantasy. "'*First*' language—lost language—the mother tongue is a sort of form lacking any content. Unattested, it can express itself only as nostalgia. . . . Nostalgia for 'Africa mater' . . . is, for many people, a nostalgia for the paradise of that first language. This creates a vacuum which is then filled by creole intervening as a kind of pseudo-mother tongue" (*La transgression*, 1:79).

40. English has no exact equivalent to the distinction between *langue* and *langage,* and I therefore retain the French terms where necessary, rather than following Dash's translation. Toumson theorizes the tension somewhat similarly in terms of a conflictual relation between the Saussurean concepts of *langue* and *parole* (i.e., the language system and the act of speech): "The subject makes its appearance at the intersection of the axes of *langue* and *parole* . . . what *parole* signifies is an intention to break away. It comes into existence in the course of a struggle, sometimes secret, sometimes overt, against domination. The speaking subject positions itself in a conceptual and concrete discontinuity" (*La transgression*, 1:79–80).

41. In *L'intention poétique* Glissant describes his relationship to the French *langue* as "my confrontation with its law. Because the connections between my community and the cultural system which it embodied have, like it or not, been those of alienation. I do not have to prove my faithfulness or conformity to it, but to force it to move in my direction; that is my way of giving it recognition" (45).

42. Priska Degras provides a useful gloss on this relationship: "It is therefore a question of inventing a new language, beyond and despite the unnameable and the multiple impossibilities that oppose creation. Though this new language cannot express exactly this unnameable, it can at least approach its meaning. . . . This effort to re-name is an arduous, uneasy, and bellicose undertaking, because its goal is to ferret out, at the very heart of the *langue,* one's own and the Other's, the multiple traps that function as innumerable obstacles to the free deployment of this new *langage*" ("Name of the Fathers," 613).

43. "There are, as we have seen, no languages or language spoken in Martinique, neither Creole nor French, that have been 'naturally' developed by and for us Martinicans because of our experience of collective, proclaimed, denied, or seized responsibility at all levels" (*CD*, 166).

44. Glissant, "Entretien avec le *CARÉ*," 17–25. The extract quoted was in answer to a question comparing the style of *La case du commandeur* to verbal delirium.

45. Ashcroft, Griffiths, and Tiffin, *The Empire Writes Back*, 38–39 (quoting Rao, *Kanthapura*, vii).

46. Ibid., 39.

2 The Lack of Language

1. This connection is made explicitly in *Le discours antillais:* "Creole is impoverished because terms relating to professions disappear, . . . because a whole series of expressions that were linked to forms of collective responsibility in the country are disappearing as this responsibility diminishes. The sociolinguistic study of terms fallen into disuse and that have not been replaced reveals that this happens because Martinicans as such no longer do anything in their country" (*CD*, 187).

2. Glissant describes "cabbalistic formulae probably inherited from the African languages: no one knew what they meant, and they had a powerful effect on the audience without anyone understanding why. It is absolutely clear to me, now, how much I was influenced by this nonelucidated presence of languages or formulae whose meaning you do not possess and which nevertheless affect you, and it is perhaps possible that one whole aspect of my theories on the necessary opacities of language comes from that experience" (*IPD*, 115–16).

3. Spivak, "Can the Subaltern Speak?," 287.

4. Ibid., 295.

5. Said, "Orientalism Reconsidered," 215; Said, *Orientalism*, 6, 7.

6. A comment that Glissant makes in a slightly different context provides a helpful gloss on this: "I believe that all peoples today have an important presence to assume in the nonsystem of relations of the Whole-world [*Tout-monde*], and a people that does not have the means to reflect on this function is indeed an oppressed people, a people kept in a state of disability" (*IPD*, 91–92).

7. The quotations from Spivak in this paragraph are from, respectively, *Post-Colonial Critic*, 43; and *In Other Worlds*, 207, 257. Her translations and analyses of Mahasweta Devi's short stories are "Draupadi" and "Breast-Giver"; see *In Other Worlds*, chs. 11, 13, 14.

The key text for Jacques Lacan's formulation of the necessarily alienated identifications of the imaginary is "Le stade du miroir comme formateur de la fonction du Je." Louis Althusser extends the imaginary into the domain of ideology and bases his construction of the ideological subject on it. See "Idéologie et appareils."

8. Michael Dash's article, "Writing the Body: Edouard Glissant's Poetics of Re-Membering," gives a detailed discussion of the ways in which these kinds of social and cultural stresses are inscribed on the body: "Even if the mind chooses to forget, the body bears the signs of the past violation. In order to break the collective amnesia of the Martinicans, Glissant focuses unflinchingly on the body" (610).

9. Derrida makes a somewhat similar connection between lack of language and loss of memory. In *Le monolinguisme de l'autre,* he argues that the "prohibition," which for the colonized subject blocks access to the French language, "by the same token [blocks] access to the identifications which make possible calm autobiography [*l'autobiographie apaisée*], 'memoirs' in the classical sense. In what language can one write one's memoirs if there has been no authorized mother tongue? How can one utter a worth-while 'I remember' when one has to invent both one's language and one's 'I', invent them *at the same time,* going beyond the surge of amnesia unleashed by the *double prohibition?*" (57).

10. Priska Degras analyzes this—and the theme of naming in Glissant's other novels—in detail in "Name of the Fathers, History of the Name: Odono as Memory." She describes "the renewed acknowledgement of a lack of something: that of the ancient Name, the Name of the *pays d'avant,* and of the Name to come, the Name of the country to be created" and argues that the Name is "the metaphor of *langage,* whose necessary invention can compensate for the lack of *langue*" (615). Suzanne Crosta also devotes a chapter of her book on Glissant to "Stratégies et enjeux de la nomination" [Strategies and Issues of Naming].

11. This triple association is commented on by Daniel Radford: "landscape, language, history . . . a single theme organized as a trinity in order to recover its trace" (*Edouard Glissant,* 33); and by Jacques André: "Glissant's writing springs from the vacuousness, the rootlessness that in the Caribbean define the territory, the language and also history" (*Caraïbales,* 113).

12. Mabi is a drink made from tree bark and ginger.

13. The important link between speech and body in Glissant's writing is addressed in detail in the second chapter, "Une pratique détournée de l'écriture: l'enjeu du corps et le recours à l'oralité," of Crosta's *Le marronnage créateur* and in Dash's "Writing the Body." (Dash's article, oddly enough, contains references to all of Glissant's novels except *Malemort.*)

14. In fact, Bhabha's analysis of the problematic construction of colonial identity implies that even the colonizer—the "original" of all the middle-class black imitations—is also caught up in and hollowed out by the dislocation of the reciprocal process of identification: "the image of post-Enlightenment man tethered to . . . his dark reflection, the shadow of colonized man, that splits his presence, distorts his outline, breaches his boundaries. . . . The ambivalent identification of the racist world . . . turns on the idea of man as his alienated image; not Self and Other but the otherness of the Self inscribed in the perverse palimpsest of colonial identity" (*Location of Culture,* 44). Derrida makes a similar point for rather different reasons: in *Le monolinguisme de l'autre,* he describes his situation as an Algerian Jew whose identity and relation to the French language is structured by his alienation from metropolitan culture.

15. Crosta, *Le marronnage créateur,* 51–54, 77–78.

16. Toumson, "La littérature antillaise," 134.

3 Subaltern Language

1. See Spivak, "Can the Subaltern Speak?"; *In Other Worlds,* sec. 3 (contains Spivak's translation of and comments on two short stories by Mahasweta Devi); "Subaltern Studies: Deconstructing Historiography"; "A Literary Representation of the Subaltern: A Woman's Text from the Third World"; and "The Rani of Sirmur." The question of subalternity is also addressed passim in Spivak, *Post-Colonial Critic.*

2. See, for instance, Gramsci, "Some Aspects of the Southern Question" and "The History of the Subaltern Classes: Methodological Criteria."

3. "[Gramsci] is concerned with the intellectual's role in the subaltern's cultural and political movement into the hegemony. . . . Yet an account of the phased development of the subaltern is thrown out of joint when his cultural macrology is operated, however remotely, by the epistemic interference with legal and disciplinary definitions accompanying the imperialist project" (Spivak, "Can the Subaltern Speak?," 283).

4. Ibid., 276–78.

5. Ibid., 279.

In *The Post-Colonial Critic,* Spivak writes: "*Representing*: proxy and portrait, as I said, these are two ways of representing. Now, the thing to remember is that in the act of representing politically, you actually represent yourself and your constituency in the portrait sense as well. You have to think of your constituency as working class, or the black minority, the rainbow coalition, or yet the military-industrial complex and so on. That is representation in the sense of *Darstellung.* So that you do not ever 'simply' *vertreten* anyone" (108).

6. "It is not a solution, the idea of the disenfranchised speaking for themselves, or the radical critics speaking for them; this question of representation, of self-representation, representing others, is a problem. On the other hand, we cannot put it under the carpet with demands for authentic voices; we have to remind ourselves that, as we do this, we might be compounding the problem even as we are trying to solve it" (Spivak, *Post-Colonial Critic,* 63).

7. Spivak, "Can the Subaltern Speak?," 292.

8. Spivak, *In Other Worlds,* 203; Spivak, *Post-Colonial Critic,* 66.

9. Spivak explains the subject-effect as follows: "I am progressively inclined, then, to read the retrieval of subaltern consciousness as the charting of what in post-structuralist language would be called the subaltern subject-effect. A subject-effect can be briefly plotted as follows: that which seems to operate as subject may be part of an immense discontinuous network ('text' in the general sense) of strands that may be termed politics, ideology, economics, history, sexuality, language, and so on. (Each of these strands, if they are isolated, can also be seen as woven of many strands.) Different knottings and configurations of these strands, determined by heterogeneous determinations which are themselves dependent upon myriad circumstances, produce the effect of an operating subject" (*In Other Worlds,* 204).

In *Post-Colonial Critic,* Spivak describes the "social text" as "a network, a weave—you can put names on it—politico-psycho-sexual-socio, you name it. . . . The moment you name it, there's a network that's broader than that . . . we are effects within a much larger text/tissue/weave of which the ends are not accessible to us" (25).

10. Spivak, *In Other Worlds,* 243, 203.

11. Spivak, "Can the Subaltern Speak?," 280; Spivak, *In Other Worlds,* 209.

12. Spivak, "Subaltern Studies: Deconstructing Historiography," in *In Other Worlds.*

13. Foucault and Deleuze, "Intellectuals and Power"; compare with "Can the Subaltern Speak?," 272–75, and passim.

Spivak, "Can the Subaltern Speak?," 276; Spivak, *In Other Worlds,* 201. In "The Rani of Sirmur," Spivak refers to the intellectual's responsibility "to inspect soberly the absence of a text that can 'answer one back' after the planned epistemic violence of the imperial project" (131).

14. "For the 'true' subaltern group . . . there is no unrepresentable subaltern subject that can know and speak itself; the intellectual's solution is not to abstain from representation. The problem is that the subject's itinerary has not been traced so as to offer an object of seduction to the representing intellectual" (Spivak, "Can the Subaltern Speak?," 285).

15. Spivak, "Can the Subaltern Speak?," 287, 286 (quoting Macherey); Spivak, *Post-Colonial Critic,* 31.

16. Spivak comments approvingly on Mahasweta Devi's short story, "The Breast-Giver": "Jashoda's story is thus not that of the development of a feminine subjectivity, a female *Bildungsroman* . . . the development of character or the understanding of subjectivity as growth in consciousness is beside the point of this parable or of this representation of the subaltern. . . . To place the subaltern in a subject-position in her history is not necessarily to make her an individualist" (*In Other Worlds,* 257).

17. "There are no autonomous dialectical relations existing between the social strata. Their relations are determined, dominated, directed by external factors, whose exteriority, however, they cannot conceptualize. They do not correspond to their status" (*DA,* 288).

18. This phenomenon has been noted by other Caribbean writers; George Lamming, for instance, is referring to the anglophone West Indian communities when he trenchantly observes: "We have had to live with a large and self-delighted middle class, who have never understood their function" (*Pleasures of Exile,* 42).

19. In *L'intention poétique,* for instance, Glissant writes: "This people *is,* it does not speak (We who speak are not its voice)" (186); and "today, to bring them to the community, to those who have no voice and whose *voice we cannot be: for the reason that we are only a part of their voice*" (191).

20. Philippe-Alain Yerro's "La trace de Gani" offers an interesting analysis of

the impossibility of the maroon as mythical hero because his struggle and sacrifice cannot be sanctioned by the people. Richard Burton's *Le roman marron* also stresses the limited historical importance of the maroons in Martinique and Guadeloupe, and contrasts this with their inflated mythical status among the islands' intellectuals. He accuses Glissant of subscribing to this myth and of giving a distorted picture of the historical reality of Martinique by claiming an unambiguously positive value for the maroon (see especially Burton's second chapter, "Edouard Glissant et l'illusion marronne"); I disagree with this interpretation for reasons given in the text.

21. On the question of political leadership of agricultural workers, Edouard de Lépine, in the introduction to his analysis of one of their major strikes, argues that the main theoretical question posed by his account is precisely that of "the instigation and the autonomy of the mass movement in these kinds of conflict, which, from the Saint-Pierre uprising (1848) to Chalvet (1974) [a cane-cutters' strike resulting in two dead and five seriously injured], punctuate the history of this country" (*La crise de février,* 19). De Lépine criticizes previous historians for their determination to find, or failing that to invent, leaders of the movement, and he concludes that "one of the original characteristics of these movements in Martinique, up to now, has been their spontaneity and the more or less autonomous position of the masses vis-à-vis the established social and political institutions (including those of their own class)" (21).

Régis Antoine, *La littérature franco-antillaise,* 25–30.

22. "It would be the first day or the second maybe, and not what was it now a morning in July 1788, for who knows July and who knows 1788 for him for me it's the first day the first shout the sun and the first moon and the first century of the country" (*QS,* 85–86).

23. For a detailed discussion of narrative shifts in *Le quatrième siècle,* see Britton, "*Discours* and *histoire.*"

24. Chapter 8 of *Le quatrième siècle* uses a similar narrative technique, as does chapter 7 of *Malemort.*

25. Spivak, *Post-Colonial Critic,* 144. Glissant makes the same point, specifically concerning Martinique, in *Le discours antillais,* arguing that the people's struggles have always been "deprived of a dimension of collective consultation . . . the Martinican 'thinkers' have therefore always found themselves committed on external issues, but never as such on the issue of the history of Martinique. Martinican action has always been historically emptied of meaning" (*DA,* 288).

26. *QS,* 55–56, 109, 117–18, 137–38, 171, 196, 232–35 (references to insurrections).

27. One possible exception to these distanced references to revolts is a first-hand account of the fighting leading up to the abolition of slavery elicited by Stéfanise from one of her suitors (196–97). This is very vivid and "close-up," but it is clearly separate from the main narrative and written in a markedly different way. Spectacularly decontextualized and disordered, it ends: "Voilà c'est la vic-

toire et l'esclavage fini, je regarde Man-Amélie couchée sa robe remontée sur la tête et la tête à l'équerre déracinée sa main sur le fusil comme un boutou elle ne crie plus n'entend plus le vacarme le bruit tous dans la rue victoire elle entend tonnerre de dieu victoire pour tous ceux-là avec elle trépassée dans la rue victoire!" [There it's victory and the end of slavery, I look at Man-Amélie lying on the ground her dress pulled up over her head and her head at right angles uprooted her hand holding the gun like a stick she's not shouting any more can't hear any more the racket the noise everyone out on the street she hears hell and damnation victory for all of them with her dead in the street victory!]. Most significantly, perhaps, the idea that abolition was a glorious victory is discredited elsewhere in the novel (as in Glissant's other novels); this cannot therefore be taken as an authoritative narrative account.

28. Spivak, "Can the Subaltern Speak?," 287.

29. In *Malemort* Silacier decides not to vote for Mathieu's party: "But I'm voting for monsieur Lesprit, even though I have a bone to pick with him. The unlucky are dropping dead with hunger, one vote's not going to change that. . . . Listen, monsieur Mathieu, nothing changes, nothing changes" (96).

30. The character of Euloge in *La case du commandeur* is another significant example of the effects of lack of political representation, again in the context of abolition. Euloge is the first black overseer on the plantation, and he allies himself ideologically with his white masters. He is against abolition because, he says, the slaves do not deserve it; and after abolition he does everything he can to help the masters recruit labor for the plantations. But he is not *simply* against the idea of liberation for the slaves; they do not deserve it, he says, because they have not fought for it but have merely been given it from above (88). The narrative voice expresses a view that is not altogether dissimilar: that abolition is not true liberation, because those who claim to speak for the slaves' cause have in fact no connection with them and the slaves themselves have no political representation: the collective narrative voice speaks of "things that we could not even imagine, 'equal rights,' 'political representation,' phrases we rolled round our mouths just for a laugh, not knowing that we would soon be carried away by their incomprehensible mechanisms" (87). Euloge "rejected these charades"; and later, he is explicitly acknowledged to have been right: "We soon saw that all the fuss about liberation was a betrayal, as the overseer Euloge had predicted" (87, 126). Ultimately, it is difficult to tell whether Euloge rejects abolition because he approves of slavery or because he realizes the emptiness of the promises abolition makes. One could argue that this ambiguity is made possible by the lack of some form of political representation for the slaves that would clarify the situation.

31. Jean-Pol Madou makes a similar distinction between a "poetics of the instant and of ecstasy" whereby the maroons are represented and a far less spectacular "poetics of duration" associated with the slaves ("Poétique de 'Quimboiseur,' parole d'esclave," 288). He argues that Glissant rewrites the Hegelian master-slave dialectic "with the aim of delimiting that which remains strictly

speaking unthinkable within it, the words of the slave, the cry of his rebellion caught at the very root of his dumb silence" (289).

32. The man involved in the real event was called Beauregard; in *Le discours antillais,* Glissant refers briefly to "the story of Monsieur Beauregard, a plantation overseer who, as a result of a quarrel with a small-time planter, became a real maroon, like in the old days, and from 1942 to 1949 held out against the whole police force of the south of Martinique, with the support—spontaneous or coerced—of the population. When he was finally tracked down, quite by accident, he chose to kill himself rather than to surrender." The conclusion Glissant draws from this incident closely echoes his remarks elsewhere on the political significance of the maroon: "But cases like these represent the dramatization of a phenomenon (the maroons) that only left traces in the collective unconscious, and not determining influences on the popular way of life" (*DA,* 70). A more detailed account of the events is given in *Le cas Beauregard* by Hermann Perronnette, the doctor who performed the autopsy on Beauregard. From this, one major difference with Glissant's fictionalized version emerges: Beauregard shot his wife rather than the man he suspected of having slept with her. Also, he was not killed in the forest but, more prosaically, behind a house in a village.

33. Mireille Rosello describes Glissant's questioning of the status of the maroon-slave opposition, relates it to the question of heroism, and suggests that moving away from this model permits a more subtle analysis of particular political situations: "Glissant's novels do not merely rethink the old binary opposition between 'the rebel' and 'the good nigger' but they question the criteria that enable a historically situated subject to decide, in relation to his or her specific situation, what makes a particular model passive or resisting, revolutionary or conservative, effective or doomed to failure. The myths of the 'hero' or the 'heroine' are constantly challenged in the texts studied here" (*Littérature et identité,* 39).

34. Perronnette describes Beauregard in similar if rather more brutal terms: "I have information which . . . authorizes me to state that [Beauregard], the daring tough guy, the womanizer, the sorcerer feared and respected by the majority of the population, was at bottom just a poor devil who became victim of his own legend; he listened to the predictions and superstitions and ended up believing that he was a hero" (*Le cas Beauregard,* 13).

35. Glissant has incorporated into the novel, with some adaptation, the true story of Pierre Just Marny, which culminated in his murdering three people and wounding three others in 1965. Marlène Hospice's *Pas de pitié pour Marny: une affaire martiniquaise* gives further details of the sequence of events and its effect on the public. She makes an explicit and interesting comparison between Marny and Beauregard (149–52): the historical differences between the 1940s and the 1960s mean that "the social and mental images conveyed by the two periods in question . . . do not engage the same social issues" (149); also, Beauregard had a very specific established social position on the plantation, whereas Marny was a

semirural, semi-urban marginal. "It has been said of Beauregard that he was the last maroon in Martinique's history. With Marny it is already impossible to be a maroon (since the maroon is dependent on the plantation system)" (152).

36. Catherine Mayaux, "La structure romanesque," 356.

37. Ibid., 357.

38. Félicité Bienvenu says of Mani's murder by the soldiers: "So then the officials covered it up with emptiness, built up the silence. It was easy, with the Marny business just beginning" (*Mah*, 151).

39. For Fanon, the absence of the *r* is a crucial feature of the racial stereotype that, for the French, defines the Martinican as non-French: "For the Negro knows that over there in France, there is a stereotype of him that will fasten on to him at the pier in Le Havre or Marseille: 'Ah come fom Mahtinique, it's the fuhst time Ah've eveh come to Fance.'" His struggle to conquer the French language is summed up in his efforts to pronounce the *r:* "The Negro arriving in France will react against the myth of the R-eating man from Martinique. . . . He will practice not only rolling his R but embroidering it. Furtively observing the slightest reactions of others, listening to his own speech, suspicious of his own tongue—a wretchedly lazy organ—he will lock himself in his room and read aloud for hours—desperately determined to learn *diction*" (*Black Skin, White Masks*, 20, 21).

40. In the last part of "Subaltern Studies: Deconstructing Historiography," in *In Other Worlds*, Spivak discusses the gender-specific aspects of subalternity and insists on the need to analyze the particular functions assumed by subaltern women: "It seems clear to me that, if the question of female subaltern consciousness, whose instrumentality is so often seen to be crucial, is a red herring, the question of subaltern consciousness as such must be judged a red herring as well" (218).

41. In the preceding chapter, the text politicizes the white man's sexual possession of the black man's woman via a pun on *colon* [planter]: "Maho n'avait jamais vérifié si sa concubine avait oui ou non été colonisée" [Maho had never checked on whether his woman had been colonized or not] (88).

42. Spivak, *In Other Worlds*, 186. Spivak translates the relevant passage as follows: "Draupadi's black body comes even closer. Draupadi shakes with an indomitable laughter that Senanayak simply cannot understand. Her ravaged lips bleed as she beings [*sic*] laughing . . . Draupadi pushes Senanayak with her two mangled breasts, and for the first time Senanayak is afraid to stand before an unarmed target, terribly afraid" (196).

43. A similar process in relation to the whole novel is discussed in detail in chapter 7.

44. See, for instance, Lacan, "L'instance de la lettre," 493–528.

45. This ambiguity also undermines Maho's status as a male desiring subject; and as such it is echoed on a larger scale by the way in which, in the course of the chapter, he moves from being an autonomous desiring subject, with Adoline as

his object of desire, to being himself primarily the object of female desire and, indeed, of female and quasi-maternal protection, as the three women feed him and keep him alive. This can be seen as a further aspect of the "de-heroicization" of the maroon.

46. *Mon corps* is commonly used in Martinican Creole as a reflexive pronoun, e.g., "Je dis à mon corps" is the equivalent of "je me dis" [I say to myself].

4 The Other's Language

1. Raymond Chassagne gives as one of the three main characteristics of Glissant's work (along with that of Césaire and Fanon): "a refusal to keep quiet about the morbidity that is prominent in the psychotic Caribbean world and the guilt of the black man perpetuated through his internalization of the referential codes of the colonial settler" ("Seuils de rupture," 62).

2. "The collective unconscious is not dependent on cerebral heredity: it is the result of what I shall call the unreflected imposition of a culture" (Fanon, *Black Skin, White Masks,* 191). It should be added that Fanon's conception of the unconscious is not that of contemporary psychoanalysis, nor is it even, arguably, strictly Freudian. Jacques André has an interesting discussion of Fanon's ambiguous attitude to psychoanalysis in his "Fanon, entre le réel et l'inconscient." André claims that, rather than seeing the unconscious as the fundamental dynamic that structures all psychic experience, Fanon reduces it to being merely a kind of false consciousness—"A veil which must be lifted, a darkness which must be lightened, an illusion which must be exposed" (113)—which it is the analyst's role to correct by bringing the patient back into touch with social reality and in particular the reality of social struggle. André does not explicitly address the question of whether such a conception of the unconscious is the *only* one that can be integrated into a socioeconomic perspective, but work by a number of later theorists suggests that similar articulations with other, less reductive conceptions of the unconscious are also possible. See, for instance, Fredric Jameson's *The Political Unconscious* or the early work of Julia Kristeva.

3. Fanon, *Black Skin, White Masks,* 12–13, 10.

Fanon and Glissant both attended the Lycée Schœlcher in Fort-de-France, but Fanon was three years older and they did not meet until they were in Paris after the war. Fanon supported Glissant's Front Antillo-Guyanais and sent a telegram expressing his solidarity to its inaugural conference in 1961, the year of his death. Glissant has described their relationship in two interviews, in special numbers of *Sans frontières* (Paris) (Feb. 1982, 38–39) and *Antilla* (Martinique) (Nov.–Dec. 1991, 38–40), commemorating respectively the twentieth and thirtieth anniversaries of Fanon's death. In the latter he praises Fanon's struggle against the mimetic drive, saying: "I think that the whole of Fanon's endeavor was directed at that: to define a new sense of humanity for the countries of the South . . . a humanity that can really think about itself and its problems in its own terms" (40).

Le discours antillais contains a brief discussion of Fanon's difficult relationship with Martinique and his dedicating himself to the Algerian cause, defining it as another example of the detour. Fanon is largely ignored in his home country, Glissant argues, because "it is difficult for a French Caribbean individual to be the brother, the friend, or quite simply the associate or fellow countryman of Fanon. Because, of all the French Caribbean intellectuals, he is the only one to have *acted on his ideas,* through his involvement in the Algerian struggle; this was so even if, after tragic and conclusive episodes of what one can rightly call his Algerian agony, the Martinican problem (for which, in the circumstances, he was not responsible, but which he would no doubt have confronted if he had lived) retains its complete ambiguity" (*CD,* 25).

4. Fanon, *Wretched of the Earth,* 31–32 (the published translation regularly translates *colon* as settler and *colonisé* as native, which is not entirely appropriate for the Caribbean situation); Fanon, *Black Skin, White Masks,* 228.

5. "Every colonized people—in other words, every people in [whom] an inferiority complex has been created by the death and burial of its local cultural originality—[places itself in relation to] the language of the civilizing nation, that is, the culture of the mother country" (Fanon, *Black Skin, White Masks,* 18).

6. Fanon, *Black Skin, White Masks,* 44, 163, 149.

It is important to note that Fanon stresses the reciprocity of black and white identifications and fantasies, which he describes as a "dual narcissism" because: "The white man is sealed in his whiteness. The black man in his blackness." Both are therefore equally and similarly alienated: "I am speaking here, on the one hand, of alienated ([deluded]) blacks, and, on the other, of no less alienated ([deluding and deluded]) whites" (*Black Skin, White Masks,* 12, 11, 29).

7. Fanon, *Black Skin, White Masks,* 58, 212–13.

8. Bhabha, *Location of Culture,* 44, 45, 74.

9. Fanon, *Black Skin, White Masks,* 21, 23, 191, 194.

10. Fanon, *Wretched of the Earth,* 41; Bhabha, *Location of Culture,* 44.

11. Fanon, *Black Skin, White Masks,* 114–15, 81, 216, 51, 154, 82 (emphasis added).

12. Ibid., 17, 38.

13. Fanon, *Peau noire masques blancs,* 26, 27, 30, 102. For the above examples, I refer to the original French text and give my own translations of the extracts I quote, since the published ones are not accurate enough. Page references are therefore to the French original. The equivalent passages in the Markmann translation are 31–38, 124.

14. Fanon, *Black Skin, White Masks,* 35, 36.

15. Conversely, however, Glissant concurs with Fanon's view that this kind of psychiatric disorder cannot be cured simply by treating the individual, as when Fanon refers to "the difficulties that arise when seeking to 'cure' a native properly, that is to say, when seeking to make him thoroughly a part of a social background of the colonial type" (*Wretched of the Earth,* 200). Daniel Maximin,

commenting on the impact of Fanon's work in Martinique, picks up the same point: "Fanon realizes . . . that madness is sometimes a sign of rebellion against the rationalizations of cultural repression. . . . Therefore, in colonial societies it is indeed those who are assimilated and not those who refuse to be assimilated that are truly sick" ("Fanon et la folie," 138).

16. The section on verbal delirium in *Le discours antillais* has not received much critical attention, although Raymond Chassagne links it explicitly to *Black Skin, White Masks* and makes interesting comments on it ("Seuils de rupture"). See also Michael Dash's summary in *Edouard Glissant*, 115–16.

17. Hector Elisabeth's article in *Acoma* cites examples of these social-scientific studies of verbal delirium. His own approach owes more to Glissant's analysis than to that of conventional psychiatrists and sociologists. Like Glissant he stresses the collective nature and the sociohistorical determinants of delirium, but he explains them rather more simplistically in terms of overcrowding and the traditional influence of groups, such as the family, on the individual. He also points out that the predominantly *verbal* nature of psychiatric disorders in Martinique can be related to the strongly oral tradition of the island (Elisabeth, "Essai d'enquête," 72, 73).

18. Chassagne usefully glosses the socially functional quality of routine verbal delirium: "This delirium is above all one of persuasion in the sense that Barthes gave to it; it is a vehicle for references and values that stabilize a given social order and that are perpetuated by the Caribbean individual at odds with himself; a delirium of representation, which replaces an uncontrollable reality with a discourse on that reality (often the outdated but functional discourse of the colonial settler). Thus in Martinique people talk a lot about Schœlcher, but slavery is a taboo subject. An artificial discourse of persuasion, a discourse of representation, hence a discourse of dramatization: one does not act effectively on reality, one plays a role, while talking about it; or if one does not speak, the discourse turns into gratuitous violence; and one turns on, without much of an overall plan or any real articulation, that 'tap of blood' that Roger Gaillard talks about" ("Seuils de rupture," 64).

19. "There will be a de-propriating function which aims to confirm, in an obsessive and reassuring fashion . . . the general ideological alienation; a reappropriating function, when the collectivity needs to externalize, in an unresolved way, the contradictions it experiences (the dim sense of unrealizable possibilities). In the first case, for instance, someone will state—violently or pathetically—that he is French; in the second case, someone will elaborate a 'contradictory' *langage* which will move towards being, in its turn, a response to the contradictions thus experienced" (*DA*, 368).

20. Dash, *Edouard Glissant*, 116. Dash's ensuing discussion of *Malemort* provides an illuminating account of its representation of social alienation and verbal delirium (116–25).

21. The orthodox, and influential, communist formulation in the 1950s and

1960s defined the problem of alienation simply in terms of the quest for authenticity. René Ménil, for instance, in "De l'exotisme colonial," originally published in *La Nouvelle Critique* (1959), contrasts the alienated writers who see their own society through the eyes of the colonizer with the "continuous effort towards the most authentic possible expression of the Caribbean man. . . . The struggle against exoticism is the obverse side of the struggle to make the truth and richness of the colonial consciousness prevail" (*Tracées*, 21–22). More recently, the notion of "interior vision," developed in 1989 by the authors of *Éloge de la créolité* (Patrick Chamoiseau, Jean Bernabé, and Raphaël Confiant), retains a similar dependence on notions of "original" authenticity, naturalness, and complete separation from what is "external": "Creating the conditions of authentic expression presupposes that we have exorcised the old inevitability of exteriority. . . . We had to wash our eyes clean: and turn upside down the vision we had of our reality in order to discover what was true in it. A new way of looking which would move what is natural to us [*notre naturel*] from its secondary or peripheral position and put it back at the center of ourselves. . . . It is in that sense that the interior vision is revelatory, and hence revolutionary" (23–24).

22. Bernadette Cailler refers in a similar sense to "discourses assimilated, used, but in part boycotted" (*Conquérants de la nuit nue*, 158).

23. Bhabha, *Location of Culture*, 86, 89. Toumson formulates the relation between European and colonial literature in terms that are strikingly similar to the ambivalence of mimicry: "If the subject's discourse bears, logically, the mark of the dominant discourse, it is also necessarily 'démarqué' [differentiated] from it. Let us interpret the verb in this precise sense: to 'démarquer' [plagiarize] a literary work is to copy it, altering the details in such a way as to mask the borrowing. From this 'démarquage' there results both a similarity and a difference, a proximity but also a distancing" (*La transgression des couleurs*, 1:113).

Extreme examples of mimicry that threatens the authority of its original in the postcolonial world are African dictators like Bokassa and Amin Dada. Thus, Glissant writes "it was the English army that *trained* Amin Dada. . . . So Amin Dada represented an absolute degree of farcical horror, but will he not also always be the rebounding image of the West's action, a reflection which destroys it by caricaturing it?" (*DA*, 196).

24. Bakhtin, *Dialogic Imagination*, 416.

25. Fanon, *Black Skin, White Masks*, 98.

26. A similar ambivalence can be seen in the way in which Lesprit uses an allusion to Racine's *Andromaque*—an apparently clear sign of identification with European culture—to frame the most explicit statement of his hostility towards whites: "Oreste loves Hermione who loves Pyrrhus who loves Andromaque. The nigger hates the mulatto who detests the white settler who abominates the French white man" (*Mal*, 85). Beneath the formal parallel of the two sentences, the reversal of the values from love to hate is in itself another way of fissuring the identification.

27. Bhabha, *Location of Culture*, 86.

28. Ibid., 88, 89, 86.

29. Ibid., 88.

30. Compare Fanon's comment that the educated French Caribbean delights in "a quest for subtleties, for refinements of language—so many further means of proving to himself that he has measured up to the culture" (*Black Skins, White Masks*, 38–39).

31. As Derrida remarks of his school days in Algeria, the model of metropolitan French as the *langue du maître* [language of the master] was transmitted through and incarnated in the nonmetropolitan schoolmasters: "The master was in the first place, and especially, the school master. The latter was thus able to worthily represent, through the universal features of the Republic, the master in general" (*Le monolinguisme de l'autre*, 73).

32. Fanon, *Black Skin, White Masks*, 153, 109–15.

33. Usually with an affectionately parodic accent: "nous osions croire par exemple qu'il [Québec] était au plein d'un ébat amoureux—comme il eût dit lui-même—avec une jeunesse consentante—mon cher une bonne de vrai à tout faire—et que cette geignarde criait aïe doudou aïe chéri—il arrêta net pour la morigéner—holà maraude, *monsieur* doudou s'il vous plaît, *monsieur* chéri—après quoi il *reprit commerce* avec la créature" [for example we ventured to believe that when he was in the midst of an amorous frolic—as he would have put it—with a compliant young woman—a real maid-of-all-work my dear boy—and she started moaning and shrieking ooh sweetie ooh honey—he stopped dead to reprimand her—Now wait a minute, *mister* sweetie if you don't mind, *mister* honey—after which he *resumed business* with the creature] (164).

34. Jean-Yves Debreuille makes a more general but similar point when he argues that "the meaning of the loss of language . . . is reevaluated, seen not so much as a long-drawn out catastrophe as a condition which allows a new, unknown, future language to mature. What the novel consists in is an 'outlined absence', the collage of 'caricatures of speech', whether those of the colonizer or those of the colonized. . . . But beneath this unfixed language another deeper language is trying to come out, a language which does not yet have words, which emerges in the cracks of their disorder" ("Le Langage désancré de *Malemort*," 327).

35. This same conflictual but intimate relationship is seen—somewhat controversially—by Toumson as the dynamic governing the production of all Afro-Caribbean *literature*. In an article on Césaire and Glissant, he writes: "In fact we propose to show that one can legitimately detect, within the dominated Afro-Caribbean discourse, a repeat of this dominant discourse. . . . Exposing the lies or the silences of the dominant discourse, the Afro-Caribbean writer struggles to effect an ideological transformation of the text of this discourse, tries to rewrite it" ("Les Écrivains afro-antillais," 116).

36. These are brand names of French underwear and children's clothes; the equivalents would be something like Calvin Klein and Babygap.

37. Chassagne describes Médellus as "the speaker who is ill from speaking, lost through speaking, and in whom the word has long been cut off from any incarnation; his daily life is merely an antiquated discursive jousting" ("Seuils de rupture," 66).

38. The buildings on Médellus's land are almost certainly inspired by Suffrin's house, which Glissant filmed in 1972, and which he describes as follows: "It was buried in a tangle of vegetation and fantastical objects, made of old pieces of wood or cut out of metal, erected like totems. On the other side of the road a piece of cleared ground supported a few worn planks, standing out tragically against the background of the sky: this was the Temple of universal brotherhood, which could be entered from all sides, and whose derisory skeleton was somehow heartrending. Today these ghostly planks, and the water pipe that represented the baptismal font, and the shack that was the headquarters of the United Nations, have been swept away by the bulldozers" (*DA*, 388).

The impossibility of "exterritoriality" can itself be seen as a determinant of Médellus's delirious speech, which, Dominique Aurélia suggests, performs the function of a kind of internalized exile: "exile, in Glissant's writing, often resides in delirium. The characters escape through their heads, so to speak, because the island imprisons them in its vice-like grip" ("La parole de l'eau," 46).

39. The fact that Lesprit says Beautemps was killed nine years later enables us to place Nainfol's murder in 1934—two years before Beautemps went on the run from the police.

40. Bhabha, *Location of Culture*, 44.

41. Sartre, Preface to Fanon, *Wretched of the Earth*, 13.

42. Fanon, *Wretched of the Earth*, 40. In the section of *Le discours antillais* entitled "Violence without Cause" (*DA*, 311), Glissant notes how Fanon's analysis of this process of self-destructive displacement is confirmed by numerous incidents in Martinican experience.

43. Fanon, *Wretched of the Earth*, 68, 73.

5 Delirious Language

1. Bhabha, *Location of Culture*, 9, 18, 12. De Certeau's "tactic" is discussed in chapter 1.

2. Bhabha's literary examples of unhomely individuals are Isabel Archer in *The Portrait of a Lady*, Bimala in Tagore's *The Home and the World*, Aila in Nadine Gordimer's *My Son's Story*, and the women in Toni Morrison's *Beloved*. He writes "but the 'unhomely' does provide a 'non-continuist' problematic that dramatizes—in the figure of woman—the ambivalent structure of the civil State as it draws its rather paradoxical boundary between the private and the public spheres" (Bhabha, *Location of Culture*, 10).

3. Freud, "The 'Uncanny,'" 225; Bhabha, *Location of Culture,* 10, 13.

4. Freud, "The 'Uncanny,'" 241.

5. Ibid., 220.

Bhabha's move from individual to collective history is a clear parallel to his treatment of Freud's analysis of fetishism, which, by transferring the structure from sexual to racial difference, he also extends from the personal to the social dimension. See chapter 1.

Bhabha, *Location of Culture,* 12, 13.

6. Freud, "The 'Uncanny,'" 226, 241, 220 (emphasis added), 245.

7. Dash points out that "both works [*Le discours antillais* and *La case du commandeur*], which are necessarily related to each other, are marked by the research into and diagnosis of Martiniquan reality that were done at the IME [Institut Martiniquais d'Études] before Glissant left for Paris as editor of the UNESCO Courrier in 1980" (*Edouard Glissant,* 126).

"Entretien avec le *CARÉ,*" 24.

8. As in Glissant's analysis of dramatizing delirium, Pythagore fulfills the social role of the individual who acts out the group's confusion. The other drinkers do not fully understand what he is saying, but they are fascinated by his questions, and they enter into "those ceremonies that we liked so much" (27–28). They sense that "Pythagore could not see what had engendered the primordial cataclysm from which we had come, or even if there had been one, and that he was only sharing with us an ignorance and a desire whose mark—we didn't know why—he had been selected to bear" (29).

9. As Maurice Roche describes Marie Celat in a review of *La case du commandeur,* "she suffers from history"; she is "not its spokesperson but the bearer of its pain" [*sans en être le porte-parole mais le porte-douleur*] (*Matin de Paris,* 26).

Freud, "The 'Uncanny,'" 226.

10. Jacques André, for instance, writes: "'Mi Celat' (here is Celat): named between the this and the that, the here and the there [*le ceci et le cela, le voici et le voilà*], in the hollow of the deictics, as far away as possible from the *proper* name. Her name invokes the empty forms of language, her character bathes in night, shadow and silence: everything in her borders on insanity" ("Un Tracé de silence," 429).

11. Bhabha, *Location of Culture,* 15.

12. Bhabha is referring here to Fanon's "On National Culture," in *Wretched of the Earth.*

13. Bhabha, *Location of Culture,* 9.

14. "If psycho-analytic theory is correct in maintaining that every affect belonging to an emotional impulse, whatever its kind, is transformed, if it is repressed, into anxiety, then among instances of frightening things there must be one class in which the frightening element can be shown to be something repressed which *recurs.* This class of frightening things would then constitute the uncanny" (Freud, "The 'Uncanny,'" 241); Bhabha, *Location of Culture,* 9.

15. Bhabha, *Location of Culture*, 9.

16. For instance, Chérubin refers to Mycéa and himself as "non-nous-en-core" [not-yet-we/us], thus naming her own sense of absence and alienation, but implying that it will not last for ever. He fantasizes about the social security office turning into a firing squad: "non-nous-encore dévalons la mort fusillés . . . dans la file devant les bureaux" [not-yet-we tumble down death shot . . . in the lineup in front of the offices]; just at this point, however, "non-nous-encore" miraculously become "non-nous-encore-mais-déjà" and get up unharmed: "but look it's not-yet-us-but-already rising up from the filthy ground at the entrance to the offices do you understand what Chérubin is saying" (195). Later he tells her: "vous êtes une femme adoressante" [you are an adorescent woman], an adjective that for her synthesizes "dorée, adorée, adolescente, caressante" [golden, adored, adolescent, caressing] (199).

17. Barbara Webb, for instance, argues persuasively that "in order to regain her sanity, Mycéa must uncover the repressed knowledge of this past . . . that manifests itself as dislocated, fragmented psyche"; the overseer's hut is the "site of recovery, the place where Mycéa goes back over the path of time" (*Myth and History*, 122). Moreover, this is coextensive with the whole of the preceding narrative: "the recapitulation of the past that takes place in the overseer's hut is the text we read and the story we must reconstruct in much the same way that Mycéa does as she plunges into the vertigo of memory" (ibid., 123).

18. For a more detailed discussion of Euloge's character, see chapter 3, note 30. Dash provides a good description of Euloge's reactionary, selfish nature (*Edouard Glissant*, 133) and emphasizes the ambivalence of his position in the novel, while giving it a slightly different interpretation from the one I propose: "the gravitational centre of the work is the realm of moral ambiguity, the inadmissible horror that the community wishes to shut out. In no other work by Glissant has the question of moral paradox been so clearly the centre of focus . . . for Mycéa and by extension for post-abolition Martinique, the overseer's cabin is a zone of inauspicious beginnings" (ibid., 132–33).

Bhabha, *Location of Culture*, 13.

19. Freud, "The 'Uncanny,'" 225.

20. Bhabha, *Location of Culture*, 12.

It is worth noting here that Freud cites *magic* as one category of the uncanny and one type of recall of the past. It is, he argues, by returning us to a primitive state of animistic belief that magic produces its uncanny effect: "It seems as if each one of us has been through a phase of individual development corresponding to this animistic stage in primitive men, that none of us has passed through it without preserving certain residues and traces of it which are still capable of manifesting themselves, and that everything which now strikes us as 'uncanny' fulfils the condition of touching those residues of animistic mental activity within us and bringing them to expression" ("The 'Uncanny,'" 240–41).

21. Just as the rhizome (couch-grass is one major example) is multiple, de-

centered, and lacking a rigid unitary structure, so the tree stands for hierarchy, centralized organization, and order—all of which Deleuze and Guattari reject in *Mille plateaux:* "We are tired of the tree. We must no longer believe in trees, in roots or rootlets, they have done us too much harm" (24). They also argue that the human mind functions, on a neurological level but also in the productivity of its unconscious, like grass rather than like trees: "Many people have a tree planted in their heads, but the brain itself is a grass much more than a tree" (24)—a formulation that has a curious resonance with Marie Celat's discourse.

Dash, *Edouard Glissant,* 170.

22. For example: "Je veux accoucher des mots dans ma gorge, que vous n'avez pas un seul entendu! Vous ne voyez pas que vous devenez transparents plus que la chair de corossol quand vous l'avez battue? Je veux crier des mots dans vos désordres, que vous écoutez sans comprendre, et vous serez aveuglés" [I want to give birth to words in my throat that not one of you has heard! Can't you see that you are turning transparent, more transparent than the flesh of the soursop when you have pounded it? I want to shout words into your confusions, that you hear but don't understand, and they will make you blind"] (*TM,* 358). The stagy quality is enhanced by presenting the dialogue as though in a play, with the characters' actions given in italics, like stage directions. Their private and intimate conversation is turned into a dramatic scene played out in a theater; the narrator tells us that "we were well aware that they were conferring in a language unknown to us, and that our very discretion put them on stage, in this theater" (347).

23. "You handle a rock, it doesn't resist. You pluck a rock, it's like torch ginger, it doesn't break" (*TM,* 369).

6 Camouflaged Language

1. For example, the riddles that Silacier asks Dlan in *Malemort* (185–86)— "Who will cross the sea?"—are on one level an amusing game but are also a way of expressing indirectly the ambivalence felt toward immigration to France. The question "and to find what?" is first of all followed by very positive evocations of France as the mother country to which they truly belong: "To find the country your country. To meet people who are more than brothers to you. To kiss the mother clay." But this list then continues with items that are to be found *not* in France but in Martinique (in other words, in their real homeland): "For pacala yam. For bread-fruit and chili. For green mango chutney and fraternity"—and then, as if realizing the mistake, the riddle continues: "But it's to go to France"— and gives a different list of reasons for going to France, which closes the whole series and, without any explicit comment, reveals the disillusionment and fear associated with emigration: "C'est pour voter pour untel. C'est pour blanchir dans là-bas. C'est pour manger salsifis. C'est pour mourir pas à pas. C'est pour orner le trépas" [It's to vote for someone or other. It's to turn white over there. It's to eat salsify. It's to die step by step. It's to decorate death] (186).

2. "Just as it stopped being a secret code [*langage du pacte secret*] without managing to become the norm and develop as an 'open' [*langue*], the Creole language slowly stops using the [detour] of imagery through which it actively functioned in the world of the plantations, without managing to evolve a more conceptual structure. That reveals a condition of stagnation that makes Creole into a profoundly threatened language" (*CD*, 127).

3. Léon-François Hoffmann illustrates "exclamatory onomatopoeia, so important in creole" with the following quotation from Francis Joachim Roy's novel *Les chiens:* "a whole range of 'Hem!', of 'Han!', of 'Ayayaye!', of grimaces, little whistles, grunts and head-shakings whereby Haitians since the far-off days of official slavery have been in the habit of communicating the most subtle nuances of their thought to one another" (Hoffmann, *Haiti*, 178–79).

Regarding the difficulty of "translating" Creole speech into written text, Glissant states "but so many different syntheses are possible, between oral and written, between deliberately constructed counterpoetics and collective songs, that we can only go on treading these roundabout paths between them" ("Entretien avec le *CARÉ*," 10, 24).

Suzanne Crosta discusses in detail the introduction of oral techniques into Glissant's literary style. See her second chapter, entitled "Une Parole détournée: l'enjeu du corps et le recours à l'oralité," in *Le marronnage créateur*.

4. The situation in *Le quatrième siècle* is more ambiguous, as I have discussed in "*Discours* and *histoire*, magical and political discourse in Edouard Glissant's *Le quatrième siècle*." See also chapter 3 of this book.

5. In his detailed analysis of *Mahagony,* Roger Ebion argues that, in common with many other Martinican novels of the 1980s, *Mahagony* is written in a "third language" that is neither standard French nor Creole but a mixture of both. The lexical items, in particular, cannot be categorized as belonging either to standard Creole or to standard French but "are a result of the contact between the two languages" ("*Mahagony,* quelle langue?," 126).

6. Glissant, "Conférence inaugurale," 8; Laroche, *Double scène de la représentation,* 45.

7. "Linguists have noticed that traditional Creole syntax spontaneously imitates the speech of the child (the use of repetition, for example, *pretty pretty baby* [*bel bel iche*] for *very pretty child*). Taken to this extreme, the systematic use of childish speech is not naive" (*CD*, 20).

8. See Gates, *Signifying Monkey,* 49, 77.

9. Ibid., 85.

10. Glissant's novels illustrate various kinds of linguistic mastery, not all of them comic. The prestige of the magic speech of the *quimboiseur,* for instance, is entirely different. Here the camouflage takes on a gnomic quality that impresses, rather then amuses, its audience—as in the imagery used by Papa Longoué, for example. Perhaps the most extreme case of this kind of magic camouflage is the series of parables and prophecies told by Gani, the nineteenth-century "pro-

phetic child" [*enfant prédestiné*] of *Mahagony,* which, as far as I can see, remain completely opaque to the reader, although not to the other characters. Finally, halfway between this very solemn, arcane discourse and the ludic exuberance of the comic examples above, there is of course the quasi-professional mastery of the traditional storyteller.

11. Creole, for Glissant, lacks precisely this capacity for self-conscious reflection on its own activities: "Creole has not been able so far to reflect on itself . . . in the host of proverbs and sayings that it communicates, at least in Martinique, there is none to provide the sort of turning of language on itself, that critical or mocking attitude to its glossary or syntax that causes a [*langue,* literally by reflection, to constitute itself as a *langage*]" (*CD,* 166).

Gates, *Signifying Monkey,* 52, 46, 66, 50.

12. Gates, *Signifying Monkey,* 14–22, 5, 6.

13. Ibid., 4. On signifyin(g) as a practice inherited from the African past, Gates writes for instance that "these variations on Esu-Elegbara speak eloquently of an unbroken arc of metaphysical presupposition and a pattern of figuration shared through time and space among certain black cultures in West Africa, South America, the Caribbean, and the United States" (ibid., 6).

14. Ibid., 75–76, 77.

15. Mitchell-Kernan, "Signifying as a form of verbal art," 325 (quoted in Gates, *Signifying Monkey,* 85–86).

One of the statements in the *CARÉ* interview with Glissant reinforces this view of a use of language that relies on intuition for its comprehension: the interviewer says of *La case du commandeur* that "the sentences are driven by a sort of rapid pulsating movement which shatters any notion of *reference* in favor of *intuition,* dream, or soliloquy" ("Entretien avec le *CARÉ,*" 10, 24, emphasis added).

16. This conception of meaning calls to mind Lacan's well-known formulation that "it is in the chain of the signifier that the meaning 'insists' but . . . none of its elements 'consists' in the signification of which it is at the moment capable" ("L'instance de la lettre," 153). This accords with Gates's claim that signifyin(g) is closer to the signifying chain of the Lacanian unconscious (see *Signifying Monkey,* 50).

17. The question of how the reader relates to Glissant's opacity has been the subject of much discussion in the critical literature on Glissant's fiction. See, for example, Albert, Cailler (*Conquérants de la nuit nue*), Crosta, Debreuille, and Radford.

Reed Way Dasenbrock makes a relevant distinction between intelligibility and meaningfulness, arguing that the "intelligible and meaningful are not completely overlapping, synonymous terms. Indeed, the meaningfulness of multicultural works is in a large measure a function of their unintelligibility for part of their audience. Multicultural literature offers us above all an experience of multiculturalism, in which not everything is likely to be understood by every reader" ("Intelligibility and meaningfulness," 12, quoted in *Empire Writes Back,* 220.) In a sense we therefore replicate as readers William Faulkner's experience as a writer—as interpreted by Glissant—when the blind spots left in his texts serve to indicate and validate the opacity of the black Other's consciousness (see chapter 1).

18. Thus, Maya Deren refers to "the waters of the abyss, the source of all life. Here is *Guinée*, Africa, the legendary place of racial origin. Here, on the Island below the Sea, the loa have their permanent residence, their primal location. To it the souls of the dead return" (*Voodoo Gods*, 42).

19. There may also be an association here with the "cosmic mirror" of voodoo, in which the soul is figured as a mirror image of the physical body; see Deren, *Voodoo Gods*, 40–42.

7 Relayed Language

1. Bakhtin develops the conception of the monologic text in *Problems of Dostoevsky's Poetics,* where he contrasts Dostoevsky's polyphonic or "dialogic" novel with the more classical type of fiction in which everything is seen from a single controlling authorial point of view. Thus, the monologic novel consists of "a multitude of characters and fates in a single objective world, illuminated by a single authorial consciousness" (9); the author has the status of "a single consciousness, absorbing other consciousnesses as objects into itself" (18); he refers also to "the unified, monologic world of the author's consciousness" (43).

2. "Subaltern Studies: Deconstructing Historiography" includes a brief section on "rumor" as a mode of communication in subaltern insurgency (Spivak, *In Other Worlds*, 211–15).

3. I have given a more detailed analysis of the progression in narrative techniques from *Malemort* through *La case du commandeur* to *Mahagony* in "Collective Narrative Voice in Three Novels by Edouard Glissant."

4. Bhabha, *Location of Culture*, 157.

5. We have seen a slightly different version of this in the relationships between Adélaïde, Adoline, and Artémise discussed in chapter 3. Another example is Eudoxie, who comments: "Toutes femmes c'est femme" [All women is woman] (*Mah*, 44), seeing herself as inseparable from other women, while at the same time experiencing her own identity as multiply split over time: "All the Eudoxies collected in my head, to give birth to knowledge. Lamented Eudoxie searching around for a smell that came off the boat with her, nobody understands the words she speaks; Eudoxie new-born in a new country . . . Eudoxie lost between the Plantation and the town . . . Eudoxie landed up in the rue Cases-Nègres, moving in with Hégésippe" (47). Therefore, when she says "the procession of women knows. Ever since the boat of the great voyage the procession of women knows" (49), it is impossible to tell whether she is in fact referring to herself alone or to the community of women slaves.

6. This discussion is based on two poems, by the Bengali Adil Jussawalla and the African-American woman M. Jin, both of which turn on the notion of the invisible or missing person. Bhabha continues, in terms equally relevant to Anasta-

sie and the position of the "author": "This change is precipitated by the peculiar temporality whereby the subject cannot be apprehended without the absence of invisibility that constitutes it—'as even now you look/but never see me'—so that the subject speaks, and is seen, from where it is *not*; and the migrant woman can subvert the perverse satisfaction of the racist, masculinist gaze that disavowed her presence, by presenting it with an anxious absence, a counter-gaze that turns the discriminatory look, which denies her cultural and sexual difference, back on itself" (*Location of Culture*, 46–47).

7. Spivak, "Can the Subaltern Speak?," 287, 286.

8. "Everyone who expressly links the problem of language to the problem of identity is in my view making a mistake, because what characterizes our time is precisely what I call the imaginary reality of languages [*l'imaginaire des langues*], that is, being in the presence of all the languages of the world" (*IPD*, 112).

9. *Tout-monde* similarly emphasizes the importance of a strategic use of language(s), of not being limited to one kind of discourse or style: "the question of the languages we use, of the way in which we use them, of the freedom we exercise in putting them into relation with other languages . . . the question of what you say is style, which is not only the man or the woman but their surroundings, their landscape and their history" (267).

10. See Spivak, *In Other Worlds*, 197–221.

11. "At the crossing of the winds, the sound of voices accompanies the written signs, arranged in a pathetic procession on the husks of plants or on the parchment; the drawing wins again. But what speaks is the unending echo of these voices. All the man of writing can do will be to consent unreservedly to the intention so often expressed by the man of speech" (*Mah*, 176–77).

12. "One would further begin to suspect that the most authoritative and potentially exploitative manifestations of writing in the narrow sense—the codes of law—operate on an implicit phonocentrism, the presupposition that speech is the immediate expression of the self. I would submit that it is more appropriate to think of the power of rumor in the subaltern context as deriving from its participation in the structure of illegitimate writing rather than the authoritative writing of the law" (*In Other Worlds*, 213).

Spivak, *In Other Worlds*, 213–14.

13. Dash stresses the mahogany's lack of stasis: "It is not the tree's tenacious solitude that provides a stable gravitational centre for Glissant's vision of time and space. Rather it releases a set of tensions, continuities and mutations that are part of a future-directed, outward-growing process. As a result this tree does not embody authentic origin or identity but is part of a series of trajectories that ultimately undermine or at least modify its supremacy and pre-eminence" (*Edouard Glissant*, 166).

Mathieu's ambiguous "sliding" between first- and third-person pronouns, analyzed above, is an example of the circulating subject. The *trame* is very close to an idea that Maurice Merleau-Ponty began to develop, in a rather cryptic note, in connection with two different novelists, Claude Simon and Michel Butor: "We no longer read I or he. Intermediate pronouns are born, a first-second person . . . this can absolutely not be understood either in classic conception of the I think or in conception of selfness as nothingness: as then I myself hold the circle of selfness, I trace it out—these uses of language can only be understood if language is a being, a world, if it's the Word that is the circle" ("Cinq notes sur Claude Simon," 6).

Bibliography

Albert, Christiane. "Temps, histoire et récit dans *La case du commandeur*." In *Horizons d'Edouard Glissant,* ed. Yves-Alain Favre, 329–40. Pau, France: J & D Éditions, 1992.

Althusser, Louis. "Idéologie et appareils idéologiques d'Etat." Trans. Ben Brewster, in *Lenin and Philosophy and Other Essays.* London: New Left Books, 1971.

André, Jacques. *Caraïbales.* Paris: Éditions Caribbéennes, 1981.

———. "Le renversement de Senglis: Histoire et filiation." *CARÉ,* no. 10 (1983): 32–51.

———. "Un tracé de silence." Review of *La case du commandeur,* by Edouard Glissant. *Présence africaine,* 121, 122 (1982): 428–29.

———. "Fanon, entre le réel et l'inconscient." In *Mémorial international Frantz Fanon,* ed. Comité Frantz Fanon de Fort-de-France, 108–26. Paris: Présence africaine, 1984.

Antoine, Régis. *La littérature franco-antillaise: Haïti, Guadeloupe et Martinique.* Paris: Karthala, 1992.

Ashcroft, Bill, Gareth Griffiths, and Helen Tiffin. *The Empire Writes Back: Theory and Practice in Post-Colonial Literatures.* New York: Routledge, 1989.

———, eds. *The Post-Colonial Studies Reader.* New York: Routledge, 1995.

Aurélia, Dominique. "La parole de l'eau." *Carbet* 10 (1990): 43–50.

Bakhtin, Mikhail. *The Dialogic Imagination.* Trans. and ed. Michael Holquist. Austin: Univ. of Texas Press, 1981.

———. *Problems of Dostoevsky's Poetics.* Trans. and ed. Caryl Emerson. Minneapolis: Univ. of Minnesota Press, 1984.

Benítez-Rojo, Antonio. *The Repeating Island: The Caribbean and the Postmodern Perspective.* Durham: Duke Univ. Press, 1996.

Bhabha, Homi K. *The Location of Culture.* New York: Routledge, 1994.

———. "The Other Question: Difference, Discrimination and the Discourse of Theory." In *Literature, Politics and Theory,* ed. Francis Barker et al., 148–72. New York: Methuen, 1986.

Brathwaite, Edward Kamau. *History of the Voice: The Development of Nation Language in Anglophone Caribbean Poetry*. London: New Beacon, 1984.

Britton, Celia. "'A Certain Linguistic Homelessness': Relations to Language in Edouard Glissant's *Malemort*." *Modern Language Review* 91, no. 3 (1996): 597–609.

———. "Collective Narrative Voice in Three Novels by Edouard Glissant." In *Caribbean Francophone Writing: An Introduction,* ed. Samantha Haigh. New York: Berg, forthcoming.

———. "*Discours* and *histoire*, Magical and Political Discourse in Edouard Glissant's *Le quatrième siècle*." *French Cultural Studies* 5 (1994): 151–62.

Burton, Richard. *Le roman marron: Études sur la littérature martiniquaise contemporaine*. Paris: L'Harmattan, 1997.

———. "Le thème du regard dans la littérature antillaise." *Présence francophone*, no. 34 (1989): 105–21.

Cailler, Bernadette. *Conquérants de la nuit nue: Edouard Glissant et l'H(h)istoire antillaise*. Tübingen: Gunter Narr Verlag, 1988.

———. "Edouard Glissant: A Creative Critic." *World Literature Today* 63, no. 4 (1989): 589–92.

Césaire, Aimé. "Et les chiens se taisaient." In *Les armes miraculeuses,* Paris: Gallimard, 1970.

Chamoiseau, Patrick, Raphaël Confiant, and Jean Bernabé. *Éloge de la créolité*. Paris: Gallimard, 1989.

Chassagne, Raymond. "Seuils de rupture en littérature antillaise." *Conjonction*, no. 155 (1982): 57–68.

Confiant, Raphaël. Review of *Le discours antillais* by Edouard Glissant. *Antilla* (July 1981): 36–38.

Crosta, Suzanne. *Le marronnage créateur: Dynamique textuelle chez Edouard Glissant*. Laval, Canada: GRELCA, 1991.

Dasenbrock, Reed Way. "Intelligibility and Meaningfulness in Multicultural Literature in English." *PMLA* 102, no. 1 (1987): 46–52.

Dash, J. Michael. *Edouard Glissant*. Cambridge: Cambridge Univ. Press, 1995.

———. "Writing the Body: Edouard Glissant's Poetics of Re-membering." *World Literature Today* 63, no. 4 (1989): 609–12.

Debreuille, Jean-Yves. "Le langage désancré de *Malemort*." In *Horizons d'Edouard Glissant,* ed. Alain Favre, 319–28. Pau, France: J & D Éditions, 1992.

de Certeau, Michel. *L'invention du quotidien*. Paris: Gallimard, 1980.

Degras, Priska. "Name of the Fathers, History of the Name: Odono as Memory." *World Literature Today* 63, no. 4 (1989): 613–19.

de Lépine, Edouard. *La crise de février 1935 à la Martinique*. Paris: L'Harmattan, 1980.

Deleuze, Gilles, and Félix Guattari. *Mille plateaux*. Paris: Éditions de Minuit, 1980.

Deren, Maya. *The Voodoo Gods*. St. Albans UK: Paladin, 1975.

Derrida, Jacques. "La mythologie blanche." In *Marges de la philosophie*. Paris: Éditions de Minuit, 1972.

————. *Le monolinguisme de l'autre*. Paris: Éditions Galilée, 1996.

Ebion, Roger. "*Mahagony,* quelle langue?" *Carbet* 10 (1990): 117–41.

Elisabeth, Hector. "Essai d'enquête sur le délire verbal à la Martinique en milieu populaire." *Acoma* 4–5 (1973): 69–83.

Fanon, Frantz. *Les damnés de la terre*. Paris: Maspéro, 1961. Reprint, Paris: Gallimard, 1991. Trans. Constance Farrington as *The Wretched of the Earth* (Harmondsworth UK: Penguin Books, 1967).

————. *Peau noire masques blancs*. Paris: Éditions du Seuil (Collection Points), 1952. Trans. Charles Lam Markmann as *Black Skin, White Masks* (London: Pluto Press, 1986).

Foucault, Michel, and Gilles Deleuze. "Intellectuals and Power: A Conversation between Michel Foucault and Gilles Deleuze." In Michel Foucault, *Language, Counter-Memory, Practice: Selected Essays and Interviews*. Trans. Donald F. Bouchard and Sherry Simon. Ithaca: Cornell Univ. Press, 1977.

Freud, Sigmund. "Fetishism." *Standard Edition,* vol. 21, 149–57. London: Hogarth Press, 1957.

————. "Instincts and Their Vicissitudes." *Standard Edition,* vol. 14, 109–40.

————. "The 'Uncanny.'" *Standard Edition,* vol. 27, 217–52.

Gallagher, Mary. "La poétique de la diversité dans les essais d'Edouard Glissant." In *Horizons d'Edouard Glissant,* ed. Yves-Alain Favre, 27–35. Pau, France: J & D Éditions, 1992.

Gates, Henry Louis, Jr. *The Signifying Monkey: A Theory of Afro-American Literary Criticism*. Oxford: Oxford Univ. Press, 1988.

Glissant, Edouard. "Assimilation ou antillanité?" Interview by Christiane Falgayrettes. *Afrique-Asie,* no. 245 (3 April 1981): 46–47.

————. *La case du commandeur*. Paris: Éditions du Seuil, 1981.

————. "Conférence inaugurale des *Carrefours des littératures européennes*" (Strasbourg). *Antilla* 562 (Nov. 1993): 6–9.

————. *Le discours antillais*. Paris: Éditions du Seuil, 1981. Trans. J. Michael Dash as *Caribbean Discourse: Selected Essays* (Charlottesville: Univ. Press of Virginia, 1989).

————. "Entretien avec le CARÉ." In *CARÉ,* no. 10 (1983): 17–26.

————. *Faulkner, Mississippi*. Paris: Éditions Stock, 1995.

————. *L'intention poétique*. Paris: Éditions du Seuil, 1969. Reprint, Paris: Gallimard, 1997.

————. *Introduction à une poétique du divers*. Paris: Gallimard, 1996.

————. *La Lézarde*. Paris: Éditions du Seuil, 1958. Reprint, Paris: Gallimard, 1997.

————. *Mahagony*. Paris: Éditions du Seuil, 1987. Reprint, Paris: Gallimard, 1997.

———. *Malemort*. Paris: Éditions du Seuil, 1975. Reprint, Paris: Gallimard, 1997.

———. *Poétique de la relation*. Paris: Gallimard, 1990.

———. "Poétique et inconscient martiniquais." In *Identité culturelle et franco-phone dans les Amériques,* ed. Emile Snyder and Albert Valdman, 236–44. Laval, Canada: Presses de l'Université de Laval, 1976.

———. *Le quatrième siècle*. Paris: Éditions du Seuil, 1964. Reprint, Paris: Gallimard, 1997.

———. *Soleil de la conscience*. Paris: Éditions du Seuil, 1956. Reprint, Paris: Gallimard, 1997.

———. *Tout-monde*. Paris: Gallimard, 1993.

———. *Traité du tout-monde*. Paris: Gallimard, 1997.

———. "La vocation de comprendre l'autre." *Courrier de l'UNESCO* 34, no. 12 (1981): 33–35.

Gracchus, Fritz. *Les lieux de la mère dans les sociétés afro-américaines*. Paris: Éditions Caribbéennes, 1986.

———. "Race/énoncé raciste/haine de l'autre/haine de soi," *CARÉ,* no. 3 (1979): 19–37.

Gramsci, Antonio. "The History of the Subaltern Classes: Methodological Criteria." In *Selections from the Prison Notebooks,* ed. Quintin Hoare and Geoffrey Nowell Smith, 52–55. London: Lawrence & Wishart, 1971.

———. "Some Aspects of the Southern Question." In *Selections from Political Writings 1921–1926,* ed. Quintin Hoare, 441–62. London: Lawrence & Wishart, 1978.

Hoffmann, Léon-François. *Haïti: Lettres et l'être*. Toronto: Éditions du GREF, 1992.

Hospice, Marlène. *Pas de pitié pour Marny: Une affaire martiniquaise*. Fort-de-France: Désormeaux, 1984.

Jameson, Fredric. *The Political Unconscious*. New York: Methuen, 1981.

Lacan, Jacques. "L'instance de la lettre dans l'inconscient." In *Écrits,* 493–528. Paris: Éditions du Seuil, 1966. Trans. Alan Sheridan as *Écrits: A Selection* (London: Tavistock Press, 1977).

———. "Le stade du miroir comme formateur de la fonction du Je." In *Écrits,* 93–100. Paris: Éditions du Seuil, 1966. Trans. Alan Sheridan as *Écrits: A Selection* (London: Tavistock Press, 1977).

Lamming, George. *The Pleasures of Exile*. London: Michael Joseph, 1960.

Laplanche, J., and J.-P. Pontalis. *Vocabulaire de la psychanalyse*. Paris: Presses universitaires de France, 1968.

Laroche, Maximilien. *La double scène de la représentation: Oraliture et littérature dans la Caraïbe*. Laval, Canada: GRELCA, 1991.

Macherey, Pierre. *Pour une théorie de la production littéraire*. Paris: Maspéro, 1966. Trans. Geoffrey Wall as *A Theory of Literary Production* (London: Routledge, 1978).

Madou, Jean-Pol. *Edouard Glissant: De mémoire d'arbres.* Amsterdam: Rodopi, 1996.

———. "Poétique de 'Quimboiseur', parole d'esclave." In *Horizons d'Edouard Glissant,* ed. Alain Favre, 285–93. Pau, France: J & D Éditions, 1992.

Marx, Karl. "The Eighteenth Brumaire of Louis Bonaparte." In *Karl Marx and Frederick Engels: Selected Works in Two Volumes,* vol. 1, 247–344. London: Lawrence & Wishart, 1962.

Maximin, Daniel. "Fanon et la folie de la désaliénation." In *Mémorial Frantz Fanon,* ed. Comité Frantz Fanon de Fort-de-France, 133–39. Paris: Présence africaine, 1984.

Mayaux, Catherine. "La structure romanesque de *Mahagony* d'Edouard Glissant." In *Horizons d'Edouard Glissant,* ed. Yves-Alain Favre, 349–63. Pau, France: J & D Éditions, 1992.

Ménil, René. "Une quête de courants souterrains." *CARÉ,* no. 10 (1983): 27–31.

———. *Tracées: identité, négritude, esthétique aux Antilles.* Paris: Laffont, 1981.

Merleau-Ponty, Maurice. "Cinq notes sur Claude Simon." *Médiations,* no. 4 (winter 1961/1962): 6.

Mitchell-Kernan, Claudia. "Signifying as a Form of Verbal Art." In *Mother Wit from the Laughing Barrel: Readings in the Interpretation of Afro-American Folklore,* ed. Alan Dundes, 73–87. Englewood Cliffs: Prentice-Hall, 1973.

Perronnette, Hermann. *Le cas Beauregard.* Fort-de-France: Desormeaux, 1979.

Radford, Daniel. *Edouard Glissant.* Série Poètes d'aujourd'hui, no. 244. Paris: Seghers, 1982.

Rao, Raja. *Kanthapura.* New York: New Directions, 1938.

Roche, Maurice. Review of *La case du commandeur,* by Edouard Glissant. *Le matin de Paris,* 31 July 1981, 26.

Rosello, Mireille. *Littérature et identité aux Antilles.* Paris: Karthala, 1992.

Said, Edward. *Orientalism.* London: Routledge & Kegan Paul, 1978. Reprint, Harmondsworth UK: Penguin Books, 1991.

———. "Orientalism Reconsidered." In *Literature, Politics and Theory,* ed. Francis Barker et al., 210–29. New York: Methuen, 1986.

Schwarz-Bart, Simone. *Pluie et vent sur Télumée-Miracle.* Paris: Éditions du Seuil, 1972.

Spivak, Gayatri. "Can the Subaltern Speak?" In *Marxism and the Interpretation of Culture,* ed. C. Nelson and L. Grossberg, 271–313. London: Macmillan, 1988.

———. *In Other Worlds: Essays in Cultural Politics.* New York: Routledge, 1988.

———. *The Post-Colonial Critic.* New York: Routledge, 1990.

———. "The Rani of Sirmur." In *Europe and Its Others: Proceedings of the 1984 Essex Conference,* ed. Francis Barker et al., 128–51. Colchester: University of Essex, 1985.

Tiffin, Helen. "Post-Colonial Literatures and Counter-Discourse." *Kunapipi* 9, no. 3 (1987): 17–34.

Toumson, Roger. "Les écrivains afro-antillais et la réécriture." *Europe* 43, no. 612 (1980): 115–27.

———. "La littérature antillaise d'expression francaise." *Présence africaine* 121/122 (1982): 130–34.

———. *La transgression des couleurs: Littérature et langage des Antilles*. Paris: Éditions Caribbéennes, 1989.

Webb, Barbara. *Myth and History in Caribbean Fiction*. Amherst: Univ. of Massachusetts Press, 1992.

Yerro, Philippe-Alain. "La trace de Gani: Dialectique du mythe et de l'histoire dans l'approche du marronnage chez E. Glissant." *Carbet* 10 (1990): 101–15.

Index

60, 61–67, 125–26, 147, 152,
154–55, 166, 168, 180, 196 n. 22,
196 n. 23, 196 n. 24, 196 n. 27
quimboiseur, 36, 61, 140, 152, 158,
209 n. 10

Relation, 9, 11–18, 19, 35, 38–39,
42, 52, 129, 177, 186 n. 1, 188
n. 10
relay, 7, 10, 163, 164–66, 167,
168–69, 171, 175–76, 178, 182
rhizome, 14, 17–18, 132, 171, 177,
178, 179, 180, 187 n. 7, 207 n. 21
Roche, Maurice, 206 n. 9
Rosello, Mireille, 6, 27–29, 198 n. 33

Said, Edward, 3, 5, 38, 186 n. 12
Sartre, Jean-Paul, 116, 182, 186 n. 12
Segalen, Victor, 17, 19
slavery, 1, 4, 6, 21–22, 26, 37–38, 58,
149–50; abolition of, 66, 197 n.
30; uprisings, 4, 62–66, 70, 196
n. 27
Soleil de la conscience (Glissant), 8
Spivak, Gayatri, 3, 17, 27, 37–38,
53–58, 71, 75, 165, 176–77, 194
n. 9, 195 n. 13, 199 n. 40; rumor,
165, 176–77, 212 n. 12. *See also*
subalternity; subaltern woman
split discourse, 94, 95, 101, 103, 104,
111, 117–18, 182
subalternity, 4, 5, 10, 18, 20, 21, 35,
39, 53–54, 55–57, 59, 61–82, 91,
118, 182
Subaltern Studies group, 56, 62–63,
176
subaltern woman, 37–38, 73–81,
170–71, 199 n. 40

subject positioning, 4, 39, 49, 55–57,
59, 76, 80–81, 164, 172, 174–76,
177–78, 182, 195 n. 16
Suffrin, Evrard, 93, 107–8, 110–11,
112, 205 n. 38

Tagore, Rabindranath, 120, 205 n. 2
Tiffin, Helen, 3. *See also The Empire
Writes Back*
Toumson, Roger, 6, 22, 50, 191 n.
39, 191 n. 40, 203 n. 23, 204 n. 35
Tout-monde (Glissant), 7, 8, 9, 10,
51, 52, 58, 59, 133–36, 137–40,
142, 153, 167, 168, 169–71, 172,
180, 212 n. 9
Traité du tout-monde (Glissant), 8, 9,
179–80, 181, 182
trame, 177–78
transportation, 1, 6, 14–15, 25, 46,
57, 120, 150, 157

verbal delirium, 10, 31, 32, 84,
90–93, 102, 119, 120, 161, 170,
182; dramatizing, 92–93, 107–9,
110–12, 118, 123–24, 206 n. 8;
pathological, 91, 92, 101, 109,
112, 118, 128, 131, 134; of representation, 92, 97, 99, 100, 101,
117; routine, 91–93, 94, 112
*Vertretung. See Darstellung/Vertre-
tung*
voodoo, 48–49, 103–4, 108, 109,
211 n. 18, 211 n. 19

Webb, Barbara, 207 n. 17

Yerro, Philippe-Alain, 195 n. 20

New World Studies

New World Studies publishes interdisciplinary research that
seeks to redefine the cultural map of the Americas and to propose particularly stimulating points of departure for an emerging field. Encompassing the Caribbean as well as continental
North, Central, and South America, the series books examine
cultural processes within the hemisphere, taking into account
the economic, demographic, and historical phenomena that
shape them. Given the increasing diversity and richness of the
linguistic and cultural traditions in the Americas, the need for
research that privileges neither the English-speaking United
States nor Spanish-speaking Latin America has never been
greater. The series is designed to bring the best of this new research into an identifiable forum and to channel its results to the
rapidly evolving audience for cultural studies.

New World Studies

Vera M. Kutzinski
Sugar's Secrets: Race and the Erotics
of Cuban Nationalism

Richard D. E. Burton and Fred Reno, editors
French and West Indian: Martinique, Guadeloupe,
and French Guiana Today

A. James Arnold, editor
Monsters, Tricksters, and Sacred Cows: Animal Tales
and American Identities

J. Michael Dash
The Other America: Caribbean Literature in
a New World Context

Isabel Alvarez Borland
Cuban-American Literature of Exile: From
Person to Persona

Belinda J. Edmondson, editor
Caribbean Romances: The Politics of
Regional Representation

Steven V. Hunsaker
Autobiography and National Identity
in the Americas

Celia M. Britton
Edouard Glissant and Postcolonial Theory:
Strategies of Language and Resistance